The Modern
Literary Werewolf

The Modern Literary Werewolf

A Critical Study of the Mutable Motif

BRENT A. STYPCZYNSKI

McFarland & Company, Inc., Publishers
Jefferson, North Carolina, and London

An earlier version of Chapter 3 appeared in Brent Stypczynski, "Wolf in Professor's Clothing: J.K. Rowling's Werewolf as Educator," *Journal of the Fantastic in the Arts* 20.1 (2009): 57–69.

LIBRARY OF CONGRESS CATALOGUING-IN-PUBLICATION DATA

Stypczynski, Brent A., 1977–
    The modern literary werewolf : a critical study of the mutable motif / Brent A. Stypczynski.
        p.   cm.
    Includes bibliographical references and index.

    ISBN 978-0-7864-6965-9
    softcover : acid free paper ∞

    1. Werewolves in literature.   2. Shapeshifting.
    3. Metamorphosis in literature.   I. Title.
    PN56.W45S79 2013
    809'.93374 — dc23   2013013037

BRITISH LIBRARY CATALOGUING DATA ARE AVAILABLE

© 2013 Brent A. Stypczynski. All rights reserved

No part of this book may be reproduced or transmitted in any form or by any means, electronic or mechanical, including photocopying or recording, or by any information storage and retrieval system, without permission in writing from the publisher.

Front cover image (iStockphoto/Thinkstock)

Manufactured in the United States of America

*McFarland & Company, Inc., Publishers
    Box 611, Jefferson, North Carolina 28640
    www.mcfarlandpub.com*

For Paul, Megan, and Dylan

Table of Contents

Introduction	1
1. It's Only in Your Head	17
2. The Disc's K-9 Unit	37
3. Wolf in Professor's Clothing	72
4. Southern Wolves	107
5. Secondary Worlds and Wolf Cousins	136
6. Variety...	161
Final Thoughts	184
Chapter Notes	191
Bibliography	207
Index	213

Introduction

The shape-shifter, particularly in its appearances as the werewolf, appears in virtually every culture in the world. References to werewolves appear at least as far back as the *Epic of Gilgamesh*, while shape-shifting figures occur in mythologies throughout history. The prevalence of these figures argues for the importance of their role in both the individual and cultural psyches, that they tell us something significant about ourselves and our cultures.

This study approaches the werewolf from the collective psyche perspective, arguing that the shape-shifter is a Jungian archetype unto itself. To achieve this goal, a continuity of themes and appearances from the classical era to the modern is necessary. The connection between modern werewolves and medieval sources is a point of particular focus as many werewolf traits that appear to originate in the medieval period greatly inform modern stories. These new werewolves bring medieval themes and views to the modern world and audience. In order to establish the continuity between time periods, a variety of the werewolf's modern guises will be explored. This also serves to display modern additions to werewolf lore as the figure evolves over time, adapting to new audiences.

The primary focus of this examination is modern literary werewolves. Those with clear ties to the werewolves of the classical to early modern periods were chosen to best demonstrate the chain of continuity. In the case of the classical and medieval periods, the connections appear between literary sources. However, most of the relevant early modern sources are non-literary in nature—trial records, treatises, and medical texts—yet, they still exert a strong influence on modern conceptions of the werewolf. Some young adult material is included as well, both J.K. Rowling's *Harry Potter* series and Charles de Lint's *Dingo* (2008). The reasons for their inclusion are many, but there are four important considerations. First, the

Introduction

novels in question, particularly Rowling's, introduce younger audiences to medieval themes that they may recognize later. These themes are presented in an updated form, that the authors build upon to delve into unexplored territory. Additionally, young adult literature, especially in the last decade or two, often leads trends in popular culture, which implies a certain degree of influence. Young adult literature is also closer to fairy tales and folklore than most adult literature. Therefore, it is closer to archetype and the collective unconscious.

Within the above goals and criteria, more detailed reasons for including particular works over others are important. One need only look at any online bookseller to see literally thousands of examples of werewolf fiction produced in the last couple decades. This is particularly true with the current popularity of the paranormal romance genre. The primary requirement for inclusion is that the shape-shifter must be a werewolf and the werewolf must change shape (or be believed to do so). That is, the change from wolf to man must be literal, not figurative. These intertwined points automatically exclude a significant body of mythology and seventeenth to early-twentieth century literature. The source in question must also be influential — Terry Pratchett, Rowling, and Charlaine Harris — or representative — Jack Williamson, de Lint, and the short stories. Finally, some admittedly qualitative judgments were made, thus the exclusion of the aforementioned paranormal romances.

Modern Werewolves

If we look at key modern representations of human-animal shape-shifting characters in modern literature, we find that they retain strong ties to their medieval forbearers and evoke similar responses in the modern audience. Such similarities imply shared social and human concerns such as where the line between nature and nurture, or between humans and other animals, is drawn. These assumptions become stronger when we note that the figures stretch back at least as far as Ovid, Petronius, and Gilgamesh and have strong associations with pre-historic, totemic beliefs. Most of these human-animal shifters are considered monstrous, within their stories and cultures, particularly Petronius'. As Malcolm South notes regarding monsters, "if [a monster] is to have a profound effect on us, it

Introduction

must reflect something meaningful about human experience and engage our emotions in a powerful way."[1] Moreover, Joyce Salisbury suggests that one reason shape-shifting figures are broadly popular and fascinating is that "[a]nimals do not abide by social expectations that bind humans. They do what they want, go where they want,"[2] especially if they are wild ones. For these reasons, modern appearances of the werewolf deserve study, not as footnotes in larger works, but on their own.

Chapter 1, "It's Only in Your Head," covers the earliest modern text in this study, Jack Williamson's *Darker Than You Think* (1948). In his conception of the archetype, Williamson takes medieval and early modern theological conceptions of metamorphosis as trickery in which a demonic entity creates an illusory wolf and makes the "werewolf" think he turned into an animal to commit crimes. Williamson mixes this concept with some New Age psychic projection ideas, a healthy dose of Darwinian evolutionary theory, and Hollywood's history of werewolf film. Ultimately, the product is a work of supernatural horror incorporating numerous elements of werewolf folklore and capturing some of the concerns of both medieval theologians (the morality of change) and later authors' fictional societies (concealment).

Chapter 2, "The Disc's K-9 Unit," offers a reading of Terry Pratchett's Constable Angua through the lens of medieval and early modern tropes because of Pratchett's fascination with fairy tales, their origins, and their logical extensions. As with all good satirists, Pratchett mocks the very traditions he uses, yet retains a serious subtext that examines myriad aspects of society. In order to explore this aspect of his work and the werewolf figure, the chapter focuses on *The Fifth Elephant* (2001) and *Thud!* (2005), two novels in which Constable/Sergeant Angua plays a major role. This chapter explains, through Pratchett's subtext, the continued popularity of the medieval tradition (as edited by the early modern period) in the modern era and discusses the adaptations that the werewolf undergoes through Pratchett's system of modernization. Angua also serves as a reminder that dogs are simply wolves that have chosen to live with man. Additionally, Pratchett notes that this character is the exception to the rule (as she at least attempts to restrain her bestial side), as with Lupin below, yielding both serious and comedic implications, both of which are important in Pratchett's writing. Not only does the figure continue from a medieval base, but it also becomes more complex as more versions and meanings

Introduction

come into play. This increased complexity weaves into the nature of the figure as a symbol of change and flux, and should be expected given that it is a mutable being capable of physical metamorphosis.

Chapter 3, "Wolf in Professor's Clothing," focuses on exactly these differences, the layers that Rowling adds to the neomedieval werewolf by both building on and becoming parallel to Pratchett's levels of meaning. The quantity and quality of narrative layering is what has drawn a number of scholars to take critical, literary, and socio-historical approaches to her work.[3] As is the case with Pratchett, Rowling's use and adaptation of her predecessors calls for critical study on its own and presents a strong case for her work's literary merit. Part of this merit comes from the fact that her primary werewolf, Remus Lupin, is one of the best modern examples of the neomedieval werewolf. Lupin is clearly constructed from a medieval mold found in Marie de France's "Bisclavret" and *William of Palerne*. That said, Rowling strays in several important ways from earlier traditions (notably that Lupin retains his friends after they discover his "condition" and that a love interest enters, rather than flees, because of his morphic ability). This chapter focuses on *Prisoner of Azkaban* (1999; Lupin's first appearance), *Order of the Phoenix* (2003; where Lupin undergoes important character development), *Half-Blood Prince* (2005; in which Lupin's background is further developed along with Rowling's conception of werewolves in general), and *Deathly Hallows* (2007; where Lupin's character develops and his son is briefly discussed). Lupin takes what Castiglione did for the elite in 1510 and makes it public in a modern world. Even though his fictional "public" is technically a hidden elite, the readers are certainly too varied in background, ethnicity, and age to be either hidden or elite. Balancing the monstrous tendencies with his sympathetic and courtly qualities creates the dynamic that is key to both Rowling's writing and to Lupin's brand of self-fashioning, which he transmits to Harry in several scenes.

Chapter 4, "Southern Wolves," argues that Charlaine Harris' approach to the figures draws from not only the oldest sources for one type of werewolf, but incorporates a post-germ theory modification of lycanthropy-as-disease for a second type. By placing both types together in the same setting and society, she adds another layer to our understanding of this representation of the archetype. Moreover, in connecting her werewolves to the general, and gradual, "coming out" of supernatural beings, Harris

Introduction

presents a transition point between Rowling-Williamson (where the figures try to remain in hiding) and Pratchett (where the existence of werewolves is common knowledge, even if Ankh-Morporkians misidentify the one in their midst). Likewise, given the werewolf's connection to eroticism and sexuality, their revelation in Harris' world can potentially be likened to the act of "coming out" in the LGBT community, thereby adding another level of meaning and hearkening back to some interpretations of Stubbe Peeter's trial records.

Chapter 5, "Secondary Worlds and Wolf Cousins," explores Charles de Lint's varied approach through *Wolf Moon* (1988) and *Dingo*. In the former, he transfers the medieval sympathetic, constitutional werewolf into a secondary world where the figure faces the Renaissance's werewolf hunting craze embodied by a hunter who becomes worse than the prey he chases. The werewolf has clear forbearers in Alphouns, Bisclavret, and Gorlagon, while his hunter has strong ties to the myriad early modern, Church-based werewolf and witch hunters. On the other hand, *Dingo* remains within the primary world, albeit one somewhat infused with the supernatural. Here he presents a rather unique take on the werewolf through twin weredingos who have to be in opposing forms — one human, the other canine — at all times, for concealment. In this case, de Lint tweaks the archetype slightly, but in a manner reminiscent of Pratchett, whose Gaspode often reminds readers that dogs are simply wolves who choose to live with humans.

Chapter 6, "Variety...," departs somewhat from the previous chapters' format to present several short stories. The purpose is to demonstrate the variety of directions that modern authors have taken with the archetype beyond those appearing in the previous chapters. Included are: Robert Randisi, Philip José Farmer, Robert Weinberg, A.C. Crispin and Kathleen O'Malley, Barbara Paul, Brad Strickland, Jane Yolen, and Larry Niven. The first four take the concealed, often sympathetic, werewolf and place him (or her) in a variety of professions. In at least one case (Farmer), werewolf newsletters are involved. Paul expands on werewolf society and brings the werewolf into the public eye, in a precursor to Harris. The last three take the werewolf into the future, using science fiction as their vehicle. In their work, we see the werewolf used for environmentalist messages, time travel, and other purposes, while retaining the tropes and theories that we are familiar with from classical, medieval, and early modern sources.

Introduction

Methods of "Taming" the Wolf

Werewolves, and shape-shifters in general, play an intriguing and complex role in the Western literary tradition, a role that has been sufficiently recognized and explored only with regards to the medieval period. Even so, much of the scholarly work on shape-shifting in literature has either focused on the historical, religious, psychological, and medical dimensions, or has been part of wider research regarding the role of monsters. Discussion of shape-changers as literary figures has been minimal, with most scholars more interested in the frames around these characters rather than the figures themselves and their fictive situations. To date, academic discussions of these figures in general, and of werewolves in particular, fall into one of five major positions: the shape-shifter as theological impossibility or monster; the "sympathetic werewolf" as a largely medieval phenomenon; the werewolf as political, postcolonial allegory; shape-shifting as a sign or symptom of insanity; or the shape-shifter as social allegory. The shape-shifter warrants attention because the representational role is fundamentally important, even if its "screen time" (for lack of a better term) in a given text is brief.

Saint Augustine presents one of the best discussions of the shape-changer as religious impossibility or monster in *City of God* (413 C.E.). In this work, Augustine acts as a commentator, elucidating passages from the Bible, other ancient sources, and current debates of his time regarding a variety of subjects. On the subject of the shape-shifter, he responds to contemporary and ancient Greek tales of "certain monstrous races of man"[4] in *City of God* 16.8. Generally speaking, his position makes use of simple black-and-white categories based on defining man as both mortal (not an angel) and rational (not an animal). Anything displaying mortality and rational thought, according to Augustine, must be a man, no matter what its outer shape appears to be. As Jeffry Massey notes, this is characteristic of Augustine's "thoughtful finagling, especially when the magic in question involved the transformation of human beings, who, as creatures made in God's image, could not be changed essentially by any but God Himself."[5] This is one of the key passages Caroline Walker Bynum references when she asserts a medieval preoccupation with creating clearly defined borders between species. The end result of this position is that, doctrinally, all stories of such creatures—notably those involving Circe, Lycaon, and the

Introduction

Arcadians — are false, the result of demonic illusion or trickery rather than actual physical change, since the essential nature of the person remains the same. That said, Augustine does insist that all shape-shifted men retain their rational minds, implying that actual physical change takes place.

The "sympathetic werewolf" as medieval, psychological phenomenon is best exemplified in Bynum's work, most notably her presentation "Metamorphosis, or Gerald and the Werewolf" (1998; reprinted in her book *Metamorphosis and Identity*). Bynum argues that a surface reading of medieval metamorphosis tales leads to discovering a medieval "commitment to species immutability."[6] However, she notes that a more nuanced interpretation of this "fascination with spontaneous generation and hybridization"[7] shows a concern with delimiting animal species-crossing. That is, many medieval authors wished to understand and control the rules and limits by which species-crossing could take place. Ultimately, Bynum maintains that the "sympathetic" werewolf is different from modern and ancient ferocious beasts both literally and figuratively, largely because the medieval versions tend to retain the rational mind, simultaneously glorifying and resisting the idea of metamorphosis (the outer shell changes, but the core humanity remains intact). Bynum's treatment of the "sympathetic" werewolf provides a useful distinction for studies of modern literary shifters. Bynum also identifies two general types of change: replacement change, where the original form or individual is effectively lost (common in modern horror), and evolutionary change, where the core identity remains largely the same even though the individual undergoes some physical change (common in Ovid, medieval literature, and modern fantasy).[8] Both of these are useful concepts for discussing modern werewolves and other shape-shifters.

The werewolf as postcolonial or political allegory has recently been posited by both Catherine Karkov and S. J. Wiseman.[9] Both scholars add to Bynum's interpretation. Karkov claims that, while Bynum is correct in her discussion of "sympathetic" werewolves, she misses or ignores the political metaphors inherent in Gerald of Wales. That is, Karkov argues, Gerald's story acts as a metaphor for the conquest of Ireland and parallels the partitioning of Ireland. The story and Gerald's *Topographica Hibernica* (c. 1188) in general, she claims, make the Irish both attractive, redeemable humans and bestial, monstrous animals, which is perfectly epitomized in the figure of the werewolf. Wiseman, on the other hand, works with early

Introduction

modern English texts about the German werewolf Stubbe Peeter (made infamous in a 1590 trial record) to resolve questions of the soul and politics. She associates the werewolf with civic discontent by viewing werewolves within a period hierarchy of species and the early modern use of the story in debates regarding civic hierarchies. That is, the werewolf becomes an allegory for civic monstrosity, namely rebellion. Wiseman notes that Stubbe Peeter has closer ties to Ovid's Lycaon than to Marie de France's Bisclavret in that, like Lycaon, Peeter is characterized as violent, cannibalistic, and deserving of punishment. The shift of influence present in Peeter, from the medieval to the classical, marks a point where the transition between medieval and early modern attitudes toward werewolves is highly noticeable.

As the early modern period evolved in Europe, ideas of self-fashioning, that is, of changing or pretending to change one's essential nature, flourished. This concept is linked to early forays into psychology, which also affect the werewolf figure. Over time, the early psychological view that shape-shifting figures are a sign or symptom of insanity is carried into the twentieth century through psychoanalysis. Although Freud deals with this issue in one of his famous case studies,[10] one of the best discussions of the werewolf as psychosis can be found in Sabine Baring-Gould's *The Book of Werewolves* (1865). Through a mixture of historical overview and collections of folklore, Baring-Gould treats the werewolf as an extinct or semi-extinct creature. He supports the idea that the folkloric and literary phenomena are cases of true shifting, while the non-fictional expressions are psychological illness. Non-fictional figures are, according to Baring-Gould, closely connected to cannibalism, hallucinations, and other expressions of the individual's "natural cruelty"[11]; in other words, lycanthropy is a form of insanity. This position is also held by numerous English sources — including Reginald Scot and James I — in the early modern period, as well as a few contemporary Continental authors such as Simon Goulart.

Related to this position, in that it considers the psychological implications of the figure, is the view that shape-changers act as allegories for society in general. H. R. Ellis Davidson's research illustrates this position and is a useful contrast to Baring-Gould's in that she sees the Nordic shape-shifter as an integral part of the social structure from whence it comes, rather than seeing the shape-shifter as an insane figure that is forced outside of its native society. Notably, Davidson ties commonly appearing forms to animals that are feared (bears, wolves) or useful (cattle, goats). These stories connect (as with some modern iterations) to initiation rites, mythology (tales of Thor and Loki), warbands (the *berserkrs*—bear-shirt—and *ulfheðnar*—wolf-coat), and shamanic practices. As one might expect, the most impressive tales involve wild creatures rather than domesticated ones. Davidson points to several sagas, including *Egil's Saga*, the *Volsunga Saga*, *Landnamabok*, and *Njal's Saga*, in which men become animals, thus displaying the pervasive nature of such fictional beings.

These five critical positions have by and large focused purely on classical and medieval fiction or modern psychoanalysis, leaving modern literary appearances of werewolves unexplored as objects of study. To that end, this work presents a detailed study of the modern literary werewolf (and, by extension, shape-shifters), as represented by numerous authors, whose combined work initially inspired this research.

Most modern authors briefly discussed above continue the medieval "sympathetic" werewolf tradition, alongside the early modern tradition of the monstrous wolf. However, none of the aforementioned authors remain solely within the older traditions. Modern authors have adapted the old forms both to discuss problems similar to those addressed in earlier literature and to introduce new issues specific to the late twentieth and early twenty-first centuries. By examining these adaptations, we can see that the shape-shifter exists as an independent archetype which, in its manifestation as the werewolf over the last century, has been put to several evolving functions that build upon, and sometimes subvert, prior traditions.

The Shape-Shifter and the Jungian Archetype

The literary werewolf operates in a complex environment involving cultural, historical, and psychological elements. The last element includes the proposed shape-shifter archetype. Carl Jung's statement that archetypes are "the contents of the collective unconscious"[12] seems especially appropriate here. Because the figure appears frequently over an extended span of time, it must serve an important purpose or seek to answer one or more significant needs. Jung notes that, like Platonic Forms, archetypes are never directly perceived by the conscious mind. Rather, they are modified as

Introduction

they move into the conscious. Therefore representations of the thing, not the thing itself, are seen. The literary realm is the perfect place to witness such representations at work in various forms. As Amy Green states, "The fluid nature of myths and folktales comprises a vital component of their lasting legacy in that they may adapt to myriad worldviews, and even perhaps the whim of their storyteller."[13] Although a Freudian perspective is certainly valid and present for the werewolf and shape-shifter — as has been well demonstrated in the extensive body of critical work focused on Charles Perrault, John Webster, and Marie de France[14] — to date the figures have not been approached from an explicitly Jungian perspective. Because they appear in every known culture around the world and throughout history, we should look at the figure from this neglected perspective, especially as an archetype independent of Jung's trickster (the archetype to which he attributes all shape-shifting). That is, shape-shifting plays a more independent role in archetypal terms than Jung expected. Jung conceived of shape-shifting as inextricably linked to the trickster. Hence all shape-shifting figures must therefore be tricksters. However, an analysis of historical and modern literature in connection with historical documents indicates that the shape-shifter is not necessarily always a trickster but is in fact a separate entity that sometimes overlaps the trickster's function. In other words: all tricksters are shape-shifters,[15] but not all shape-shifters are tricksters.

To begin, some definitions are necessary. The most important terms related to this archetype are "werewolf" and "shape-shifter." There are a variety of academic definitions for both terms, such as Kirby Smith's defining "werewolf" as "a person who, either from a gift inborn or from the use of certain magic arts of which he has learned the secret, is in the habit of changing himself into a wolf from time to time."[16] Smith refers to this definition as simply one kind of werewolf, a "constitutional" werewolf. He identifies a second type as "the involuntary werewolf, whose transformation was unavoidable, owing to the curse or charm of some outside power."[17] However, for the purposes of this study "werewolf" (from the Anglo-Saxon *were-wulf*, literally "man-wolf")[18] will be defined as a figure that can assume the shape of a human and a wolf, yet is never truly either one. The other major term, "shape-shifter," will be defined as a figure, whether human or otherwise, that is capable of altering its physical appearance without the aid of make-up, surgery, or prosthetics, often crossing species, gender,

Introduction

and racial boundaries. This alteration can be as minor as changing to give the appearance of age/youth or as major as changing from a man to a bird. For both terms, my working definitions are meant to be as inclusive as possible without being so broad as to be useless.

Based on these definitions, then, the shape-shifter archetype is, at its core, characterized by the ability to change form. This trait is the most obvious one. The ability to change forms is also the physical manifestation of the shape-shifter's principal psychosocial role: crossing boundaries. The existence of the shape-shifter displays a cultural need for boundary-crossing figures that can reinforce new and old definitions even as society enters a phase of change that is simultaneously frightening and attractive. This capacity possesses clear positive and negative attributes. Although crossing boundaries can help society and the individual evolve, it can also cause the social structure and individual psyche to collapse. In both cases, the shape-shifter archetype represents mutability. It stands to reinforce old definitions while simultaneously proposing new ones, and it paradoxically presents stability by means of its very mutability — all of which applies to Terry Pratchett's (feudalism to modernity), J.K. Rowling's (childhood to adulthood), Charlaine Harris' (blissful ignorance to frightened knowledge), and Charles de Lint's (childhood to adulthood in *Dingo*) respective works. The ability to cross boundaries and divisions recalls the tension inherent in neomedievalism, thus making the shape-shifter an ideal representation of the phenomenon. Not only does the archetype represent a tension between time periods, it also crosses the boundaries between genres — fantasy and police procedural (Terry Pratchett); fantasy and mystery (J.K. Rowling); fantasy, mystery and modern romance (Laurell K. Hamilton) — and audiences — as with Rowling's bridging the age gap between children and adults. Genre crossing creates its own tension for readers, publishers, and booksellers thereby having the potential to affect the audience's view of these categories and their place in society.

However, what defines the shape-shifter archetype is what the figure does rather than how it appears. Manifestations of this archetype function as civilizing figures, whether by scaring the audience into obedience or by providing an example of good behavior. For earlier, agricultural, audiences the archetype's fearsome qualities come from the human-to-animal changes, especially when men metamorphose into predatory animals. This particular transformation does not necessarily cause fear in the modern

Introduction

audience, although the close relationship between domestic dogs and wolves, for instance, could be a subconscious source of concern for the modern audience. While the human-to-animal shape-shifter, especially the werewolf, remains a staple of the horror genre, human-to-human[19] or alien-to-human transformations in such works largely replace the human-to-animal as a source of fear and uncertainty. The former types act through displaying instability and hybridity where we seek solidity. The human-to-human or alien-to-human shifter exposes the façade that exists in most human relations, that which maintains the divide between public and private persona. Thus, "the potential to shift external shape also provides the means to reveal the innermost traits of a character."[20]

The shape-shifter also serves as a reminder of humanity's past and bestial nature, largely in the form of human-to-animal shifts, which evoke a fear of the supernatural or, potentially uncomfortable, reminders of our close connection to the animal world. At the same time, these manifestations provide a sense of connectedness with nature and open up the nature-versus-nurture debate. Because of their dual nature, "the creatures they become provide the reader with insight into the darkest, most flawed aspects of their personalities."[21] For example, Marie de France's Bisclavret and *William of Palerne's* Alphouns exemplify nurture ascendant, while Rowling's Fenrir Greyback exemplifies nature triumphant. Jeffrey Jerome Cohen notes that monsters "are disturbing hybrids whose externally incoherent bodies resist attempts to include them in any systematic structuration,"[22] and who almost always escape to the unclassified margins of society. Although Cohen discusses monsters in general, his observation is especially apt for this archetype because the more we try to classify types of shifters (or archetypes), the more they adapt to evade those very categories.

In this way, the shape-shifter is related to the trickster archetype. Like the trickster, the shape-shifter is both human and bestial and therefore shares an affinity with the part of the psyche that Jung calls the shadow. That said, the shape-shifter does not have to be bestial; it can be a supernatural magician like Thomas Malory's Merlyn and Edmund Spenser's Archimago. The shape-shifter is independent of the trickster in that it does not normally, or solely, work through the application of pranks, as is often the case with the Native American Coyote or Norse Loki. Rather, most shape-shifting figures come from a standard set of possibilities: (1)

Introduction

they are the victims of other characters' cruelty; (2) they exist because of aid from a demon; (3) they are ethically neutral agents with little concern for society or humanity; or (4) they act to reinforce society. Although the trickster almost always incorporates a lesson, whether explicit or implicit, in his/her story, this is not necessarily the case with the shape-shifter. In many cases, the shape-shifter is used simply to instill fear, either of the unknown or of the bestial side of the audience.

The shape-shifter is also related to the trickster in that they are both agents of change. In archetypal terms, the shape-shifter reminds us that mutability, both replacement and evolution, is a constant in life. Depending on its manifestation, the shape-shifter, especially as the werewolf, can represent social or political change (as is the case with Marie's Bisclavret), biological evolution (as with Jack Williamson's werewolves or Hal Clement's alien shape-shifters[23]), or psychological change (John Webster's Ferdinand or Rowling's Remus Lupin). In every manifestation, the shape-shifter acts to herald, to cause, or to draw attention to the moment of alteration. How the individual reacts to the shifter's appearance and message — with fear, excitement, or trepidation, for example — determines how the person responds to the mutability the figure represents.

The proposed archetype also has a variety of other traits, some of which it shares with representations of monsters in general. Shape-changers act to justify categories and categorizations even as they work to break such classifications. Shifters appear as signs of a constantly mutable world that changes socially, physically, and individually (on the part of its inhabitants). As David Gilmore notes, they (meaning monsters) work to "expose the radical permeability and artificiality of all our classificatory boundaries, highlighting the arbitrariness and fragility of culture."[24] This fragility appears in many forms. For instance, according to Michael Chelik, cannibalism (an artificial boundary between the civilized and the wild) is a key trait that appears in many tales involving the shape-shifter archetype, in part because the shape-shifter develops in its earliest form at an evolutionary transition point between semi-vegetarian apes and carnivorous apes.[25] Tied into the construction of the archetype is the fact that, according to Irving Massey, at least in the medieval period if not today, "[m]etamorphosis [...] is about a reconciliation [...] of the damned with the divine," the illogical animal with the reasoning human.[26] That is, metamorphosis is about achieving the balance between the falling angel and the rising ape, to paraphrase Pratchett's suggestion.[27] As with most subjects of literary criticism, the archetype also has transgressive erotic undertones, especially when it appears in werewolf stories and sixteenth-century witchcraft trials — with witches turning into cats to enter their victims' bedrooms — but then, to paraphrase Irving Massey, what has not been given such connections? That is to say, erotic connotations are certainly not unique to the shape-shifter.

However, building out of the erotic connotations, we can see that the proposed archetype is interested in beginnings, birth, and re-birth, much like the multi-morphic Shiva and Durga of Hindu theology. Shape-shifters act upon their socially transgressive impulses, thereby providing a vicarious psychological release. Said impulses include wildness, violence, nudity taboos, bestiality (in both senses of the term), social bonds (medieval representations are commonly associated with marriage), adultery, and rape. In this way, the theriomorph (human-animal shifter) also functions to separate humanity from excessive violence, as in the cases of rape and mass-murder present in the trials of Jean Grenier[28] and Stubbe Peeter (or Peeter Stubbe). By blaming the transgressive violence and sex on the beast, the human part of the individual is absolved even as it is punished. This role as psychological release valve brings the archetype into a closer relationship with the shadow, that part of the psyche made up of all the socially transgressive impulses. The shape-shifter archetype allows the shadow to be vicariously exercised or exorcised, thereby helping the individual to come to terms with the shadow and maintaining the social structure by releasing some of the pressure created by the collective shadow.

Within this rather broad characterization are many potential categories for the archetype's manifestations. Among the most important and common of these are: human-to-human (Malory's Merlyn), human-to-animal (Marie de France's Bisclavret), non-human (Shakespeare's Puck, also a trickster, who uses an inherent talent), magical transformations (Spenser's Archimago, who uses spells), and cursed shifters (Alphouns in *William of Palerne*). The human-to-human, non-human, and magical shifters share the most traits with Jung's trickster. Many use their abilities to fool and play pranks on those around them, some more benignly than others — for instance, Puck is more benign than Archimago. The human-to-animal figures (such as the werewolf) and the cursed ones tend to draw the shape-shifter away from the trickster into an archetype of its own

Introduction

because, in many cases, they are more interested in removing their curse or recovering their lost human shape than in trickery or changing society. This is not to say that shifters do not make use of trickery to achieve their goals, but rather that their goals and those of the Jungian trickster are not generally the same.

Among cursed and human-to-animal shifters, the most common in the English and European literary traditions is the werewolf. In one form or another, werewolves are insinuated into European literary history from their earliest appearances in the Near Eastern *Epic of Gilgamesh*, Petronius' *Satyricon*, and Ovid's *Metamorphoses*.[29] This manifestation of the shape-shifter continues through the Middle Ages, in the works of Gerald of Wales and Marie de France among others, to subtly inhabit the early modern period, as evidenced by Webster's and Perrault's works. Moreover, werewolves especially litter the modern literary landscape from Stephen King to J.K. Rowling, as Charlotte Otten has partially shown in her anthology *The Literary Werewolf* (2002).

The werewolf manifestation appears in virtually every Western culture, in both the New and Old Worlds. This intercultural appearance makes the werewolf much more common as an iteration of the shape-shifter than any of its cousins. Other appearances — including werecows and werebears, werejaguars, weretigers, and selkies — are often limited to specific geographic regions (Scandinavia, Central/South America, Asia, and the British Isles, respectively). Only the werewolf appears to move throughout most world cultures without regard to national or cultural boundaries. The werebear is a close second, appearing in some North American stories as well as Scandinavian and Russian tales. This prevalence of the werewolf is probably due in large part to the fact that wolves of one breed or another were once common to every region. Since wolves prey on domestic animals, there is a nearly universal fear of the wolf in agricultural societies throughout history. Because it is such a widely spread figure, the werewolf is also the most widely varied manifestation of the shape-shifter in its traits, in audience responses, and in how authors employ the figure.

This study argues for the presence of the proposed shape-shifter archetype based on modern werewolf appearances, with the assumption that earlier appearances have been investigated at considerable depth by others.[30] The archetype is, in the simplest terms, a figure that can change forms. It

Introduction

thereby represents a crossing of boundaries. It serves to question and reify the social structures that police transgressive acts, and it provides a vicarious psychological release valve for the shadow. In order to establish this figure as an archetype, this study presents a tradition of modern manifestations and functions that reflect psycho-social concerns and build upon a much longer tradition. Ultimately, the work demonstrates that the proposed archetype has adapted to remain relevant to the modern psyche and society.

1

It's Only in Your Head

Augustine Meets Freud

Jack Williamson presents, in 1948's *Darker Than You Think* (*Darker*), a very clear modern expression of the lycanthrope as archetype in the Augustinian and early modern views. He weaves a story that recreates the debates about the nature of humanity to which Augustine responded, employs the medieval theological impossibility of true shape-change, and incorporates the Augustinian theory of illusory change that influenced European theological thought on the subject for centuries. While he mostly reflects Augustine, there are elements of Ovid and Gervase of Tilbury in his werewolves. However, he does keep the medieval secular tradition of the sympathetic werewolf in mind, although his protagonist, Will Barbee, arguably, does not necessarily end as a sympathetic character. Nor does Williamson directly reference any particular tales from the medieval period. At the same time, Williamson uses early modern views of lycanthropy as insanity — based in melancholy — combined with the period's tendency to conflate the witch and the werewolf. The figure is treated as a typically early modern monster bent on cannibalism, murder, and base desires. A small, Eastern European legend regarding the relationship between werewolves and vampires from the early modern period also sneaks in to add a couple layers of meaning to Williamson's work. Like Terry Pratchett, Williamson also brings modern cinematic lore to bear, specifically the relationship between werewolves and silver (which, as a metal associated in western mythology with the moon, hearkens back to Gervase). There may even be intimations of potential influence of World War II Nazi propaganda, regarding the failed Operation Werewolf, present in the work.[1]

With the plethora of werewolf material present prior to the 1940s, one might wonder if Williamson has anything to add to the mythos and archetype. He moves beyond his predecessors in a variety of ways. Perhaps the most important is that he applies new scientific and semi-scientific theories, as well as some pre-scientific ones, to the old legends and tropes. Specifically, Williamson's werewolves are informed by Darwinian evolution, Heisenberg's uncertainty principle, and Freudian psychoanalysis. This addition is the most important aspect of Williamson's writing, in terms of his werewolves. He essentially presents one of the earliest attempts to provide a, fictional, scientific rationale for the archetypal creature. This presentation has its origins in both the enhanced place of science in the post–World War II world and in Williamson's own attempt to legitimize his preferred career path: writing science fiction (SF). The choice to use psychoanalysis to legitimize the genre becomes ironic in that the first psychiatrist Williamson saw at the Menninger Clinic told him that writing SF was a symptom of neurosis and that he could be cured of the urge to write in the genre as part of his treatment.[2] Interestingly, Jungian psychoanalysis is never directly addressed in the novel, despite its potential. This absence is likely due to the fact that Williamson was undergoing psychotherapy as he wrote the earliest versions of the book, and his therapist was a Freudian. Thus, not only does Williamson present an expression of the shape-shifter archetype, he also provides limited commentary on Freudian analysis, even if the latter is colored by his own somewhat negative experience as a patient.[3]

Ultimately, Williamson's werewolves, and the term should be used somewhat broadly here, serve as part of Williamson's own therapy as he discovered his identity and place in society. As part of the author's therapy, the werewolves play with the idea of not fitting into society, and suggest a reason why certain individuals never quite seem to mesh with the rest. In the process, they provide a commentary on the science of psychoanalysis and, in so doing, bring the scientific to the legendary, or, to loosely borrow from Will Barbee, bring the new magic to the old. Thus, they create a link between the past and present. In Williamson's world building, the werewolves represent a link even further back to prehistory, connected to the modern world via myths, archaeology, and genetics. Finally, the werewolves are used to evoke pure fear and horror, a descent of man into darkness and inhumanity with an element of moral relativism. Even so, the undercurrent of self-discovery and, ultimate, acceptance of the shadow — or a Jungian failure as the shadow becomes dominant — direct the action of the narrative.

1. It's Only in Your Head

Sympathetic Devils

Williamson marks a point where the Ovidian werewolf—Lycaon—becomes cemented in the modern consciousness. The monstrous, cannibalistic figure known for bloodthirst and ferocity entered the literary and fictive realm of the modern era through nineteenth-century horror stories and the early days of film. As noted by Caroline Walker Bynum, "Ferocious, hairy, dripping with blood, a devourer of human beings, the werewolf of Pliny, Ovid, and Petronius is, like the werewolf of modern TV and folk story, an emblem of the periodic eruption of the bestial from within the human."[4] Williamson approaches this connection between his modern werewolves and the mythological with two allusions. First, he foreshadows heavily as Will Barbee first meets April Bell—his lead werewolf—and is reminded of Circe within minutes of their introductions. Throughout the course of the narrative, Bell nudges, cajoles, ridicules, and pushes Barbee into his changes of shape, filling Circe's role, although as a guide and teacher rather than punisher and executioner. Much later, Barbee and Bell invade the lab of their enemies (also Barbee's former friends) to find themselves confronted with a medieval tapestry depicting the Norse myth of the Fenris Wolf (a speaking, intelligent wolf, although not truly a werewolf). The presence of the partial tapestry underscores one of the novel's themes: that mythology conceals reality within its stories, but said stories are generally dismissed in the modern world.

While the Ovidian werewolf continues in *Darker*, Saint Augustine's discussion of lycanthropy has a greater influence. Augustine's *City of God* contains his arguments regarding the werewolf and other stories of shape-changing that were circulating in the fifth-century C.E. His theories and attempts to come to grips with the werewolf of legend shaped the thoughts of witch hunters and werewolf trial judges well into the seventeenth-century.[5] Perhaps the most important element of Augustine's theories was that only God can transform beings, any other transformation is, therefore, the work of demons and, thus, only illusion. Exactly how these illusions work, Augustine leaves open—this becomes the subject of much discussion in the early modern period. His work becomes the basis for the psychic projection werewolf, based on the "belief that the souls of certain individuals can leave their bodies in the shapes of beasts or birds, and that the body must not be moved during the soul's absence [which] is widely attested in

European folklore."[6] This belief forms Williamson's werewolves who go to sleep and send their "mind webs" out in the shape of various animals, usually wolves. While walking the town in his wolf shape, Barbee is completely invisible to police officers and drivers, thus establishing the wolf shape as a spirit or soul shape.[7]

As he attempts to deal with werewolf beliefs, Augustine delves into the definition of humanity. First, he states, "whoever is anywhere born a man, that is, a rational mortal animal, no matter what unusual appearance he presents in color, movement, sound, nor how peculiar he is in some power, part, or quality of his nature, no Christian can doubt that he springs from [Noah]."[8] Later, Augustine states that in the case of transformations, the "mind did not become bestial, but remained rational and human," therefore there was no real change.[9] He does note that this theory leaves room for the soul to leave the body while the body sleeps. This is characteristic of what Jeffry Massey calls Augustine's "thoughtful finagling, especially when the magic in question involved the transformation of human beings, who as creatures made in God's image, could not be changed essentially by any but God Himself."[10] On one hand, Williamson's werewolves appear to fit perfectly within the Augustinian definitions and place of shape-changers: they apparently cast their souls out into the world while their bodies sleep, they retain their faculties of speech and reason, they seem to remain mortal, and God is not involved (apparently), so their changes must be illusion and they must be human, by Augustine's definitions. However, April Bell, in her role as demon-guide, tells Barbee, "You're free tonight, and all your human inhibitions are left behind with your body on the bed."[11] In other words, she claims that something inherent in humanity, something that separates humans from other animals, is left behind when they change forms or cast their "souls" forth to use a more theological perspective. Thus, Williamson's werewolves are, perhaps, not human, even though they fit within the simplest definition Augustine creates.

Defining the differences between man and beasts is an important issue for both the medieval secular writers — Marie de France and the anonymous authors of *William of Palerne* and *Arthur and Gorlagon*—as well as the theological writers — such as Augustine and Gerald of Wales. If the boundary between man and animal is erased, as in the case of the werewolf, then man may appear to be ultimately irrational and immoral. This is also true for Williamson's exploration of the figure. Throughout the narrative, the question of humanity and inhumanity is central for Will Barbee as he is exposed to his inhuman abilities and nature. He arguably retains some measure of his humanity by refusing to kill Sam Quain, but this only occurs after he has been directly responsible for the deaths of two of his other friends and is involved in the murder of Rowena Mondrick, his former mentor's wife. The question is not only applied to Barbee himself, but to his associates, as April Bell is repeatedly described as "some wild creature, unfettered and shy"[12] or in other ways akin to a wild animal, even before Barbee or the reader knows that she can take an animal's form. As we see, Bell has already resolved this question for herself, she embraces her inhumanity. However, Barbee struggles with the social and ethical differences between "true humans" and *Homo lycanthropus*, as Quain calls the "lost" species. Throughout his changes, there is evidence of Barbee's growing inhumanity, such as when he and Bell run into Rowena's dog Turk while changed. Barbee notes that the dog's scent "steeled him with a racial hatred"[13] that is clearly not part of the "true human" psyche.

Part of the reason for Barbee's reaction is his shift toward a different genetic heritage. Like Bisclavret, Alphouns, and Gorlagon,[14] Barbee is, at least initially, a sympathetic figure. His descent into apparent madness via another's agency combines with the backstory that he was mysteriously dropped from Dr. Mondrick's cadre of close, trusted, students to evoke the audience's sympathy. Even after the first attempts on Sam Quain's and Rowena Mondrick's lives, the sympathy remains as both the reader and Barbee wonder if the attempts were merely part of a dream. However, by the end there is little room to see Barbee as a sympathetic werewolf. That said, like the sympathetic werewolves of the medieval secular tales, Barbee is a concealed nobleman (Bisclavret) or prince (Alphouns and Gorlagon). In this case, he is referred to as "a Black Messiah — the Child of Night,"[15] a savior of the concealed race once thought to have been exterminated by "true" humanity. Unlike his predecessors, Barbee does not necessarily represent the best of chivalry and nobility in his role as the concealed prince. Rather, he, in keeping with the paradoxical nature of the archetype, represents the demise of the social structure and the birth of a new society. The fact that the new society favors beings known to themselves as witches and known to "true" humans as monsters segues Will Barbee and April Bell into the early modern period's influence.

Monsters, Witches, and Werewolves

While the influence of the medieval period on Williamson's werewolves is minimal, in some cases even a bit of a stretch, the early modern views of the beings had a significant impact on his work. The influence is very likely indirect — through the early modern era's influence on eighteenth-century conceptions and early cinema — but is definitely present from Williamson's connection of his werewolves and madness to his concern with the mechanics of transformation. Even the focus on the monstrosity of the werewolf and its association with cannibalism, although rooted in the classical era, have their early modern alterations present in *Darker*.

A survey of, mostly Continental, early modern sources[16] shows a tendency to conflate the werewolf and witch during the period. Nearly all treatises on witchcraft have at least a few sentences on lycanthropy, arguing the relative status of werewolves and witches. As Jane Davidson notes, "[f]rom the late fifteenth through seventeenth centuries, witchcraft authorities debated whether witches could also be werewolves. Others thought witches transformed themselves into wolves, but did not become werewolves themselves."[17] Given that not all accused werewolves were also accused of being witches, the crucial point of definition was often whether the creature caused harm to humans. Williamson continues this hazy dividing line between the witch and the werewolf, perfectly in keeping with the blurring of divisions caused by the archetype. Early in the narrative, Bell identifies herself as a witch, a separate species from humanity, but interbred.[18] Shortly thereafter, she appears as a white "she-wolf" to guide Barbee through his first change.[19] She appears to have complete control of the situation, even when Barbee resists and attempts to ignore her while he adjusts to his changed shape. In this respect, Bell acts in the role of the demonic agent of change, in the early modern conception of the figure. Most early modern werewolf trials involve the accused werewolf being led into his (and they are almost always male) life as a werewolf by some other party, who typically introduces him to a demonic being that effects the change. In this case, Bell is both guide and demon as not only does she help Barbee change form, her "heirloom" — a white jade pin in the shape of a wolf — is used to help Barbee focus for his first change. However, Bell does eventually abandon Barbee, leaving his spirit to find his body alone. Upon rejoining with his body, Barbee believes the entire previous evening's actions to be but a dream. The latter is in keeping with the early modern tradition which held that all shape-changing must be illusory, as per Augustine. The Continental sources were split, though, between the "werewolf" being deceived into thinking he wore a wolf's shape and the "werewolf" being put to sleep by a demon that then wreaked havoc in a wolf's shape and somehow implanted the memories in the sleeping mortal (perhaps another example of "thoughtful finagling" in the Augustinian tradition).

The question of how demonic illusion was achieved spoke to a greater interest on the part of early modern writers in determining how shape-shifting might work. In part, this interest was a response to a desire for control, but it was also the result of the (re-)emerging sciences. As Norman Smith argues, the monster "then, though it differs from the normal, nevertheless conforms to natural and understandable laws."[20] Like his predecessors, Williamson seeks to codify exactly how his werewolves, his monsters, work and what rules they must abide by. There are two categories of laws for Williamson's creations: the change and vulnerabilities. Both are, of course, essentially elements of the world building that is necessary for any modern writer of fantasy, SF, or horror.

The basic elements of Barbee's and Bell's transformations seems to follow the theory presented by Simon Goulart (1607): "the soules taken out of the bodyes, enter into these fantasmes or visions, running with the shapes of Wolves: then when the worke enterprised by the Divell is finished, they returne into their bodyes which then recover life."[21] Initially, the first part, "the soules taken out of the bodyes," is difficult for Barbee but becomes progressively easier. At first, he describes the change as "[t]here was a curious, painful flux of his body — as if he had twisted into positions never assumed, had called on muscles never used. Sudden pain smothered him in darkness [...] And suddenly he was free. Those painful bonds, that he had worn a whole lifetime, were abruptly snapped."[22] His second change is easier, more fluid, and he actually sees his body left behind on the bed.[23] His third change is completely unconscious and involves no effort whatsoever; likewise, his return to his body is fast and easy.[24] The freedom he experiences with later, easier metamorphoses, however, does come with its restrictions.

While she is teaching Barbee to use his abilities, Bell states, "Ours is a precious and useful power, but it has its limitations and penalties attached. If you fail to regard them, you can very easily destroy yourself."[25]

One of the most important powers and limitations is that "[m]ost men can't see us [...] But dogs have a special sense for us and a special hatred. The savage man who domesticated the first dog must have been an enemy of our people."[26] Bell later explains the three greatest weaknesses of the werewolf-witches: silver, sunlight, and fire. She explains all three as vulnerabilities based on Heisenberg's uncertainty principle combined with theories of molecular vibration. According to her premise, sunlight's vibrations interfere with the spirit-soul's cohesion as does fire's. Likewise, silver, she claims, is deadly due to its vibrations. Thus, despite their great powers, Williamson's werewolves follow certain rules that limit their abilities. For similar reasons, their magical powers are limited to affecting chance — or probability — and causality. In addition to restricting the werewolves' abilities, the requirement that events have a certain probability of happening in order for their powers to work also affects Barbee's ability to accept what is happening. Because there is a good chance that his former mentor could have died from an allergic reaction and that his former friend could have driven off the road, Barbee has trouble determining whether they were murdered or simply died due to accidents of chance. If the latter is the case, he decides, then he is descending into madness.

This connection between mental illness and werewolves is one that stretches back at least to the sixteenth-century. Reginald Scot (*The Discoverie of Witchcraft*, 1584), King James I ("Men-Woolfes," 1597), John Deacon and John Walker (*Dialogicall Discourses of Spirits and Divels*, 1601), Robert Burton (*Diseases of the Mind*, 1621), Thomas Blount (*Glossographia*[27], 1661), and Robert Bayfield (Τῆς Ἰατρικῆς Καρπος or *A Treatise De Morborum Capitis Essentiis & Prognosticis*, 1663) argue that lycanthropy is a mental disease. This perspective is picked up by James I in his treatise on demonology as well as virtually every early modern English source. The view of lycanthropy as madness was so pervasive in England that it entered popular culture, as evidenced by Ferdinand in John Webster's *The Duchess of Malfi* (1614; V.ii.8–18). Invariably, these early modern sources attribute lycanthropy to melancholy. To quote Goulart, "there be Licanthropes in whom the melancholike humor doth so rule, as they imagine themselves to be transformed into Wolfes."[28] Will Barbee is clearly open to the potential for excessive melancholy as his former mentor cut him from the "inner circle" for unexplained reasons. Thus, Barbee settles for a reporter's position at a local paper while all of his friends join Mondrick

1. It's Only in Your Head

on archaeological digs around the world, including the extremely important dig in Mongolia that leads to the novel's plot. As noted, he sees the events around him as signs of his own madness, which leads to checking himself into a mental hospital. Rather than being treated at the hospital, his symptoms are enhanced by both the head psychoanalyst and April Bell. There are also, in this lycanthropy-as-madness line, some clear connections to Webster's Ferdinand both in Barbee's killing nearly every member of his makeshift family — Dr. Mondrick as father, Rowena Mondrick as mother, the rest as his siblings (only Sam and Nora Quain survive) — and his repressed interest in Sam Quain's wife — if we see her as a stand-in for Barbee's sister in this adoptive family (to parallel Ferdinand's desire for his sister).

Webster is not the sole direct connection between early modern views and Williamson. Barbee and Bell have the trial of Jean Grenier (1603) to thank for their animosity toward dogs, to some degree. According to a girl in a nearby village, Grenier said that "he had sold himself to the devil, and that he had acquired the power of ranging the country after dusk, and sometimes in broad day, in the form of a wolf [...] he had killed and devoured many dogs, but that he found their flesh less palatable than the flesh of little girls, which he regarded as a supreme delicacy."[29] Interestingly, like Barbee and Bell, Grenier worked after dusk — for the most part — and had a taste for attacking dogs. One can easily imagine Grenier attacking a canine exactly as Barbee is described assaulting the Quains' pet. Likewise, Bell was very willing to attack their young daughter, although she was restrained by Barbee who still retained a great deal of his humanity. Focusing the cannibalistic tendencies of werewolves on young girls will appear later with J.K. Rowling's Fenrir Greyback as well.

Barbee and Bell also share some of the traits that Henri Boguet (1590) identifies. Boguet argues, in favor of Kramer and Sprenger, that it is impossible for the body to survive without the soul. Thus, we return to Goulart's assertions as necessary to make the psychic werewolf work. However, Boguet also posits the theory that all werewolves eat men and share wounds between forms. The latter is important because it becomes the primary means of identifying werewolves in both trials and fiction for the next three or four centuries. Barbee shows evidence of Boguet's wound theory as he awakes from his first change — both the tooth he injured in wolf form by biting Rowena Mondrick's silver bracelet and the hand-paw that was scratched by the Quains' dog appear when he returns to his body as well.[30] Barbee, of course, dismisses the idea that they are the same wounds and invents what he considers to be logical reasons for both injuries. All of this occurs after his first change, but before his final transformation.

Barbee's final transformation is an important one in European folklore. According to some stories, mostly from Eastern Europe, that seem to have originated in the early modern period or slightly earlier, the vampire and werewolf become conflated. Some tales explain this conflation by saying that every vampire is a dead werewolf. The same idea is at work with Williamson's werewolves. Sam Quain explains to Barbee that *Homo lycanthropus* "had learned to like the taste of human blood, and they couldn't exist without it."[31] Admittedly, this statement alone does not indicate that the werewolves are also vampires, since cannibalism is closely linked to lycanthropy throughout history. However, the werewolf-witches are also described as having "delicate bones and pointed ears and long, rounded skulls ... and pointed, peculiar teeth."[32] The delicate bones would be less indicative of werewolves, even though the other traits are often shared by both creatures in folklore. After his death, though, Barbee survives and his ability to change becomes true shape-shifting as the "mind-web" is freed from the body permanently. Bell tells him, "You're a vampire now, and you might as well learn to like it."[33] She then notes that in this form, Barbee is practically immortal and invulnerable, except for sunlight and silver (and whatever nameless device Mondrick and Quain dug up in Mongolia). The link between werewolves and silver is obvious as it has become part of our common folklore, but dates to sometime after the early modern period. Sunlight, on the other hand, is more in line with our vampire lore. In some cases, the two join together in vampiric lore—e.g., in Charlaine Harris' Sookie Stackhouse series. Regardless, the two form a connection between the vampire and werewolf that hearkens back to early modern European folklore.

Archetype and Ancient Monsters

As with all literary werewolves, Williamson's work within the shape-shifter archetype. His wolves fill the archetype's role in producing fear and acceptance of the bestial, affinity with the shadow, crossing boundaries,

1. It's Only in Your Head

the paradox of stability via mutability, and an interest in rebirth. Because of the almost unique nature of *Darker*, Williamson adds a search for identity and role of the archetype in his own therapy to its more common uses.

Humanity's simultaneous fear of, and interest in, the bestial side of its nature comes to the forefront in Will Barbee. This is not surprising, as Edith Benkov has noted, "Part-man, part-beast, the dual nature of the werewolf epitomizes the dilemma of humankind."[34] This is indeed Barbee's problem, as humanity's representative. However, in the scenario Williamson creates, not only is the nature of humanity at question, but what parts of that nature are truly human. Because of the interbreeding between *Homo sapiens* and *Homo lycanthropus*, both Mondrick and Sam Quain use the latter's genetic influence as the source of everything negative in "human" nature. Quain argues, "We aren't all human — and that alien inheritance haunts our unconscious minds with dark conflicts and intolerable urges that Freud discovered and tried to explain."[35] He later adds that people in prisons and asylums are victims of this split heritage. Thus, humanity's bestial side is explained away as the result of a mingling of human and non-human lineages — all the negative aspects come from the non-human, presumably leaving the rare saint as a "pure" human, although Quain suggests that saints may be closer to the inhuman, due to their miracles. The bestial is therefore both feared and accepted, albeit grudgingly and as an alien intrusion.

Because he is fascinated with psychoanalysis, Williamson connects these "dark" impulses with Freudian theories. Quain claims that Freud recognized the problems, but could not account for them. However, we can argue that Freud's one time friend, Jung, accounted for such impulses. The werewolves in question, as at least partial representatives of an inhuman species, have a close affinity with Jung's shadow. When they are changed, they are free to undertake all sorts of socially transgressive behaviors, as is common with the shifter archetype. The first such behavior we see is wildness, exhibited by Barbee's sense of freedom from restraints during his first experience in animal form. In fact, the lure of the wild allows him to ignore April Bell's call and commands for some time. Once he responds, though, the pair fall into typically early modern werewolf behavior that also suits the shadow: true (often bestial) violence. The end result is an injured Mrs. Mondrick and two dead dogs — Mondrick's Turk and the Quains' Jiminy Cricket. The attack on Mrs. Mondrick represents not only bestial violence, but also a severing of Barbee's social bonds. Breaking the bonds of society is a common trait of the shadow, and is multilayered as Barbee helps to murder almost all of his friends. A lesser represented social behavior that is violated by the werewolf-witches is the nudity taboo, even more in force during the 1940s. This is only violated when April Bell takes her projected state while retaining her human shape. She appears naked as a psychic projection twice, the first time due to lingering weakness after the failed first attempt on Rowena Mondrick's life.

Crossing society's boundaries is perhaps the simplest and least concerning boundary breaking that Williamson's werewolf-witches do. Obviously, they cross the boundary between human and beast. They also straddle the boundary between the human and inhuman, or alien. As Williamson creates these werewolf-witches as a hybrid of two species, two races inimical to each other, they cross the gaps that separate species. These gaps are, perhaps, even more important today than they were in 1948. Given the rapid advancements in genetics, genetic engineering, and related fields, not to mention medical transplants, hybrid human-animals are increasingly common, from the man with a pig's heart to experiments with growing replacement human ears on lab mice. Moreover, the werewolf-witches move fluidly across the chasm that separates the present and the pre-historic past — over 100,000 years ago. This both becomes disturbing and interesting for the characters, and possibly the audience, as it questions established history and archaeology. It also presents a sort of historical and physical basis for Jung's theory of the collective unconscious, that place where archetypes develop and reside. Because, according to Jung, the collective unconscious is the source of all our culture-crossing myths, legends, and other tales, it can be a daunting concept to fully grasp, but Williamson provides an easier explanation via the concept of race memory as aided by myth and legend.

Williamson's modification of history and prehistory is a good example of the archetype's paradoxical ability to achieve stability through mutability. We commonly think of history as stable, unchanging. However, we also know that our understanding of history and archaeology are constantly changing and are moderately mutable as new discoveries are found that better hone or reshape our understanding of the past. On the fictional scale, the werewolf-witches become a conservative factor in the modern world. They use their powers of mutability in order to maintain the status quo, at least until such time as they feel they can openly overthrow "true" humans.

Mutability also connects the werewolf-witches to the concept of rebirth. On the broadest level, the werewolves herald a rebirth of legends and folklore in the modern world. More importantly for the plot, the werewolf-witches precede the rebirth of a species, one that will likely recreate its glory days, when it ruled over humanity's ancestors. At the smallest scale, we have Will Barbee's rebirth as a werewolf-witch, then his literal rebirth from death into what Bell calls a vampire.

Rebirth in literature, of course, can speak to figurative rebirth as well. In this case, both the writer's and reader's search for identity and the writer's individual therapy are important. Shape-shifting figures are excellent representations of the search for identity since they move through two or more physical forms. They become nebulous in terms of identity because of the change of outward appearance, that by which others come to immediate conclusions regarding the person. As in the cases of Bisclavret and Alphouns from the medieval period, a number of Williamson's characters have their true identities concealed beneath false outward appearances. The four notables here are Barbee, Bell, Dr. Glenn, and Rowena Mondrick, all of whom have significant amounts of the *Homo lycanthropus* lineage. Bell tells everyone that Glenn and Mondrick possess relatively strong lines, but the reader only sees Barbee and Bell change shape. Unlike Bisclavret and Alphouns whose concealed identities are hidden by the animal shape and used to reinforce the social structure, Barbee's and Bell's true identities are masked by their human appearance and used to undermine the "true" human social structure, in favor of their own ancestry. Dr. Glenn attempts to awaken Barbee's identity, just not in the way that Barbee expects — by pushing him to use his werewolf-witch abilities, rather than by making him a more "true" human. The struggle for identity, torn as it often is between fear and desire, directly reflects Williamson's own experiences with psychoanalysis, as more fully explored by Alan Elms.[36] Perhaps most importantly in his analysis, Elms concludes that Barbee displays Williamson's own "avoidant personality" and strikes against those who socially reject him. As shown in the previous section, this personality is, in Barbee's case, explainable as the result of melancholy, at least for early modern audiences.

Darker Wolves

Williamson, like his predecessors, employs the werewolf for numerous purposes and explores different mechanical aspects. He also creates his own unique take on the werewolf and shifter, adding elements that reflect his own society, history, and concerns. Perhaps the most important reflection is his focus on introducing scientific explanations for the werewolf—referencing Darwin, Heisenberg, and Freud primarily. Use of Heisenberg introduces the concept of uncertainty into Williamson's discussion of the archetype. Likewise, his inclusion of Freud opens up the questions of social acceptance and self-discovery, both of which can be linked to horror and fear.

The focus on scientific theories present in *Darker* makes sense when we look at both the theories Williamson uses and the socio-historical context of the book. Despite being formulated in the nineteenth century, Darwin's theories of natural selection only came into acceptance in the early-twentieth. This was also when Heisenberg's uncertainty principle was being developed (1920s) and Freud's psychoanalysis came into being (1917's *Introduction to Psychoanalysis* or *Vorlesungen zur Einführung in die Psychoanalyse*). All three were either new theories, just coming into their own, or both during the eight years from *Darker's* first version (1940) to its published form (1948).

Darwin's theory becomes useful for Williamson and starts to move the novel from the fantastic into the science fictional because Williamson can use natural selection as a plausible explanation for his werewolves. During an extended Platonic dialogue — in which Will Barbee acts akin to Plato's interlocutors, typically making noncommittal noises or asking for clarification — Sam Quain explains the prehistory of *Homo lycanthropus*.[37] Barbee, correctly, translates the name as man-werewolf; Quain, incorrectly, "corrects" him to translate the name as man-wolf, then adds that witch-man would be a better name. Regardless, Quain explains the species' existence as an ice age era evolution. He claims that, during an ice age, humanity had to adapt to survive and this created numerous offshoots of the species (and entirely new species). According to Quain's legends, the werewolf-witches "overran the world" some 400,000 years ago. They were then wiped out by "true" humanity that adapted, again using Darwinian natural selection and some unnatural selection based on Darwin,

1. It's Only in Your Head

and domesticated dogs to help them fight. However, the *Homo lycanthropus* species, Quain notes, survived through crossbreeding with "true" humans by passing on the recessive genes. Thus, there are a few in every generation who possess the werewolf-witch genes in sufficiently active quantity to use the abilities inherent in the species. Darwin's theory also informs the werewolf-witches' social structure, as Bell tells Barbee that he will rule them until a stronger one comes along; thus the strongest — the purest lineage — survives, rules, and passes on the most pure bloodline. The species takes knowledge made possible by Darwin's theory and uses it to selectively breed "throwbacks" among humanity in order to increase the chance of a purified bloodline. They do not leave all to chance, though. Because they can manipulate probability, the werewolf-witches use Heisenberg's theory to manipulate the genetic codes of the unborn to enhance the chances of a more genetically pure offspring.

The werewolf-witches' psychic projection is justified via Heisenberg's uncertainty principle, to some degree. Basically, Bell explains that they can pass through matter because of the gaps between atoms and the space between sub-atomic particles. Because, she argues (using Williamson's understanding of quantum physics), there is always uncertainty regarding either a particle's position or its momentum, one or the other is open to manipulation. The werewolf-witches therefore use probability, and the linkages that probability creates, to practice their "magic" (I place magic in quotes here because it is effectively advanced physics, rather than supernatural in origin). Bell further notes that all objects, all matter, all energy, produce vibrations — adding Nikola Tesla's work on vibrations to Heisenberg — and that the werewolf-witches can take advantage of such vibrations. However, in seeking a scientific rationale for his werewolves, Williamson adds that silver is deadly to them due to "the wrong vibration [...] the electronic vibrations of silver clash with ours."[38] Likewise, Bell explains that "fire is the last resort [...] because the vibrations are so deadly to us."[39] Here we see a new addition to the archetype as Williamson applies, in some cases new, scientific theories to his werewolves. Elms argues that part of Williamson's reasoning was to legitimize his writing to his therapist, but it is also likely that he was trying, as a science fiction author, to apply realistic laws to a fantastic, often psychological, entity.

Despite the pseudo-scientific rationale, *Darker's* werewolves are still psychological, psychoanalytic, entities. They are representatives of the shadow, for Jungians. They are a representation of the primal, the bestial. But, the shifters are also a scapegoat or release valve, as it were. The violent, bestial tendencies (murder, rape, cannibalism) are easily explained in the werewolf as the animal side ascendant, which the audience can then deny in itself. In Barbee's case, this is readily apparent. He is always in an animal shape when he commits his murders, not counting Rowena Mondrick's, in which he was technically a framed bystander. Because his acts of violence were always committed while wearing an animal's shape, he can and does brush them off as merely a dream when he returns to his human body. The mechanism of change, its method, reinforces the view that everything that happened was a dream — Barbee lies down, he goes to sleep, his spirit ("mind-web") leaves his body in animal shape, his spirit returns, he wakes up. Who is to say that Barbee is not simply dreaming? Once the corpses start piling up, even Barbee cannot explain them away as mere coincidence. Then, he has to face the shadow, face his bestial interior, and deal with it. Interestingly, even though he is confronting the Jungian shadow, Barbee does so through a Freudian therapist, Dr. Glenn. Elms has, through Williamson's own biography and admission, presented the evidence that Dr. Glenn was based on Williamson's own therapist, as a commentary on psychoanalysts in general.[40] What exactly the piece says about psychoanalysts is buried in Williamson's inclusion of Dr. Glenn in the worldwide conspiracy of werewolf-witches, for Glenn is himself one of them. Glenn, under the guise of treating Barbee, actually attempts to slowly bring Barbee's latent lineage to the fore and teach him to use his new abilities — in a sense, making Barbee's condition worse rather than better, since Barbee wants to become "normal."

As with any change, the ability to break — or the idea of breaking — the hierarchical boundaries of society evokes fear of the unknown, a fear that is inextricably tied to an innately human sense of wonder and curiosity regarding novelty. That fear, though, also creates and responds to uncertainty. For Williamson, and Barbee, the uncertainty goes beyond Heisenberg's quantum physics. Obviously that type of uncertainty is present, and exploited, as Bell states, "All our power lies in [the] control of probability, and we must strike where it will serve."[41] Probability, as discussed above, connects to the uncertainty in physics. Williamson's uncertainty, though, especially with his werewolves, also includes the question of what it means to be human and social uncertainty. Because the werewolves appear human, they could be anywhere and anyone. There are some continuances that show the line between werewolf and man, though. As S.J. Wiseman notes of the early modern period, Peeter Stubbe's trial shows that "the wolf shape compromises the human status of the shape changer so that only after his return to human form can he recognize and repent of the atrocities he committed."[42] Barbee demonstrates exactly this trait as he allows his humanity to slough off while in his beast shapes. Once he returns to his formerly sleeping body, remorse returns, reinforcing his humanity. Even so, he has to wonder, as does the reader, where the line between man and beast lies; especially after his human body is killed, leaving his "mind-web" to roam free with no actual return to human form. He can take the shape of a human, but the fact that his human body is gone permanently places Barbee in an inhuman state. The fact that Barbee, and others, have a certain amount of non-human genetic lineage also adds uncertainty, as one asks exactly how much of so-called "human nature" really is human and how much comes from this other species. Moreover, because his were-wolf-witches effectively control society, from the shadows and indirectly, there is nothing that Williamson's characters can rely upon. Mondrick and his students find they cannot tell anyone about their discovery without risking assassination. Barbee learns that even the place that seems to offer succor from what he thinks is his descent into madness and alcoholism — the Glennhaven psychiatric hospital — is, in fact, run by one of the were-wolf-witches.

Social uncertainty leads to the question of fitting in, socially. In fact, one might ask if one even wants to be socially accepted. The werewolf represents a failure of society in some fashion. As Leonard Barkan argues, "Metamorphosis is an outward sign that the ties that bind [society and individuals] have been loosed."[43] The most obvious "loosening" of social bonds comes in the division between Barbee and his former friends, and the fact that he kills or is complicit in killing, all but one of them. If we consider Elms' and Williamson's argument that *Darker* is about Williamson's experience with psychoanalysis, then we have to consider Williamson's problems fitting into society, or at least his perception that he did not fit in. Perhaps the clearest sign that his werewolves do not fit in is the reaction of dogs. Williamson demonstrates, several times, that dogs can detect and hate his werewolves. First, there is Rowena's dog Turk who practically attacks Bell.[44] This is followed by several minor instances of unhappy dogs, culminating in all the farm dogs around Glennhaven reacting to Bell's changed presence. Acceptance by society's pets, specifically dogs, is a key symbol. After all, since their early domestication, canines have often been referred to as man's best friend. If the dog hates someone, then there is probably a reason why, something that sets the person apart from the rest of society. In Barbee's case, their reaction is to his "true" species which is tied to his ultimately following the "Child of Night"—a Satan-like figure that evokes the early modern werewolf trials in which Satan or one of his representatives meets with the prospective werewolf and gives him a device to cause the change, usually an unguent or paste; in Barbee's case this device is Bell's wolf pin that acts as a catalyst. The werewolf-witches, further, provide a reason that some people feel they do not fit in society. According to Williamson's legend building, those people generally have a high percentage of active *Homo lycanthropus* genes that the rest of humanity unconsciously responds to. In addition to providing a reason for social misfits, the mingling of genes also presents a reason for all the ills of humanity and absolves humanity in the process.

This absolution via inhuman genetic lineage, however, does not help the subject deal with the issue, at least in Jungian terms. The subject must confront the shadow through an often fear inducing process of self-discovery in order to come to terms with the bestial. Or, as David Gilmore suggests, the "mixture of human and animal is a direct consequence of a profound ambivalence shared by all people: a simultaneous terror and fascination with the beast within, the impulsive need to both deny and acknowledge that, no matter how exalted, we humans are members of the animal kingdom and heir to violent instincts."[45] The werewolf allows both sides of this terrifying fascination to be explored. In Williamson's case, the werewolves provide a scapegoat for the more animalistic attributes of humanity. Quain tries to deny the bestial shadow side of human nature, claiming that violent instincts come from the *Homo lycanthropus* genes, and he ultimately fails in his goal to fight against the shadow's representatives. Barbee, on the other hand, clearly fears his animalistic urges, but also acknowledges them. However, he too fails because he embraces the shadow, letting it take control. Neither Quain nor Barbee manage to successfully complete their self-discovery. Rather, Barbee's eventual acquiescence to the werewolf-witch genes "represents an unleashing of, or a capitulation to, those powerful non-rational forces which can impel a man to violent and cruel acts that transgress against accepted norms of civilized behavior."[46] We see the shadow ascendant in Barbee during his first change, he explains that "[n]o longer was he imprisoned, as he had always been, in that slow, clumsy, insensitive bipedal body. His old human form seemed utterly foreign to him now, and somehow monstrous."[47] Although this passage focuses on Barbee's physical change, he undergoes a simultaneous psychological change that the physical reflects, with the trappings of society, the social bonds, being sloughed off.

The werewolves' changes are not only a reflection of the struggle within humanity. Williamson's werewolves are also very much present for the horror and fear factor. Clearly Barbee views his actions in animal shape with horror when he resumes his human form, as previously discussed. But, the fear goes beyond the personal. His actions with Bell, a sort of shadow war, are at their heart acts of terror — or a guerrilla war, if one takes the *Homo lycanthropus* side. They murder those who would expose them in part to keep their secret and in part to warn off any other "true" humans who might acquire enough information. Their tactics are typically wolfish — separating individuals from the herd — and are designed to evoke fear in their targets. Of course, the threats fail in this case, or there would be no plot. Had Dr. Mondrick heeded the warning sent via the attack upon his wife that left her blind, there would be no story. Had Quain and Spivak heeded the warning that was Mondrick's murder, there would be no story. Even so, all three fear for their lives, but this fear galvanizes their resolve to see things through. Here we can see Williamson's werewolves demonstrating to the audience that fear can be a good thing, it can be a powerful motivating force. Alternately, they show that an emotion most see as negative, or a drawback, can be turned around and used for positive motivation. We will see something similar with J.K. Rowling's Remus Lupin later.

From Terror to Law

In *Darker Than You Think*, Jack Williamson presents Will Barbee and his internal narrative to the audience. Barbee is one of the early self-reflective werewolves, that is werewolves given to introspection and internal thought in both shapes. Despite the third person narrator, Barbee effectively narrates his own story, unlike the medieval or early modern werewolves. In this respect, he is a predecessor of Terry Pratchett's Constable Angua who takes the self-reflection a step further, as will be discussed in the following chapter. However, while Barbee, at least in theory, exists to subjugate humanity, Angua rejects the superiority of werewolves over humans. Both, though, serve to reinforce the status quo, Barbee through transgressive acts that keep werewolves concealed and Angua through upholding the law of the land.

Even with his modern conception — and Barbee cannot exist in a pre–Freudian world — Williamson still presents werewolves with clear and strong early modern roots in monstrosity and psychology. Like many early modern writers, he emphasizes the mechanics of change using the science of his day to justify his werewolves' abilities. For his part, Pratchett takes this interest in mechanics, but turns from the scientific explanation to folklore. Pratchett also removes most of the early modern and early film influence to bring the werewolf back to its medieval and classical roots, updated for the modern world.

2

The Disc's K-9 Unit

Pratchett's Werewolves

Throughout his writing career, Terry Pratchett has continuously used his novels to argue in favor of the power of stories, the literary venue for archetypes. From a witch/fairy godmother's attempt to make the world fit fairy tales (*Witches Abroad*) to the importance of telling a story at the right time (*Thud!*),[1] this firm belief has lurked, sometimes more blatantly than others, beneath the surface humor and satire in all of his novels. Approaching the entire corpus of Pratchett's Discworld work — currently including thirty-nine novels, fourteen printed theater adaptations, four collections of maps, seven short stories, twenty miscellaneous works, and three novels rumored to be in production[2] — is a daunting task. Even attempting to summarize the body of his work is a task best left to its own book. Surprisingly, save for the work of a few individuals (notably Andrew Butler and Andy Sawyer), Pratchett has not generated as much scholarly commentary as his significant and complex corpus might be expected to stimulate. His subject matter ranges through pieces written for young adults and adults to his relatively recent Discworld books for a younger audience — *Where's My Cow?*, *The World of Poo*, *The Amazing Maurice and His Educated Rodents* and the Tiffany Aching series. The range of his work includes such issues as gender equality (*Equal Rites*), the power and artificiality of fairy tales (*Witches Abroad*), religion and faith (*Small Gods*), jingoism and national fervor (the aptly named *Jingo*), the benefits and drawbacks of the Internet (*The Fifth Elephant* and later Ankh-Morpork focused books), the power and danger of a free press (*The Truth*), the role and power of music and celebrity (*Soul Music*), and racism and ethnic cleansing (*Thud!*). Along the way, Pratchett not only references a great store of archetypes, myths, legends, and folklore, but also pays homage to various literary notables and pop culture celebrities. Among these individuals and works are Shakespeare's *Macbeth* (*The Light Fantastic*), *Phantom of the Opera* (*Masquerade*), *Doctor Faustus* (*Eric*), Robert E. Howard's Conan (*Interesting Times* and *The Last Hero*), the Mad Max movie series (*The Last Continent*), and even Ian Fleming and Neil Gaiman (through Messers Pin and Tulip in *The Truth*).[3] Of this impressive corpus of work, two novels stand out for their portrayal of the werewolf archetype: *The Fifth Elephant* and *Thud!*

The links of influence between this popular writer of fantastic fiction and the tradition described in the introduction is not necessarily a scholarly, or documented, set of explicit references but rather the conscious development of "timing" in his storytelling. Pratchett employs this "timing" to subtly reintroduce old tropes into new stories. Each traditional trope and archetype appears in a new story that reflects major issues or cultural trends that are occurring in our own world. Further, in evoking traditional literature, legend, folklore, and popular culture, he taps into the influence and power that he sees in stories as well as the collective unconscious. Thus, we should not be surprised to find that Pratchett introduces werewolves and other manifestations of the shape-shifter archetype into the Disc. As Caroline Walker Bynum states about the medieval period, shape-shifting is about process and story.[4] Because of this role, Pratchett's werewolves naturally undergo a continual metamorphosis from their first appearance to subsequent ones and they appropriate medieval and early modern traditions in an effort to re-fashion the werewolf archetype to "speak" to modern readers. After all, Pratchett is a self-described "vast consumer of folklore"[5] who sets his stories in "the largely imaginary world of Discworld."[6] In this case, he uses the phrase "largely imaginary" because so much of the fictional world is drawn from everyday Earth.[7]

His werewolves are no exception, nor is it surprising that werewolves provide a focus for some of his satirical novels. As Jeffrey Jerome Cohen noted in his study of monsters, "The co-option of the monster into a symbol of the desirable is often accomplished through the neutralization of potentially threatening aspects with a liberal dose of comedy."[8] In the case of his werewolves, Pratchett neutralizes their threats by reminding the reader that the differences between wolves and dogs are minimal, especially throughout both *The Fifth Elephant* and *Thud!*

This same comedy is employed so that, as Amanda Cockrell contends, "we don't notice what serious stuff he is talking about until it's at our throats,"[9] namely Pratchett's discussions of, and commentaries on, racism, nationalism, religious fundamentalism, and the continuous technological revolution. The last of these four is the most important in that the technological revolution is not only daunting in and of itself but it is also a symptom of another of Pratchett's continual themes: the inevitability of change. This idea that change is both unavoidable and constant becomes a problematic topic due to its implication that stability and rest are impossible. Within this tension between constant change and the desire for stability is Pratchett's comic tone in the form of the werewolf, a figure that itself struggles with the same tension. To cope with the problems inherent in both theme and figure, Pratchett introduces comic moments as his characters attempt to do "the best [they] can in a labyrinth of mirrors."[10] At the same time, this comic tone allows Pratchett to conduct socially relevant discussions in a non-threatening fashion, much as Samuel R. Delany did in the 1960s.[11] In other words, the comedy attempts to address the tension between the old and the new in a disarming manner.

Specifically dealing with werewolves, Pratchett draws from such "serious" material as Marie de France, Albert the Great, and *William of Palerne*. In an inversion of Marie de France's *lai*, Pratchett presents the exception to the rule first — the sympathetic werewolf—then introduces the ferocious part of the population, as I demonstrate below. However, this apparent inversion, seen in a cultural context, is not truly an inversion since Pratchett's readers are already familiar with both the *garvulf*[12] and the *bisclavret*.[13] Because the former is more readily apparent in folklore and film, Sergeant Angua is introduced as the exception to the cultural rule and Marie's order of introduction remains intact. Pratchett also consciously draws upon Gerald of Wales to provide subtle hints and clues, as discussed later in this chapter. He adapts medieval criteria for bestiality versus humanity. For the most part, save in Angua's brother Wolfgang, he bypasses early modern traditions in favor of blending the medieval literary and early-twentieth century film traditions that better inform his storytelling and modern reactions to the archetype. Moreover, his werewolves are clear manifestations of the shape-shifter archetype as it evolves through the twentieth and into the twenty-first centuries. As part of this evolution, Pratchett uses his werewolves primarily to discuss racism and ethnic animosity, the nature-versus-nurture debate, and social building. He does this through Angua, an expansion of the figure not only as a female police officer (although she is a noblewoman), but also as a self-reflective werewolf—a figure that is unique to the modern, post–Freudian/Jungian era—and her family.

Bisclavret's Influence

Two Discworld books that focus on the werewolves are *The Fifth Elephant* (*Elephant*) and *Thud!* Of the two, *Elephant* presents the most involved and detailed look at werewolves through Sergeant Angua and her family, the von Überwalds. *Elephant* is also Pratchett's most obvious employment of classical and medieval elements such as losing clothing, breaking social structures and associations with cannibalism, transforming off-screen, and interrogating the medieval criteria for humanity.

Like Petronius' and Marie de France's, Pratchett's werewolves lose their clothing when they transform. Most presumably remove whatever they are wearing before changing forms, but this is never explicitly stated. Unlike what we find from classical and medieval sources, Pratchett's werewolves think about this necessity and form different opinions of it, which fall along gender-based lines. Sergeant Angua and her mother, Serafine, embrace clothing—the one as uniform, the other as finery, both as a sign of humanity and civilization. In fact, when she is wolf shaped, Angua "kept clenched in her jaws the little leather bag that was a friend to any thinking werewolf, such a creature being defined as one who remembers that your clothes don't magically follow you."[14] This bag contains a lightweight change of clothes and a bottle of mouthwash. Her father—Guye Ruston von Überwald, more commonly called "the Baron"—and brother—Wolfgang (Wolf)—eschew clothing when possible. The Baron rarely wears more than a tattered dressing gown and always appears uncomfortable in any clothing. But he also spends most of his time "changed" into wolf shape. Wolfgang, at least around the family castle, wears nothing, claiming that nudity represents purity, thus clothing is unhealthy.[15] For Wolfgang, the animal side is stronger and better than the civilized. Indeed, he uses the word "civilized" in many variations as a sneering insult. His one concession is that he dons a military-style uniform for official functions outside the castle.

This mix of militarism and savagery is representative of Wolfgang's roots in the classical and medieval traditions not due to the discussion of clothing, or the connection to Petronius' soldier-werewolf, but also through cannibalism.[16] There are a number of moments in *Elephant* where Pratchett implies that Wolfgang and his pack engage in cannibalism. Only once is this explicitly stated, the other moments all involve allusions to what happens when someone loses "the Game"—an event in which a pack of Überwald's werewolves choose a victim and chase him or her through the woods. The clearest statement of what happens to losers comes from Wolfgang, who says that the question of monetary reward does not occur if the victim fails to outrun the pack.[17] The obvious implication is that losers are eaten by the pack, supported by Captain Carrot who tells Angua, "If he *lost*, then your father had him for dinner out in the woods."[18]

The combination of militarism and wildness also ties Wolfgang to Marie de France's fables, especially since he is a member of the nobility. Here, Wolf is a reflection of Marie's use of wolves as representatives of nobility gone awry. Like these fable wolves, Wolfgang works with his pack of werewolf relatives to bring down the existing social structure in Bonk[19]— a three way balance—swinging it in his own favor. Although there is no central authority figure, such as a king, for Wolf to oppose, the balance of power itself acts as an authoritarian status quo that can be fought against. His sister, Angua, on the other hand, acts as an agent of the law with her own mismatched, heterogeneous pack to uphold the social balance and the existing structure of power. What is telling here is that Wolfgang's associates are a homogenous group. Not only are they all werewolves, but they are also all relatives—Angua names a sampling: Uncle Ulf, Aunt Hilda, Nancy, and Unity. They are all representatives of the rising power, the single species rebels who wish to take over. Angua's "pack" is a more diverse collection of individuals—a dwarf (Constable Littlebottom), a troll (Constable Detritus), and several humans—who represent a cross-section of the species living in Bonk and Überwald in general. The only Überwaldian species not represented in this makeshift pack are the vampires, none of whom join the Watch until *Thud!*, and the Igors, who join the watch soon after *Elephant*. This is important in that Wolfgang's pack is homogenous (both in terms of species and their origin the same family) while Angua's is heterogenous, drawing from numerous cultures and species.

Pratchett's portrayal of the werewolves also bears some resemblance to Albert the Great's discussion of wolves although the religious concepts attached to werewolves do not appear in his work. Both through Angua (the *bisclavret*) and Wolfgang (the *gar vulf*), they are shown to be fierce, cunning, crafty, and social. These qualities appear during the two Games that are shown in the narrative, the first involving Mister Sleeps the initial ambassador, the second involving Commander-Duke Vimes, Angua's boss. Their social nature continuously comes to the forefront as well, sometimes more subtly than others. Wolfgang's socialization is rather blatant in that he only appears in the company of others — his family, his pack, or social events; in contrast, Angua's socialization is a little less obvious, although still noticeable. When she travels from Ankh-Morpork to Bonk, in wolf shape, she does so with a variety of wolf packs, but this is only a temporary arrangement. For long term sociability, we need to look at the fact that Angua attaches herself to a close knit sub-community, the Watch. In both *Elephant* and *Thud!*, she is constantly surrounded by fellow watchmen, and usually the same core group: Fred Colon, Nobby Nobbs, Vimes, Captain Carrot, Cheery Littlebottom, Detritus, and (later) the vampire Sally.

Initially we might suggest that many of these connections and those that follow could be subconscious or inadvertent. However, Pratchett hints that he knows what he is doing in *Elephant*. In a brief moment in which none of the werewolves are present, nor any discussion of them occurs, Constable Visit-The-Infidel-With-Explanatory-Pamphlets takes a moment to quote a prophet Ossory,[20] named for the Irish kingdom that was home to Gerald of Wales' werewolves.[21] Taking this subtle clue, present in a narrative focused on werewolves, and adding Pratchett's clear understanding of folklore, it is a reasonable assumption that any connections between his werewolves and earlier conceptions of them occur consciously.

While the actual allusions to medieval writers in Pratchett's work are interesting, the narrative devices that he chooses to use are of greater interest and importance regarding his werewolves. Pratchett deploys two major medieval narrative devices regarding the shape-shifter archetype: off-screen transformations and their appearance during times of transition.

Like Bisclavret, Alphouns, and Gorlagon, Pratchett's werewolves change shape "off-screen." Even though this is not always literally true, since they sometimes shift forms where others can see them, they are effectively off-screen because the other characters rarely watch. Even when Pratchett chooses to have a character change on-screen, as it were, he uses vague language to describe the transformation, unlike late-twentieth cen-

2. The Disc's K-9 Unit

tury film and horror fiction. There are only eight points where Pratchett mentions a werewolf changing shape in *Elephant* and only one in *Thud!* The first of these occurs when Seraphine von Überwald tells her husband to Change when he comes inside, at which point, "the wolf gave her a look, and strolled behind a massive oak screen at the far end of the room. There was a ... noise, soft and rather strange, not so much an actual *sound* as a change in the texture of the air."[22] The baron steps out from behind the screen a short time later. The second involves Angua and a wolf friend of whom is said that when she returned later, "Angua was human again — at least, Gaspode corrected himself, human *shaped*."[23] A while later, traveling with the wolves and Carrot, she returned to the pack, still fixing her shirt after changing shape again off-screen.[24] All three of these incidents fit within the medieval tradition, as represented by Marie de France, *William of Palerne*, and *Arthur and Gorlagon*.

The other five do not fit in so neatly, but are still effectively out of sight. The first of these occurs when Wolfgang and his pack are chasing Vimes during the Game. After running for a time, the wolves catch up with Vimes. In order to taunt him, "Wolf took a deep breath. The other werewolves, sensing what was going to happen, looked away. There was a moment of struggling shapelessness, and then he was rising slowly on two feet."[25] In this case, it is the other werewolves who either do not want to see the moment of transition or have some respect for privacy. Vimes watches, but he does not relate any notable details, rather leaving the process to the audience's imagination. He has another chance to describe the change when he is attempting to drown a member of the pack. At that point, "it *Changed* ... It was as if the wolf shape became small and a man shape became bigger, in the same space, at the same time, with a moment of horrible distortion as the two forms passed through one another."[26] This is the clearest description of the lycanthropic transformation that Pratchett ever presents. While he refuses to provide as much detail as many horror writers, in some ways the vague descriptions are more horrifying and effective because they leave room for the reader to apply his or her imagination to the process. This is the climax of Pratchett's description of the transformation. From that point forward, his descriptions become highly vague again, such as "there was a sudden moment of morphological inexactitude,"[27] "in midair he changed into a wolf" (and back again),[28] and "When werewolf fights werewolf, there are advantages to either shape.

It's an eternal struggle to get a position where hands beat claws [...] The mind has to fight its own body for control and the other body for survival."[29] In *Thud!* the only transformation is simply described as "She went back to human to get down; claws were fine, but some things were better done by monkeys."[30] During this scene, Angua is alone with no witnesses to her transformation; when she shifts again in this scene, the vampire Sally is present but is not noted as watching.

As with the medieval sources they reflect, the description of these transformations can remain nebulous because the transformation itself is not what is important to the character, the author, or the audience. The fact that the character *can* transform is what is important. It is this ability, not how it looks when it is used, that calls up the questions regarding transition, humanity, and identity that are so central to werewolves in particular and the shape-shifter archetype in general. The specifics of the transformation might be important to a writer in the horror genre, but even then leaving the appearance vague, as most of the descriptions in *Elephant* are, can produce the desired effect much better than a fully detailed gory description.

On a related issue, Pratchett's werewolves, like their medieval ancestors, appear at times of transition and change. Just as Marie's and Gerald's appeared and became popular during a time of social change,[31] the characters in *Elephant* herald a significant social transition. They also appear on the cusp of a major technological transition, the introduction of the clacks — a semaphore tower system that mimics the telephone or internet — to Überwald. This technological innovation brings about obvious social and economic changes as information passes from one end of the continent to the other within a day, linking solitary and insular Überwald to the rest of the world. At the same time, a moderately progressive dwarf king is elected, causing another social shift that more conservative elements in that society oppose, by working in league with Wolfgang.

Likewise, as *William of Palerne* and *Arthur and Gorlagon* became popular in the fourteenth century, a time of considerable social, economic, and theological change wrought by the Black Death,[32] the characters in *Thud!* are involved in a highly significant social and quasi-theological transition that reflects similar changes in our own world (as will be discussed later). In this case, the shifter archetype appears to help bring about peace and social understanding between the Discworld's dwarfs and trolls, who had been at war since the dawn of both races. This transition involves the message of the dwarf "god" Tak (but dwarfs are not religious) and the dying words of the hero/semi-divine B'hrian Bloodaxe as well as one of the quasi-god-kings of the trolls (this one is named Diamond; the current one, who is active in the narrative, is Mr. Shine), all of whom call for peace and understanding between the two races. The game for which the novel is named serves here as a shared middle ground, safe territory in which the two races can meet, talk, and socialize. For both races the transition is one of borderline religious significance, revising creation stories that dwarves and trolls held with religious reverence, not unlike the evolution-creation debate that forms an issue in our own society. In the case of the events in *Thud!*, the debate centers on history versus religion, much as the science versus religion debate in our own culture involves history, or rather pre-history. This connection is tied strongly to Pratchett's discussion of timing and story. In this way, unlike the fourteenth century's introduction to the Reformation, Pratchett's key werewolf helps to usher in a religious and social reunion rather than being a sign of difference and monstrosity.

As with any socio-theological changes, questions of identity arise for those whom the transition affects and thus cause the archetype to manifest. One of the key elements of identity is the cultural definition of humanity. When we look back to medieval definitions of humanity, we find the four criteria identified by John Block Friedman as used by teratologists in the later part of Middle Ages: clothing, diet, speech, and choice of weapon(s), sometimes adding reason. If we apply these criteria to Pratchett's werewolves, the sample characters rest on both sides of the human-animal divide. As discussed above, the werewolves' views regarding clothing are varied — for the Baron they are an unwanted necessity; for Wolfgang they are a sign of weakness; for Seraphine clothing is a sign of respectability, self-fashioning, and means of hiding the wolf; and for Angua the Watch uniform is a means of controlling the beast within through self-fashioning. Diet also produces mixed results — the Baron and Wolfgang occasionally eat people; Angua not only never eats people but pays for the chickens she otherwise steals in the city; and the reader is left with little knowledge of what Seraphine eats. There are implications that the baroness hunts and eats raw game, though, since Lady Sybil (Vimes' wife) thinks that the food tasted like the cook had never even attempted cooking before, as Sybil unsuccessfully has, and that "she'd seen the kitchens, when Serafine had given her the little tour, and they'd just about do for a cottage."[33] In these ways, and those that follow, we see most of Pratchett's werewolves unleashing or capitulating to the non-rational forces that a medieval audience assumed direct a beast's actions. Meanwhile, Angua resists these influences to the best of her ability, even to the point of resisting them for others near the end of *Thud!* where she prevents Vimes from acting upon such urges.

Speech is a clearer indicator in that all of the werewolves do possess the ability to speak, after a fashion, while in their wolf shape. They also prove to have the ability to speak to wolves while in their human shape. This faculty is most clearly shown when Angua, in wolf shape, claims Carrot to save him from the wolf pack she travels with, growling *"Hmine"* to indicate that the vocalizing wolf was her, and to note her non-wolfish nature.[34] She and her mother perform similar speech actions elsewhere as well. Even this fairly clear indicator of humanity is only a single step forward, and not a very large one. The human-animal question, for a medieval audience, becomes problematized when we address the question of choice of weapon(s) and use of tools. Angua, as a member of the Ankh-Morpork Watch, automatically straddles the border even before taking her species into account. Going back to Friedman's argument regarding humanity, all members of the Watch carry the sword that ties them to the upper classes, the civilized people. But they also, because of their job, carry a truncheon or club, placing them in the non-human or sub-human strata of the medieval socio-biological hierarchy. This puts the Watch in the middle ground occupied by the shifter archetype, and provides one reason for Angua's presence among them. She becomes a representative of the borderline place the Watch occupies regardless of the species of individual members. Vimes places the werewolves squarely in the non-human category, though, when he considers Wolfgang and his pack. He explains to himself that werewolves did not use weapons. He recalls that, despite her socialization, Angua paused before reaching for her sword. Vimes concludes that a manmade weapon would never be the first choice for a werewolf.[35] Of course, since he immediately gets involved in an unarmed fight with a werewolf, his own position on the scale is also questionable at that point.

All of these criteria for humanity versus bestiality return to the core question of identity. As Bynum says of medieval werewolf tales, "Behind these fantastic stories lie probing, parody, and evocation of that glorious, inexplicable, and (to postmodern eyes) totally improbable thing: identity"[36] whether the identity question involves the mind-body, inner-outer, or biological-social. In the case of Pratchett's archetypal werewolves, we see this crisis of identity most clearly in the character of Sergeant Angua. Since she is a self-reflective werewolf, she provides a unique perspective in both *Elephant* and *Thud!* The identity crisis is non-existent for the male members of the family, as evidenced in *Elephant*. Angua's brother embraces both morphological sides of his being, although he sometimes has trouble deciding which form is appropriate. He breaks the human-animal binary by accepting himself as the hybrid werewolf. Their father, on the other hand, largely embraces the wolf while their mother appears to accept the wolf so long as it remains controlled by the trappings of human civilization, in other words, a dog. We may initially think that Seraphine then has come to terms with her shadow and exerted control over it. But, she has not done so: she merely hides the shadow because she has not undertaken the psychological search or meditation necessary to truly reconcile the shadow.

Angua, contrary to the other werewolves, appears constantly struggling with the human-beast identity problem. She wrestles with her shadow in an honest attempt to tame it. This occurs in large part because Angua has left the society that the rest of her family inhabits. In effect, she resembles Gerald's werewolves, if he had met them in London instead of the Irish wilderness. She becomes the civilized, tamed werewolf that, unlike Gerald's, works to reinforce the status quo (even as she, by her species nature, breaks down an important wall) instead of introducing unsettling doctrinal questions. Rather than remaining at home where werewolves are a fact of life and expected to act in certain ways, she went to the big city and experienced a different way of looking at things.[37] During her travel from Bonk to Ankh-Morpork and back, she was required to travel through wolf territories, which enhanced a certain sense of understanding of her borderline place, as she tells Carrot, that humans hate the wolf part of werewolves (as monsters due to false or exaggerated stereotypes) while wolves hate the human that drives the wolf-formed werewolf (presumably due to its extra viciousness).[38] For Angua, the problem of identity is compounded with the fact that Pratchett never lets the reader forget that there is only a marginal difference between wolves and domestic dogs. For the moment, it suffices to say that in general Angua plays the part of the loyal dog, in much the same way as Bisclavret, Alphouns, and Gorlagon relate to their chosen humans — king, William, and brother-king respectively, which is especially apt as Carrot may be the rightful king of Ankh-Morpork.

Discworld's Renaissance

The influence of early modern views regarding werewolves on Pratchett's work is minimal. He does not connect his werewolves to his witches indeed they have separate story arcs that have not yet intersected in any significant way. Nor does he connect his werewolves to madness, at least not in the way that early modern demonologists did, since his werewolves actually change form rather than simply believing that they do. On the other hand, Wolfgang and the Baron certainly have their own sort of madness, but this has no notable effect on their status as werewolves.

That said, his werewolves do have a few similarities with early modern conceptions of the werewolf and monster. The von Überwalds are connected to the author's and audience's interest in beginnings, change, and creation. Most of these beginnings and acts of creation are involved with social and technological change. In another connection, while the religious element leaves along with the ties to witchcraft, like the early modern werewolf, Pratchett's are generally considered monsters, at least outside the cosmopolitan cities such as Ankh-Morpork. There they become mere curiosities, or useful tools and friends as in Angua's case. This attitude ties Ankh-Morpork even closer to London given Anglo-Scottish academic approaches to lycanthropy during the early modern period. Likewise, according to Pratchett as in all the classical to early modern sources, a werewolf's bite does not transmit werewolfism on the Discworld. While they differ as to the causes of lycanthropy — madness or consorting with demons versus genetics — they do agree on that point. Pratchett, at least in *Elephant*, is also interested in describing the mechanics of his werewolves, or the rules that govern their existence and behavior, just as many early modern demonologists were obsessed with the mechanics of lycanthropy in their own era.

Of the four major werewolves that Pratchett presents, Wolfgang is the closest to the early modern Continental version. He even has some ties with the moralized uses to which English authors put the werewolves of their own era in that he provides a threat within society which acts as a rallying point for otherwise disparate segments of the nation. That is, Wolfgang functions to threaten the social and political body through his half-baked plots, due in part to his position as the baron's son and the fact that his plots, if successful, would drastically shift the balance of political power in his homeland. *Elephant* focuses on Wolfgang's transgressions of the rules and mores of society. Angua appears for balance, another werewolf acting as a representative of law and order (along with Vimes) to uphold both the rules and society as a whole. In this way Wolfgang functions in the same way as Webster's Ferdinand in that he becomes a metaphor for social ills (inbreeding of the aristocracy), loss of values (Angua tells Carrot that her father played the Game by the rules while Wolfgang does not), and social depravation or degeneration.

There are an equal number of aspects that work against the early modern concepts beyond those already noted. For instance, Pratchett's werewolves do not require any external tools to change their shape. The fact that they are forced to change within a few days to either side of a full moon is the trade off, either Pratchett knows Gervase of Tilbury's theory or he drew that aspect from later cinematic sources. Unlike the early modern sources, Wolfgang needs to be in his wolf shape for his execution. Were he not in that shape, the execution would take a different and perhaps much less effective form. Because of this, Wolfgang loses his chance to recognize his transgression and repent, even though Vimes very vocally goes through the arrest procedure. Finally, unlike Boguet and other early modern sources, only in a few cases are there outward signs by which a human can detect a Discworld werewolf.[39] As Angua says, because wolves have a foolproof sense of smell, especially compared to that of humans, "I can pass for human, but I can't pass for wolf."[40] This ability to pass, to pretend to be human or "normal," is one point where we see the modern threat and edge of fear that the werewolf evokes in some modern audiences as well as the negative effect of self-fashioning by which the monster can pass as a normal part of society.

Like many early modern accounts or more recent horror fiction, Pratchett never actually shows his werewolves killing anyone, though the reader knows many of them have done so. This in itself provides a layer of fear response, but no more than we would expect from any other villain (and only the villainous werewolves kill people). So, in our post-agricultural society, what then causes the werewolf to remain a staple of the horror and fantasy genres? In a post–1960s world in which organized terrorism is commonplace, the individual who wishes to destroy society and can pass undetected becomes a significant source of fear. The roots of this role can be seen in the early modern period through Catholics in England and the Germanic states or Protestants in Spain and France, those who look like everyone else but wish to attack the perceived foundations of society. In much the same way, the modern literary werewolf (especially the female werewolf) questions many of the binaries and divisions upon which society is built, threatens invisibly from within, whether advertently or not, as is the case with both Wolfgang and Angua.

Angua, Wolfgang, and the Archetype

Based on the aforementioned roots, we can see that Pratchett's werewolves exhibit many of the key characteristics of the greater shape-shifter archetype, including their role as civilizing figures, as reminders of humanity's bestial nature, as signs of the mutable world, as representatives of the nature-versus-nurture debate, and as figures connected to the Jungian shadow. Whether consciously or not, Pratchett presents multiple sides of each aspect of nature-nuture, especially in *Elephant*, that work to explore and dissect the archetypal traits through a process of comparison.

The previous discussion of medieval and early modern continuances in Pratchett's werewolves already touches upon their role as civilizing figures. However, there is more to this aspect of the archetype and its expression in these works. Clearly Wolfgang serves as did the wolves in Marie de France's fables, the monster that acts as an example of the forbidden and socially unacceptable. He civilizes the audience by first performing anti-social, uncivilized actions, then by being punished for his transgressions. In this case, it is important to note that his transgressions against civilization were punished while he wore the form of the uncivilized. Not only does this wolf form and means of punishment (being executed while playing fetch) act to "other" Wolfgang (a nobleman effectively disowned by the nobility), thereby making him a scapegoat representing all the problems of Überwald's society, but it lets the audience, both

2. The Disc's K-9 Unit

fictional and real, know that society was threatened by a beast, the wolf simultaneously beyond and within its borders. The human, the urban, is kept intact.

His mother, on the other hand, acts to civilize in a different way. Even while she is being intimidated by her son and turned toward his purposes, she attempts to maintain some degree of civilization within their family and home. Seraphine undertakes this mission through the use of clothing — see her attempts to keep her husband and son dressed, cited above — and the other outward trappings of culture and refinement such as the finishing school she attended with Lady Sybil and her attempts to maintain a level of decorum in her home (including her requirement that her husband be in human form when he is inside, which does not always happen). In the latter case, more often than not she is forced to rely on social niceties of speech and social gatherings rather than cuisine and decoration — the former discussed above, the latter being shown in the minimalist furniture and lack of expected decorations around the castle (no armor or swords on the walls, for instance). Because of these limitations and the fact that they are simply a thin veneer, Seraphine ultimately fails to civilize anyone, even her own husband and son. Her daughter, though, makes the same attempt on a larger scale. By the very nature of her profession, Angua functions as a civilizing force. Since she works to enforce the various rules and structures that make society possible, she acts to civilize others on a broader scale than her mother, and with fewer restrictions. Because of this, and because Angua honestly and actively attempts to control her own wild, bestial side, Pratchett allows her methods to be successful — for instance, every time she and Wolfgang fight each other, he turns and flees, showing civilization triumphant, especially demonstrated when Vimes finally, and "accidentally," executes him. Wolfgang's continuous defeats and ultimate execution place him as the representation of the archetype that allows for violently transgressive acts, both in his attempted fratricide and disruption of the social order. In this way, due to his execution, the audience can vicariously attempt both acts, safely within the realm of fiction and fully understanding the consequences.

Even with this civilizing factor, the werewolves, as with all human-animal shifters, function to remind the audience of humanity's own bestial nature and the inevitability of change. This aspect is clearly demonstrated by the very nature of the beasts, as it were. To paraphrase Angua's statement, humans hate werewolves because they sense the beast within. Of course, that very beast also attracts people to werewolves and the archetype. Another obviously demonstrated trait that is worth mentioning again is that these werewolves, through their hybrid human-beast nature, act as signs of a mutable world. They appear during times of social, political, technological, and theological change and work to either help or hinder that social evolution. Werewolves, and other shifters, appear at such times to represent our ambivalent feelings regarding points of transition — the simultaneous attraction and repulsion that these historic moments evoke. Because Pratchett's werewolves represent the police (Angua) and the nobility (her family; also a reference to the Ossory werewolves),[41] they fulfill the archetype's paradoxical role as a point of stability within their own mutability. That is, these unstable creatures represent structures that maintain order, even as they are directly involved in effecting a social evolution. For the purposes of *Elephant* and *Thud!*, the technological and social change invoked may be likened to that caused by the explosion of the Internet while the socio-theological change in *Thud!* can be represented by the fall of the Soviet Union. Although both are imperfect analogies, as most analogies are, they will work well enough for our purposes. Just as the rampant expansion of the Internet has created ambivalent feelings — excitement at the connectivity and information access potential mixed with fear and concern regarding privacy and predators — the Disc's clacks call up similar excitement and concerns. Likewise, as the fall of the Soviet Union brought about a historic moment when former rivals became, at least for a time, friends, *Thud!*'s revelations bring together two old enemies in an atmosphere of trepidation (including concerns about trust) and excitement (the knowledge that one is part of a deeply historic moment). Again we see the archetype manifesting at a point of rebirth and new beginnings. In *Elephant*, this is the beginning of a new social order and rebirth of a society that involves greater equality across five different species and political ideals (not counting the Igors). *Thud!*'s beginning, rebirth, is more fundamental, and thus we see more ambivalence regarding the change, in that it brings about a new relationship between two otherwise irreconcilable species, or nations.

This ambiguity translates itself into the debate over the influence of an individual's nature versus upbringing. Once again, Pratchett presents arguments from four major directions in *Elephant*. Most of Angua's family appears as an even mix of inherent, wild, nature and learned behavior —

the Baron acts upon his werewolf nature by spending most of his time as a wolf and follows learned behavior, for instance through upholding the traditions of the Game. Seraphine generally leans toward the upbringing end of the continuum, and it is a sliding line rather than a hard binary in Pratchett's treatment. Wolfgang mixes both, as a combination of his parents, but tends toward the nature side as there is little to account for the degree of his wildness based on the behavior of his parents and sister. Angua, like her brother, moves toward the nature side of the spectrum, although in a different way. Rather than connecting with her nature as a werewolf, something she does her best to control, she does what she can to tie herself to her nature as an individual. This comes out especially well in *Thud!* In the case of all four werewolves, Malcolm South's assertion that "fabulous creatures reflect both the dark and the bright side of human nature"[42] rings true.

Not only does South's claim partially explain the role of Pratchett's werewolves, but it also explains their affinity with the Jungian shadow. Wolfgang has clearly embraced and been consumed by this aspect of his psychology, giving in almost entirely to the anti-social behaviors that make up the shadow. His parents, on the other hand, deny their shadows, using traditions, animal shape, and the veneer of civility to cover up and excuse this darker side. The only family member who accepts this aspect of her psyche, realizes its purpose, and attempts to deal with it is Angua. Throughout both *Elephant* and *Thud!* she acknowledges the darker, anti-social, side, but does what she can to fight it off or channel it. Like Vimes whose shadow is personified in *Thud!* as the Summoning Dark, Angua struggles with her internal darkness. While Vimes creates his own mental persona—the Watchman, or Guarding Dark—Angua uses various small things to keep the uncivilized side at bay, for instance, she pays for any chickens she "steals" around the city or elsewhere because animals do not pay for their food.[43] In this way, she becomes psychoanalytically healthy while her relatives remain in need of assistance.

Lycanthropic Mechanics of the Disc

Like many earlier writers, Pratchett is interested in the rules, limits, and mechanics that govern his werewolves. He is very concerned with the morphology and physiology of his werewolves, at least as regards their transformations, as a means of discussing both their otherness and similarity to his human audience. This interest appears in the classical and medieval authors — the insistence upon rituals or clothing — in a less systematic or obvious way than some of the early modern writers, but it is still a long tradition. The tradition continues throughout Pratchett's work, and later Rowling's, alongside an interest in the rules and limits of magic, witchcraft, and other important aspects of his "largely imaginary" world. The rules governing Discworld's werewolves, at least those currently featured, fall into three categories: abilities/vulnerabilities, reproduction, and the effects of long term Changing.

Pratchett indirectly mentions several different abilities his werewolves possess, from regeneration to the obvious shape-shifting. The two he most directly discusses are what happens when the werewolf loses control of his or her shifting, and the sense of smell. What happens when a werewolf who can Change loses control of his ability? Pratchett answers that question through Wolfgang. Just before he and Angua attack each other, Wolfgang is described as having wolf ears rising from a human head, a mane of hair, and patches of fur tufting his skin, "the rest of him ... was having trouble deciding what it was. One arm was trying to be a paw."[44] This scene, including the fight, shows that, according to Pratchett's conception, a certain amount of conscious or unconscious control is necessary for the werewolf to maintain a given shape. It also speaks to Wolf's psychological turmoil, his hybrid nature and instincts finding morphological expression.

Of equal importance, though, is the werewolf's sense of smell, especially given Angua's job. In this respect, Pratchett describes Angua as seeing with her nose: throughout the entirety of *Thud!* he uses the verbs "see" and "smell," in various conjugations, interchangeably for her. The reader is told, during an investigation that "Angua tapped her nose. You couldn't argue with a werewolf's nose,"[45] even if she is in her human shape. This particular trait, which can be overcome,[46] is virtually a necessity for her role in the Watch, where it is typically used to investigate crime scenes, and therefore to police society's rules and norms.

Even werewolves' regenerative abilities are limited, as Angua explains to Vimes that because he did not attack Wolfgang with silver or fire, it likely hurt considerably but he would survive because they heal very fast.[47]

This echoes an earlier thought that Vimes had when he was told that Überwald's dwarfs do not mine silver: "where you got werewolves, didn't you need silver?"[48] This reflects a more modern sensibility, probably drawn from the horror genre, both literature and film, rather than the earlier written sources. It is also a necessity in that transgressive werewolves need to be punished, so they must have some exploitable weakness.

Reproduction is another important area that Pratchett touches on, both notable moments question how the lycanthropic ability passes on genetically. In the first, Angua tells Carrot and the audience that a werewolf who lacks the ability to Change is referred to as a yennork.[49] She explains that fairy tale monsters originate with these werewolves because they are "[p]eople with a *bit* of wolf and wolves with that extra capacity for violence that is so very human."[50] In addition to creating more layers of Wolfgang's villainy — he killed their yennork sister and drove away their yennork brother — Pratchett's inventiveness works to heighten the reader's suspension of disbelief. It does so because the post–Darwin reader presumably knows that sometimes certain traits are not genetically passed down to children, even if both parents share them, though the potential remains for the next generation. Therefore, the modern audience understands that lycanthropy could be one of these traits and this makes the manifestation of the archetype more acceptable to the audience. The other moment involves Vimes considering Angua's relationship with Carrot: he notes his uncertainty about the result of human-werewolf breeding, suggesting that their children may simply have to shave more often near the full moon and sometimes get an urge to chase carts through the street.[51] This concern is also, indirectly, raised by medieval authors as demonstrated by Bisclavret's wife and her reaction to learning that her husband was a werewolf. On one hand, her response could be considered in light of the introduction to the *lai*, in which werewolves are described as bloodthirsty beasts. On another, it could be concern for any children she might have with her baron-husband. Similar concerns are also raised by Rowling, as we will see later.

In Pratchett's conception of the archetype, the Change can occur whenever the werewolves wish. However, his work reveals certain problems with reverting from one shape to the other or remaining too long in one form granting preference to one side of the hybrid nature. Regarding the former, he writes, "For a second or two after Changing, they're not entirely up on current events."[52] A few seconds of disorientation make sense, further acting as a means of suspending disbelief, while the mind adjusts to the new body. Interestingly, this particular drawback is ignored during the fight between Angua and Wolfgang. But, the more important aspect, for Pratchett and the archetype, involves the identity problems associated with remaining in one shape for too long. He provides ample evidence of the degenerative process caused by remaining a wolf for extended periods of time through both the Baron and Wolfgang. During the Baron's introduction, he is shown acting dog-like and responding to questions in single word growls because of spending too much time Changed in his wolf form. He is also seen in his human shape attempting to act like a wolf or dog in that he tries to scratch behind his ear with his leg and forgets how to use utensils. Both he and Wolfgang are described as being very hairy in their human shapes as well. Whether this is due to Changing often or because they are males is unclear — Angua and her mother do not share this trait, but also do not Change as often in the narrative. Wolfgang, for instance, is described as being noticeable by "the slight lengthening of the incisors, the way the blond hair was so thick around the collar,"[53] but again, this may be due to his father's genes or being male. Vimes provides the last comments on the effect of spending too much time Changed, stating that whichever shape the werewolf was in, (s)he started to slowly lose the skills and benefits of the other form. Eventually, the human mind begins to lose control after a time as a wolf.[54]

These rules are important both for the suspension of disbelief through continuity — thereby making the archetype more acceptable to the modern audience — and because they return to the early modern idea that monsters of all sorts conform to certain rules. With a subject as broad in folklore, mythology, and legend as the werewolf, each author picks and chooses which rules his or her werewolves will follow from the past and whether new rules will be added to the old, as we will see again with Rowling, Harris, and de Lint in the next chapters. These rules, especially for Pratchett's werewolves, function to determine or frame the core issue of identity and nature. That is, they denote and transgress the boundaries of the self-identification problem inherent in werewolves of all types. They guide the discussion and help form the forum in which that all important debate occurs.

Of Wolf and Dog

One of the other ways in which Pratchett deals with the dual nature of the werewolf archetype is that he constantly reminds the reader that the line between wolves and dogs is a thin one. As the talking dog, Gaspode, says, "I could've *bin* a wolf, you know. With diff'rent parents, of course."[55] This approach simultaneously heightens the potential threat of the werewolf and provides a comedic effect that neutralizes the threat. The threat is increased because the audience is familiar with domesticated canines, and being reminded that there is minimal difference between the canines in our homes and those in the wild can be unsettling. On the other hand, when Pratchett's werewolves react like the dogs we see in homes around the world, the comedic effect then disarms the threat.

Reminding the audience that wolves and dogs are not all that different is something that Pratchett returns to many times during both *Elephant* and *Thud!* This reminder is more pronounced in *Elephant* largely because there are more werewolves present and they are the central characters. The balance between human and animal that the werewolf and the dog represent in *Elephant* is displayed to the audience notably through the characters: Vimes, Gaspode, the Baron, and Wolfgang. The concept makes its appearance in Vimes' thought regarding Wolfgang: "but something between a human and a wolf has a bit of dog in them."[56] This statement is supported by Gaspode who claims that dogs are more vicious than wolves.[57] The latter statement refers to the aforementioned violence that Pratchett, through Angua, says is particular to humanity. Since dogs have picked up some human traits via domestication and training, according to Pratchett's view, they themselves can be considered partial werewolves and are certainly hybrid creatures. Thus comes the nastiness Gaspode refers to and his thought, "This is me [...] stuck between the humans and the wolves,"[58] exactly the same position in which Angua and the other werewolves find themselves. Through this sort of statement and his constant hints that domestication actually makes canines more threatening, Pratchett subtly increases the potential threat represented by his archetypal werewolves. If, he implies, we find werewolves threatening because they are part man and part beast, should we not also find the domestic dogs we live with equally threatening? After all, his talking dog "took it as an article of faith that there was in all dogs a tiny bit of wolf."[59]

Since most of Pratchett's audience has likely never seen a wolf before, but is probably familiar with threatening dogs, the wolf and werewolf as threat become more relevant.

Even as he asks this difficult question, Pratchett undermines the threat posed by his werewolves. The thin line between wolf and dog, we find, works both ways. Just as the dog can seem wolf-like, fierce, and nasty, the werewolf can appear quite puppy-like. For instance, after greeting Vimes, the Baron releases his visitor's hand to throw himself on the floor, where the family dogs proceed to leap on him, and presumably wrestle.[60] Vimes, we find, refers to the canines as dogs simply because they are indoors, acknowledging that he would probably refer to them as wolves if they were outside. During the same scene, Pratchett shows the von Überwalds reacting like dogs to certain words, such as having problems saying the name "Vetinari," due to the "vet" part. Because of this, when Vimes next uses the Patrician's name, he put "a slight stress on the first syllable and [heard] the growl on cue."[61] Likewise, whenever the word "bath" is used around the werewolves, Pratchett makes sure to note that they grimace, yelp, growl, or otherwise react negatively. Although these traits and reactions might not be amusing or disarming in and of themselves, coming from a pair of nobles, both of whom are "monstrous," they cause the audience to relax for a moment. The reactions are what we would expect to see in our household pets; therefore, when the baron and baroness wince at "bath" or "vet," we smile or chuckle and they become less threatening. This disarming effect continues when Littlebottom tells Vimes, "Werewolves like to sleep in front of the fire at night, sir."[62] Then, just as the audience becomes comfortable with the amusing baron and his wife, Pratchett introduces the von Überwald family motto—"Man is a wolf to man" which has relevance, in its Latin form, in our own world. This brings the audience back to the seriousness of the plot and position that the main characters are in, although soon after bringing us back, Pratchett uses Lady Sybil to allow another smile and reminder of dog-like qualities as she tells Vimes that werewolves, like dogs supposedly, hate cats.[63]

The combination of threat and disarming amusement (a paradox worthy of the archetype) also appears in *Thud!* through Angua, usually in relation to receiving praise or showering. Those reactions, due to her self-reflective role, are shown in the context of self-identification, rather than being performed by characters whose thoughts the audience does not see. Because of that key difference, Angua's dog-like responses and attributes will be discussed later.

Pratchett takes these traits beyond their amusement level, even beyond the level of neutralizing the potential threat of lycanthropy through humor. In *Elephant*, these dog-like traits that provide disarming amusement also serve as tools used by the everyman, as represented by Vimes,[64] to execute Wolfgang for his social misbehavior. After assuring himself and everyone else that Wolfgang is guilty of social misconduct and that he is resisting arrest, Vimes produces a flare or firework tube and preys upon the werewolf's domestic dog traits. He feels the device jerk as the powder inside combusts and watches the flare slowly tumble from the tube with smoke trailing in a spiral. "It looked like the stupidest weapon since the toffee spear."[65] Wolfgang zigzags beneath it, his face split in a grin, and gracefully leaps into the air to catch the flare in his mouth. Then the device explodes. Here we see Pratchett taking the very qualities he used for humorous effect earlier and twisting them. Rather than merely being a source of amusement, they become a source of identification with the monsters that fit within society. Since the audience can recognize the canine traits, a point upon which the audience can sympathize with Wolfgang is created at the very moment his character is removed from the narrative. The traits then gain another layer as they become a defense against the monster that threatens society. In case the reader missed the significance of the scene, Vimes refrains from such James Bond-style comments as "fetch," although he considers a few. Then, to further underscore the point, Pratchett adds a character telling Vimes that he obviously had no way of knowing that Wolfgang would instinctively try to catch the flare because the more dog-like traits inherent in the werewolf could clearly not be known to a resident of the city, where they supposedly lack werewolves.[66] This is despite the fact that Pratchett wants it clear that Vimes *did* know about those qualities, a fact made abundantly obvious by his earlier calculated references to baths and vets.

This presentation of similarities becomes part of something greater as Pratchett puts his werewolves to a variety of uses. When he expands the role that they play, the wolf-dog dynamic present in his use of the archetype slides smoothly into discussions of racism and related issues.

Werewolves at Work

Over the course of several novels, Pratchett's werewolves challenge, adapt, or expand a variety of major issues beyond those covered by medieval and early modern lycanthropes. He employs werewolves to discuss: racism and ethnicity, self-reflection, expansions on the nature-versus-nurture debate, and social construction — the latter of which occasionally involves comparisons to vampirism. These become the core issues that Pratchett returns to whenever his werewolves, especially Angua, appear.

The role of werewolves as archetype in Pratchett's discussion of racism and ethnicity is rather complex, since he plays not only with human-werewolf relations but also with wolf-werewolf relations. Both cases are used to highlight issues of racism and ethnicity and discuss how or why it functions. Tied to this issue is that of multiculturalism, an integral connection since the one usually follows or precedes the other. On that aspect, we turn to Angua because, as Cockrell writes, "[t]he Watch [...] skewers the pitfalls of multiculturalism with gentle understanding in its officers."[67] This is especially the case in *Elephant* and *Thud!* in which politics and racism are major themes. Both texts require the audience and the characters to see Angua as something more than just a handy sleuthing nose or Sergeant Detritus (a troll) as more than a simple battering ram. At the same time, *Thud!* presents Vimes, and Angua, being forced to deal with a vampire joining the Watch in the interests of political correctness and diversity — a sort of multi-species version of affirmative action.

More directly related to racism, we look at Wolfgang and Angua in their relations with others, both human and wolf, as well as Angua's employment. David Buchbinder has already noted that Wolfgang "has an attitude toward non-werewolf kind that echoes Nazi master-race ideology (complete with a cult of exercise and nudity)"[68] that is evident not only in these two areas but also in the military uniform (made for a non-existent military) he wears to the dwarf reception. Speaking with regard to Seraphine, with whom she went to school, even the likable and positive Lady Sybil adds a layer to this discussion of racism, telling Vimes that everyone knew about her nature, but in those days no one would even think of talking about it because (a) it was not done and (b) it would be impolite.[69] On one hand, the language she uses mimics some of that used during the pre–civil rights era in the U.S. It can, however, also be read as language used when discussing a disease. This ambiguity is, I think, intended, though less so than we will see with Rowling. The ambiguity creates a strong link between the Discworld's view of werewolves and our world's treatment of ethnicity, such as current discussions regarding immigrants in the British Isles.

As part of this discussion, Gaspode and Angua make attempts to justify prejudice directed at werewolves by both humans and wolves. Gaspode argues from both perspectives, as befits his position as a dog between the human and the wolf. He explains to Carrot, "People don't like wolves that can think like people, an' people don't like people who can act like wolves."[70] Unpacking this assertion calls up a variety of questions, since Pratchett has previously asserted that: humans possess an extra potential for violence and that dogs, being partially human, are "a lot nastier than wolves." If those two are the case, what exactly is Gaspode saying? The first half of the statement makes sense based on Pratchett's other assertions. That is, people clearly dislike and fear any wolf that possesses that extra, human, capacity for violence because it makes the wolf more threatening. Not only that, but it also acts as a reminder that humans possess the capacity for cruel violence, while the wolf pack prefers to expend as little energy as possible and bring down prey swiftly, without intent to cause pain or suffering. The second half, though, becomes problematic until we apply humanity's perception of wolves rather than scientific reality. Because humans, in general, do not wish to appear vicious and fierce, at least after the advent of civilization, these traits are transferred to the wolf, or other animals, and deemed bestial. The characteristics are then dubbed "anti-social" and those who possess them are effectively cast out of society, unless the traits are channeled into entertainment or the military. Even then, limits are put in place — sports rules, codes of conduct — and society as a whole reacts when the limits are violated. The desire to forget and ignore our own violent heritage and the shadow aspect of our psyche has clearly been present for centuries, as evidenced by medieval and early modern attempts at denial such as Gerald of Wales' attempt at transference (shifting the bestial away from the English to the Irish) or use of the Plinian races to move bestiality away from Europe as a whole. It can also be seen in our own world if we employ Jane Yolen's replacement technique.[71] If we remove troll-dwarf, for instance, and insert Serb-Croat, Greek-Turk,

The Modern Literary Werewolf

Hutu-Tutsi, Irish Catholic-English Protestant, Sunni-Shi'ite, we see our own stereotypes of violence being created to justify acts of even crueler violence, as mirrored in Pratchett's writing. However, this is only one layer of Pratchett's application of the archetype to racism.

Gaspode and Angua both argue the wolf side as well. Gaspode's brief foray into this aspect of prejudice is to say quite simply that wolves hate werewolves because they smell wrong. Wolves, he notes, are very particular about things smelling the proper way.[72] The position he expresses is that, since humans do not like werewolves, even when they look human, it makes sense that wolves would not like werewolves, even when they look like wolves. This argument returns to the aforementioned assertion about wolves that think like people, rephrased by the reader as "Wolves don't like wolves that can think or act like people." Since, in Pratchett's world, most of the mammals have some degree of intelligence and at least limited access to reason, this chain of logic makes sense within the narrative. Left solely to Gaspode's view of the relationship, though, the prejudice seems largely unreasoned, illogical, and summed up as werewolves "smell wrong." Angua presents a better, more rational, explanation. She eventually tells Carrot that "it's always wolves who suffer when werewolves get too powerful."[73] Werewolves, she says, are intelligent enough to avoid hunters and traps. Vampires, she adds, ignore wolves. Werewolves, though, occasionally hunt wolves. While Pratchett never explicitly explains why they hunt wolves, the implication of previous statements indicates that the reason is the human part of their psyche, the part that hunts not for survival but for pleasure and simply to kill something. The same can be said of the Game, since neither Wolfgang nor the Baron need to maintain the Game for survival purposes. As nobles, they have access to power and food, but they continue the Game in part to remind the populace of their power and in part because of that streak of uniquely human nastiness that both Angua and Gaspode allude to, at least according to Pratchett's implications.

Ultimately, Pratchett sets himself firmly on the side of racial or species co-existence through an exchange in which Detritus says he has never shaken hands with a king before. He adds as an afterthought that he has never done so with a dwarf either. Cheery takes exception and says they shook hands once, prompting: "'Watchmen don't count,' said Detritus firmly. 'Watchmen is *watchmen*.'"[74] While this exchange passes between a troll and a dwarf, it can just as easily be applied to any of Pratchett's hybridized Watch characters. Pratchett's message is clear: while racial prejudice exists in the wider world, there are some places, some sub-cultures, in which it either is being eradicated or has been erased.[75]

A related trait that Pratchett helps introduce, compared to classical through early modern sources, is that his primary werewolf is self-reflective. This post-psychology, post–Freudian trait allows the reader to appreciate the werewolf's thoughts and views, as well as speech about herself, rather than just his or her actions, as was the case with the earlier sources. For instance, on the prejudice issue above, Angua reflectively muses, "When werewolves make trouble, it's the *real* wolves that always suffer. People'll kill anything with fur."[76] Most of these thoughts, whether vocalized or internalized, are related to her construction of identity, as we might expect, and they vary from commentaries on werewolves to humans to vampires, the three most important species that come into her mind throughout the narratives.

Much of the reflection on werewolves involves her identity as a being split between two worlds and known as a monster, an integral part of the archetype. With this in mind Angua states, "We're not nice people, Carrot. We're all pretty dreadful."[77] That she includes herself in this generalization is interesting in that, from her introduction in *Men at Arms* through *Elephant*, Angua has worked for the Watch and has been in the group of characters that, if not exactly good, at least try to do what is best for society, whether society wants their help or not. Even so, at that point, Pratchett shows Angua identifying herself with a base, stereotyped, nature rather than with what she has accomplished since leaving Bonk. Much of her self-reflection needs to be viewed with some skepticism. For instance, she claims that werewolves always leave their prey an opening to run through,[78] to preserve the chase, even though her actions during what amounts to a sting operation with Corporal Nobbs at the beginning of *Elephant* show otherwise. There is some justification for her apparent contradiction of words and actions since she tells Carrot, "Being two things at the same time, and never quite being one ... we're not the most stable of creatures."[79] In this single statement, Angua reflectively states the core problem and nature of the shape-shifter archetype in general and werewolves in particular: the instability that is simultaneously exciting and frightening for both the individual and society.

This duality is also central in the use of the werewolf as a focus for expanding the nature-versus-nurture debate. In the case of the werewolf, the duality means that the animalistic side cannot be expunged. Instead, that natural side becomes controlled, tamed, and subordinate to society through learned behaviors. But this characterization oversimplifies a complex relationship presented indirectly even as far back as Ovid and Petronius. Due to Angua's self-reflective moments, questions of controlling nature through upbringing or vice versa are explicitly spelled out for the reader, as are the gut level responses evoked by the lycanthropic figure. While these latter responses are greatly tempered, based on the popularity of werewolves and wolf-like beings in both the literary and cinematic horror genre, I think it safe to say that they are still present.

Throughout her appearances in the Discworld books, Angua is depicted as constantly struggling to either subsume her bestial side or balance the wolf with the human. Usually this works, though there are some uncontrollable aspects, such as when she states that she needs to sleep in a dog bed for the seven days around the full moon.[80] Associated with this Change is what Pratchett calls pre-lunar tension (PLT), an obvious analogue to pre-menstrual syndrome (PMS), since his primary werewolf is female (although his male werewolves also suffer through this state). While the lunar induced Change is uncontrollable, at least Pratchett's werewolves have a choice in how they spend that week[81] without the need for external aid, unlike Rowling's as we will see later. The problem comes to a head with Angua's thoughts, such as "She ought to have at least another day! [...] Bits of her body *wanted* her to become a wolf, right now."[82] In order to combat this uncontrolled Change, Angua finds other ways to escape the werewolf nature, as she and others see it. The aforementioned paying for chickens is one of these attempts. Another method is, as Carrot muses, that Angua is very concerned about being clean. He notes that this trait is uncommon for werewolves.[83] Many of her werewolf traits come to light along with Angua's early appearances, but many of her attempts to master these urges come later. The chicken and cleanliness passages appear after her character is well established in the series, shortly after she and Carrot develop a romantic relationship. The debate reaches its apex during *Thud!*, though, due to the introduction of Constable Sally, the new vampire watchman.

With the introduction of Sally, Pratchett decides to play with the

2. The Disc's K-9 Unit

recent resurgence in popular culture of vampire-werewolf animosity, drawing from medieval eastern European legends[84] and modern movies.[85] The very first scene involving both characters features Angua thinking, "All she could do was grin and bear it and fight down a pressing desire to rip out the girl's throat with her teeth."[86] Unlike some other modern recapitulations of this animosity, Pratchett does indeed make it a natural, biological, instinct rather than a socially understandable one. Instead of constructing a history fraught with revenge or other social conflicts, he takes a biological route, implying that the animosity exists because both species compete for the same prey: humans and, presumably, dwarfs. The fact that neither werewolves nor vampires require human prey, especially since Pratchett introduces a league of vampires reminiscent of Alcoholics Anonymous but regarding blood, does nothing to curb the competition. Interestingly, this animosity does not appear in *Elephant*, although there are also no scenes in the book that show werewolves and vampires together, even if one scene implies that a vampire might have helped Wolfgang.[87] The hunting methods employed by the two species add to the problems — the suave, debonair vampire versus the animalistic werewolf. Because of this, Angua reminds herself, "Don't start believing you're stupid and hairy. Think clearly. You *do* have a brain."[88] This relationship acts as a window into the civilized-savage tension that the werewolf archetype represents, that which humanity does its best to balance on a daily basis as well, though not so obviously as the literary werewolf.

The vampire-werewolf relationship is not the only window that Pratchett opens into the werewolf-human psyche. Another returns to his reminder of the thin line between wolf and dog, wild and civilized. This aspect generally takes three forms: reception of praise, expected behavior, and dealing with baths. In *Thud!* each of these forms occurs in relation to Carrot or Sally and all of the incidents appear in the form of Angua's internal or external speech.

The first two areas where the wolf-dog dynamic appear tend to overlap with each other and can be summed up in two scenes: in the first, Angua receives praise from Carrot (her superior officer and significant other) and in the second, she pauses to share her thoughts regarding vampires. Once Carrot praises Angua for finding a particularly useful clue, Pratchett tells us that "under her flesh, she felt her tail want to wag. She wanted to lick his face. It was the dog part of her thinking. You're a good dog. It was important to be a good dog."[89] There is the potential for some gender related commentary here, unless the critic recalls that in *Jingo*, Vimes, also known as "Vetinari's terrier," tells Angua that everyone is someone's dog. What is more important is that the general reaction is not unique to Angua, nor to Pratchett's werewolves. The specific manifestation of the reaction is certainly unique to Angua, but virtually every other character in the books responds to Carrot in the same general way. Therefore, her specific reaction is a manifestation of the werewolf's canine nature, but it is also a representation of a typically human response to both a charismatic leader and a loved one. The fact that she does not act upon the urge is also significant for the archetype in that it shows that natural impulses can be restrained when necessary.

In the second instance, Angua thinks about werewolves and their relation to vampires. During this introspective moment, she thinks, "Never mind that, because everyone *knew* that a creature that was a wolf and a human combined was a kind of dog. They were *expected* to behave."[90] Beyond acting as another reminder about the dog-wolf divide, this thought reveals a perception that the civilized is supposed to outweigh and overrule the wild. The human part is supposed to influence the wolf and create a being that behaves socially and maintains the niceties and laws that keep the social structure running. Ironically, since people are perhaps unique in the animal kingdom in being able to act either selfishly or with the interests of the pack in mind, the wild wolf part is more likely to be the socially responsible aspect of the werewolf. This hearkens back to Gaspode's comment about dogs being nastier than wolves because of their association with humans. The thought also reveals a probable reason for Pratchett's primary werewolf to join the Watch. If a werewolf is supposed to be a kind of dog and dogs are supposed to behave (contrary to everyday evidence), then where better for that reasoning, sentient, dog to work than the police? This structure also, in Angua's case, provides a level and source of discipline that her brother lacks at home. Therefore, in Angua's case, positive self-fashioning wins out over nature. Whether she would agree with this assertion is another matter, since when she is corrected by Sally about the nature of her relationship with Carrot — that she is his, not the other way around — her response is simply, "It's a werewolf thing. We are what we are!"[91] On the other hand, Wolfgang and the Baron clearly personify the nature side of the equation, as the vampire Margolotta ironically

2. The Disc's K-9 Unit

suggests to Vimes that she feels for Seraphine, claiming it would be difficult for a werewolf to realize she was raising a monster. Then she notes that the baron is easy to please — a simple bone amuses him for hours.[92]

One of the last ways in which Pratchett deals with nature-versus-nurture through the wolf-dog dynamic is with Angua's reactions to showering. Her initial reaction, when questioned by Sally about her reluctance to shower — after both spend a night tramping through mud filled tunnels — is "It's full moon, okay? The wolf is a bit strong."[93] In keeping with Pratchett's minimal triumph of nurture over nature, she does eventually step in, pretending that the shower is merely falling rain. However, afterwards, she thinks, "The important thing now was to remember to use a towel and not to shake herself dry."[94] Pratchett resists the scene, as does Angua, thus showing nurture triumphant.

Perhaps the proverbial final word on the wolf-dog divide is Angua's thought about werewolves:

> Well, they were just sad monsters, weren't they? Never mind that life was a daily struggle with the inner wolf, never mind that you had to force yourself to walk past every lamppost, never mind that in every petty argument you had to fight back the urge to settle it all with just one bite.[95]

This particular thought is another reminder of subconscious, biological thinking mastered (at least briefly) by the conscious, socialized part of the psyche. The triumph of the socialized over the shadow occurs through constant struggle. There are, however, points where Angua plays with the subconscious instincts of others through her abilities as a werewolf to aid her position as a watchman.

Both of the major scenes where the audience sees this effect come when Angua attempts to keep someone immobilized after tackling them in her wolf shape. In the first instance, Done It Duncan, having just been caught purse snatching, notes, "Something right by his ear started to drool. And there was a long, very long drawn out growl, not changing in tone at all, just unrolling a deep promise of what would happen if he tried to move."[96] Here Angua takes up the stories, fears, and collective unconscious reaction that werewolves, and wolves, evoke in people and uses them to her advantage. She appeals to this deep seated, one might say genetic, impulse later, in order to keep Vimes safe from himself. In that scene, after tackling him, "Angua drooled. The hair along her spine stood out like a saw blade. Her lips curled back like a wave. Her growl was from the back of a haunted cave. All together, these told the brain of anything monkey-shaped that movement meant death."[97] Not only do these scenes evoke deep instinctive responses, which help to explain the audience's simultaneous fascination with and fear of the werewolf and archetype, but they move into a corollary to the wolf-dog dynamic. The scenes serve to remind the audience that just as the wolf became the dog, the monkey that the wolf hunted became the human. Moreover, the impulses that drove the monkey are not, according to Pratchett, extinct and are not buried all that far down in the human psyche. Based on these scenes, and the wolf-dog dynamic that Pratchett constantly refers to, the werewolf also functions as a symbol of evolution, a concept that Pratchett has referred to numerous times throughout the series and clearly assumes his audience accepts. This assumption builds a community out of the audience, just as his werewolves serve to build a society in the novels.

Part of any society is a shared sense of justice and order. Edith Benkov could have had Angua in mind when she asserted that the werewolf was a "[s]ympathetic character whose 'beastliness' will both serve justice and restore a certain order, albeit one which is different from that at the outset of the tale."[98] She was talking about Bisclavret, but the statement is even more applicable to Pratchett's Angua. In both *Elephant* and *Thud!*, Angua is portrayed as a sympathetic character. She uses her wolf side to serve the Watch, the representatives of law and order. Both tales involve her working with others to undermine an older social order in favor of a newer, more modern one (supplanting a feudal state with an emerging Athenian democracy in *Elephant*). The old order in *Elephant* is Überwald's feudal clans of werewolves and vampires that claimed large territories (likely for prey) while the new order allows for the country's dwarfs and humans to have a say in the national government.[99] The laws of the new order allow for enforcement which reins in the depredations of the old order, as represented by Wolfgang and his pack. Admittedly, the old order did create the present society through its depredations, especially the Game, which Wolfgang tells Vimes is the source of initial funding for most of the businessmen in the country.

The form of social building practiced by Wolfgang and his father, though, and that which Angua eventually takes part in through *Elephant*, follows David Gilmore's formula of appearance for the monster. Initially the monsters — the werewolves especially — appear from the shadows and are disbelieved or discounted. Wolfgang restarts the Game, without the traditional rules, but is largely ignored by the populace of Bonk and is effectively encouraged by his parents. The depredation and destruction perpetrated by the monster leads to an awakening in the community. This awakening is represented in the person of Tantony, one of Bonk's watchmen, with Vimes acting as a catalyst. Eventually, the community reacts and unites under a hero-saint. This particular point is a tricky one for *Elephant*. The community in Bonk does not publicly unite as such. However, various members secretly help the hero-saint, represented by a conglomerate of watchmen — Vimes, Carrot, and Angua — in keeping with Pratchett's favoring an ensemble cast. In this way, the Ankh-Morpork Watch in general, and Angua in particular, work to build a new society out of the old, even if that society is initially held together by fear of a particular individual. Sally's appearance in *Thud!* provides evidence that the new society flourishes, since she arrives as a vampire and member of the Bonk Watch, ostensibly coming to learn from Vimes and his heterogeneous family. The fact that she also comes to the Watch as a spy for the dwarf king adds evidence for a working society left in Angua and her compatriots' wake.

The community in Bonk is not the only society built or reinforced by Pratchett's primary example of the werewolf archetype. By the very nature of her role as a watchman, Angua acts to build and influence Ankh-Morpork's social fabric through enforcing the rules by which that society defines itself and works. She also helps to create a sub-society in the Watch itself, involving a collection of disparate elements from humans to werewolves, dwarfs to trolls, gnomes to gargoyles, golems to zombies, vampires to Nobbses[100] and even a Feegle. This sub-community acts as a hybridized pro-diversity society in and of itself, which serves as an example for the society that contains it. As Pratchett said through Detritus, species, race, and ethnicity do not matter to this society because "Watchmen is *watchmen*."[101]

Watchmen to Teachers

In Pratchett's hands, the late-twentieth and early twenty-first century manifestation of the werewolf archetype comes to represent racial and ethnic minorities and social builders. As the figure evolves to deal with these traits and issues, Pratchett never loses sight of the long tradition that brings the werewolf into the modern day. His werewolves have clear ancestors among the medieval sources, from Bisclavret and Alphouns to Gorlagon and the werewolves of Ossory. They share the medieval avoidance of explicit on-screen transformation and continue the medieval and early modern quest for identity, especially for a human identity as different from, or encased in, that of other animals. At the same time, he draws from early-twentieth century cinematic sources and the subconscious as represented by the connections between his werewolves and the shape-shifter archetype. Even though he largely ignores the early modern tradition, certain echoes can still be found, such as his interest in the mechanical and psychological aspects of how werewolves work and the rules that govern them.

A significant part of Pratchett's popularity around the world is his storytelling method, use of older traditions, and tapping of the collective unconscious. Readers find various things that they recognize from folklore, fairy tales, legends, myths, literature, popular culture, and our own world in his work. His readers enjoy this sense of familiarity and the game of finding his sources. As an example of this relationship with his readers, Pratchett relates an incident from a book signing in which an Indian family approached him: "Did I know, the mother asked, that the world turtle is part of Hindu mythology? Er, yes, I said ... er ... did they mind? They beamed and said no, that was fine, and now would I sign their books?"[102] The fact that his readers work to unpack the various sources Pratchett draws from enhances his importance as a writer. In the process of unpacking his sources, his readers incidentally unpack the various serious subjects and positions hidden beneath the layer of humor which the satirist uses to convey his lessons regarding ethnic tension, social problems, change, and story.

Pratchett's archetypal werewolves move beyond these traditional roots, not only through the representations they embody, but by the methods they use to achieve the same goals. From Angua's self-reflection to Pratchett's constant reminders of the close link between wolves and dogs, these methods serve as a reminder of the narrow line between humans and other animals in ways that the earlier sources do not employ. We see similar methods in another late-twentieth and early twenty-first century author,

2. The Disc's K-9 Unit

J. K. Rowling, and her werewolves, as represented by Remus Lupin and Fenrir Greyback. Even so, the methods vary even more, as do her werewolves' functions. Although Angua works to shape society by catching and punishing transgressors of the social rules, Lupin works to pass those very rules on to others at a young age through his work as an educator. This difference creates a modified social dynamic: whereas Angua occasionally employs leaping on transgressors and tooth-and-claw fights, Lupin remains level headed and denies his violent, bestial side, at least when the audience actually sees him. Where Pratchett's lessons come from the educating author through a police officer, Rowling's come through an educator who remains both borderline pedantic and slightly aloof at the same time as he befriends both the title character and the audience.

3

Wolf in Professor's Clothing

Margins and Medievalism

J. K. Rowling presents one of the clearest examples of the sympathetic werewolf and lycanthrope as archetype in modern literature. True to its form, Rowling presents the paradoxical archetype through the conflicting figures Remus Lupin and Fenrir Greyback. In her exploration of these characters and the archetype, she works through or with the inherent tension between Freudian and Jungian approaches within the figure. Like Pratchett, to whom she has been compared, Rowling also incorporates significant classical, medieval, and early modern roots in her werewolves. However, unlike Pratchett, she minimizes the pieces of modern cinematic folklore that she adds to the creatures — for instance, silver has no significant effect on her werewolves nor do they possess special healing powers but they do transmit their condition through bites.[1] That said, as with most of the serious issues she introduces,[2] Rowling discusses her werewolves with a certain amount of humor. Beneath the marginal position in which Lupin and Greyback are placed, both as characters and in their fictional world, there are clear connections to the long tradition of werewolves and the archetype stretching back to Petronius' soldier and Ovid's Lycaon. At the same time, she draws upon Marie de France, *William of Palerne*, and *Arthur and Gorlagon* in that her werewolves appear in force during multiple points of transition. They also reflect the monstrous werewolves of the early modern period as they display Rowling's characteristic focus on the mechanics or rules of her fictional world and connect her work to early modern views of self-fashioning.

Two of the most important aspects of Rowling's writing are the layering effect undertaken in her narratives and the role of the margins. The first is most obvious in the variety of readers she has attracted over the span of the Harry Potter series, from children the age of her main characters

3. Wolf in Professor's Clothing

to older audiences. One of the important, and academically interesting, literary sub-layers is her incorporation of classical, medieval, and early modern texts, themes, and ideas in an otherwise modern fictional world (as the books take place from 1991 to 1998). This inclusion can be seen from the quasi-medieval wizards with their misunderstanding of technology — case in point, Arthur Weasley's fascination with the "fellytone" and plugs, which he has studied for years and barely understands — to such beings as Fluffy the three-headed dog and brief comments about chimerae. The other aspect mentioned above is the importance, role, and interest in the people she places as marginal figures. Although the eponymous title character and his friends — Hermione Granger and Ron Weasley — are clearly the central characters, since the stories are told from Harry's point of view, the marginal characters become just as central, if not moreso, in the minds of Rowling's readers. Among these characters are Harry's low grade nemesis Draco Malfoy, his friend Hagrid, and his surrogate father figures Sirius Black and Albus Dumbledore. Two figures straddle both roles (marginalized characters born of earlier material) more than any of the others: the werewolves Remus Lupin and Fenrir Greyback.

Although Rowling's werewolves return to these earlier traditions and continue to remind us that the monster is, in Joseph Andriano's words, "the familiar Self disguised as the alien Other,"[3] they move beyond the limits and previous functions werewolves have served. Like Pratchett's, Rowling's werewolves are used to discuss intolerance, prejudice, and racism. But as archetypal figures they move beyond that point to bring up questions of morality and moral paradox. They also function as metaphors to discuss diseases such as HIV/AIDS and multiple sclerosis. Lupin brings to bear the role or nature of respect, friendship, and mentoring both as Harry's school teacher (a role he never sheds, even in the last book, four years after he has resigned from Hogwarts) and his parents' friend. Lupin personifies the positive aspects of the shape-shifter archetype and exemplifies a healthy relationship with the shadow while Greyback personifies the archetype's negative aspects and the individual that has been consumed by his shadow. Perhaps even more importantly, and tied to questions of paradox, this stereotypically violent figure acts through Lupin as a peacemaker and voice of civility more often than not. The combination of intolerance and civility also allows Lupin especially to both support and question socialization while he serves to complicate perceptions of key characters such as Ron, Severus Snape, and Mrs. Weasley. In the process, the juxtaposition of Lupin and Greyback serves to continue M. Kratz's theory that werewolves "articulate an assumption about the possibility of losing one's humanity"[4] and the internal struggles necessary to retain control of said humanity.

Lycaon and Bisclavret Modernized

Although proving that Rowling was aware of the classical and medieval werewolf traditions as she created her characters may be effectively impossible, there are some strong pieces of circumstantial evidence that imply familiarity. Heather Arden and Kathryn Lorenz argue that her possible familiarity with the medieval tradition comes from her time studying French at the University of Exeter.[5] This, however, does not appear as conclusive, or as worthwhile a path to pursue, as letting her characters speak for themselves. If we look closely at both Remus Lupin and Fenrir Greyback, the only named werewolves in the books, a variety of connections to the medieval tradition are readily apparent. One simple point is that Rowling preserves Marie de France's organization of appearance: the *garvulf* is discussed by reputation first, then the exception to the rule, the *bisclavret*, arrives, before the *garvulf* appears in person. The most important connections that display Rowling's continuation of the shape-shifter archetype and werewolf tradition are their similarities to the tales — notably those of Petronius, Ovid, Marie de France, and *William of Palerne*— combined with the fact that both the two named werewolves and the single unnamed one appear, as in the medieval cases, at major points of transition. As we should expect from Rowling's body of work, the latter points are heavily multilayered.

Akin to the medieval tradition, Rowling's werewolves have, as Andriano says about monsters, "come to reflect our various emotions, anxieties, ambivalence" about the wild and our relationship to it.[6] These emotions and anxieties are no less worrisome today than they were millennia ago, especially when we see medical procedures involving animal organs transplanted into humans or discussions of cloning for medical purposes. Lupin and Greyback function to reintroduce the questions and thoughts raised by the aforementioned authors and texts using the terms of humanity and

3. Wolf in Professor's Clothing

bestiality. Both figures contain the principles in varying amounts, with Lupin acting in a manner more befitting Alphouns or Bisclavret while Greyback speaks to Lycaon and Petronius' werewolf. Both, however, have moments in which they cross into the other's territory. The mirroring line is hardly fixed, especially in Lupin's case as the series develops.

The two werewolves, for the most part, remain on their own side of the divide. In both cases, Adam Douglas' assertion that "one notable feature of [Gerald of Wales'] telling of the story is that his werewolves are innocent victims"[7] is equally applicable to Rowling's tale. The description of Lupin's contracting lycanthropy, told in *Harry Potter and the Prisoner of Azkaban*[8] and repeated in part in *Half-Blood Prince*, show him to be an "innocent victim" since he was bitten as a child through no fault of his own. While we are not told of Greyback's origins, presumably his story was similar in general points, if not in details. His preference for targeting children, such as Lupin, may be a sign that he himself was attacked as a child.[9] After they had this undesired condition thrust upon them, the two victims took themselves in different directions. Lupin became a teacher, much like Bisclavret and Alphouns, while Greyback became bestial and, quite possibly, a man-eater, as happens with Lycaon and Petronius' soldier.

If we take the latter case first, we find similarities between Petronius' soldier-werewolf and the Lupin-Greyback hybrid figure. As with Petronius, Rowling's werewolves become potentially man-eating wolves and turn bestial in their wolf form — for example, Greyback manages to channel his violence only by positioning himself before he changes shape and Lupin is stripped of most, if not all, of his civility and control when he changes around humans. These werewolves are also, like Petronius', feared by the public and subject to monstrous reputations involving violence and cannibalism, though with the addition of a focused threat toward children. Presumably both werewolves lose their clothing when they change shape. However, this can only be proven with Petronius, who specifically states that the soldier-werewolf removes his clothing. Rowling remains quiet on this matter either: because she does not consider it an important point, because she minimizes discussion of most clothing,[10] or because she is reticent to come close to anything involving direct sexuality beyond basic dating.[11] Since we only see a werewolf change shape on-screen once — Lupin — and never see one revert back to human form, this particular point remains speculative. That said, given her use of previous traditions, the loss of clothing during the transformation seems likely, but Petronius' ritual in the graveyard is not present.

Likewise, the association of lycanthropy with divine displeasure is not present with Rowling as it is with Ovid. There are certain similarities between the two, though. Despite the lack of divine involvement, both Lupin and Greyback presumably did not know the change was coming and were taken by surprise. Like Lycaon, how they react tells the audience a great deal about their individual characters. Perhaps the most important similarity in this respect is that, like Lycaon, Greyback embraces his bestial form and that aspect of his nature. That is, he, like Lycaon, gives in to his shadow and gives free rein to the anti-social, bestial aspects of his psyche. He apparently adapted quickly, as Lycaon did, and discovered ways to use this otherwise undesired ability to his favor. Greyback chooses, like Lycaon, to use this change to inspire fear in those around him. He revels in threatened violence, as shown when Lupin explains Greyback's tactics to Harry in *Half-Blood Prince* or the threats he levels both in that work and in *Deathly Hallows*, which will be discussed in greater detail with his early modern ancestors. On the other hand, Lupin rejects the animalism implicit in the new shape. He resists the urges Lycaon and Greyback gave in to, he strives to master these urges and is generally successful at doing so. He has come to terms with his shadow by his first appearance, and has learned to control that part of his psyche to some extent, partially with the aid of James Potter and Sirius Black. Only once during the narrative does the audience see his control slip. Ironically this occurs when he is surrounded by three recently come of age children, including his best friend's son: Harry. Whether he loses control off-screen, such as when he is attempting to bring the werewolf community away from Greyback, we cannot say for sure. The fact that he is described as being haggard, prematurely greying, and run-down every time Harry sees him during the two year and book period that he performs this work could argue for either a retention or loss of control. If the latter occurred, though, it is doubtful the audience would know since all of the audience's information comes from Harry and Lupin would hardly tell Harry, of all people, if he lost control.

Although these classical roots are present and important to note, Lupin has a much stronger tie to the medieval werewolf tradition. Marie de France's Bisclavret is a near perfect example of Lupin's ancestry in that

3. Wolf in Professor's Clothing

there are many strong parallels between the characters. Initially both characters are the exception to the rule, that is both authors first present entirely vicious and anti-heroic stereotypes of werewolves then introduce and focus on sympathetic examples for their readers. Marie transmits this information in a straightforward method at the outset. Rowling waits to some extent, although she subtly refers to the *garvulf* reputation that her werewolves are part of throughout the first two books. When Lupin appears in the third book, he is presented as a *bisclavret*, a tame, courtly werewolf. In fact, Amy Green notes that "Remus is more than just exceptionally polite; his civility and deference to others borders on domestication."[12] This point is debatable, as will be discussed later. In both cases, no figure appears to physically support the negative stereotype — at least not for some time in Rowling's case. Eventually, Greyback is introduced and certainly fits the *garvulf* stereotype, but he does so long after Lupin, the positive image, is well established. This ancestry has already been noted by some scholars, such as Arden and Lorenz who state, "Werewolves that presage Professor Lupin appear in Marie's 'bisclavret' and also in the anonymous 'Melion.'"[13] Likewise, with one exception, Lupin transforms off-screen, out of the public eye, exactly like Bisclavret. Both figures, as has been previously discussed by others regarding Bisclavret,[14] act to civilize others around them through their own examples of courtly and socialized behavior. Inextricably tied to their courtly, social examples, both characters have befriended their king or social or military leader — Bisclavret's nameless king and, for Lupin, Dumbledore who could have been a political leader and is certainly a guerrilla military leader from *Order of the Phoenix* through his own death as well as Harry who takes over the second role, to a degree, as the face of the resistance.

Like Bisclavret, Lupin acts to evoke pathos due to his situation, just as the audience feels sympathetic toward his predecessor. As in the case of Harry, the reader feels indignation and anger due to Lupin's resignation after his secret is revealed. In much the same way, Marie's audience is intended to feel Bisclavret's sense of betrayal when his wife traps him and remarries. Because Lupin reappears over a longer narrative, the evocation of pathos develops during his continued involvement in Harry's story. This sense increases as it reaches a false peak in *Half-Blood Prince* when he explains that he has been pretending to join the werewolf who bit him.[15] However, the true peak of Lupin's pathos comes in the final novel where he achieves Harry's dream of having a family, only to lose both his wife and his own life during the final climactic battle.[16]

Lupin's participation in this final battle, at least partially motivated by a sense of justice, is connected to the lineage he shares with *William of Palerne's* Alphouns. Both tales include characters who seek justice for various acts. Alphouns serves this role first in saving the eponymous character from an unjust murder plot. The fact that the audience is never told what happens to the uncle who was plotting to kill William is unimportant to the story. After that rescue, the werewolf ensures that William is raised in a royal court, even if it is not that of his parents. Through his actions, he ensures that the injustice enacted upon himself by his stepmother is rectified so that both he and William are returned to their rightful places. Due to the actions of this werewolf, both unjust crimes are undone or foiled and two legitimate and just rulers are returned to their respective thrones. In this way, the proposed archetype appears again in order to reinforce old definitions and reify the social order through his brief transgression.

Similarly, Lupin acts as a force of just action in Harry's tale. Initially, he works to ensure that Harry is not unjustly and irreparably harmed by the dementors in the Hogwarts train. Later, he reminds Harry to behave judiciously toward Severus Snape because Snape is a known confidant of Dumbledore and did his part during the last war within the wizarding community, even though neither he nor Harry like the other professor. Of greater importance, though, is that Lupin helps Harry to see that justice is done in discovering Sirius Black's — his friend and Harry's godfather— innocence in the matter of Harry's parents. As part of this process, he works with Black to expose the actual perpetrator, Peter Pettigrew (another school friend of both men), and attempts to bring him to trial for his crime. Perhaps the most important aspect of the latter act is that Lupin causes Black to halt his attempt to kill Pettigrew himself. Although the act itself is of some importance, the motive has greater significance. The point at which Lupin convinces Black is when he states, "You owe Harry the truth, Sirius!"[17] This statement finally recalls Black's sense of what is right and just to the point that, after explanations are done, his position shifts so he is convinced that only Harry has the right, as the most injured party, to dispense justice in Pettigrew's case. Here we see the werewolf acting in its archetypal role to civilize others and police the standards of society.

3. Wolf in Professor's Clothing

Black's vigilante justice is replaced by Harry's decision to work within society and let Pettigrew stand trial before a court.

The Black-Lupin-Pettigrew scene is a significant point of transition for the characters, the target readers,[18] and the series. Thus, it is a perfect moment with which to connect Rowling's modern werewolves to the medieval tradition. Medieval werewolves appeared and regained popularity at moments of social, political, or religious transition. This effect prompted Caroline Walker Bynum to state, "We read [...] not in order to understand the tradition (an academic enterprise) but in order to understand [...] ourselves."[19] This is no less true for the modern werewolf audience, in Rowling's case. Like the medieval archetypal werewolves, her's appear at a point of transition. As we should expect from Rowling, these transitions are multi-layered. The first time Rowling's werewolves appear in person is during *Prisoner of Azkaban* in which Remus Lupin is introduced. This particular part of the series contains many significant turning points. On a very basic level, *Azkaban* is the text that contains Harry's thirteenth birthday, a significant transition point for many British and American children, the beginning of their teenage years. The shift to Harry's teenage years, like most transitions, is a grey, mutable area in which he, his friends, and the target audience of the narrative are moving between childhood and young adulthood. Into this stage of life, Rowling injects two of James and Lily Potter's best friends, one of whom happens to be a werewolf (and the other can willingly turn into a dog).[20] Both figures become mentors for the rest of Harry's early teenage years.

Although Harry's age is a significant transition point, it is not the only one present in *Azkaban*. The series undergoes a serious shift during the course of the narrative. My choice of the term "serious" to describe the change is done with purpose, and with no intent to present a pun on Black's name. While the series before *Azkaban* had its serious moments, for the most part it is lighthearted with everything returning to happy normalcy in the end. *Azkaban* signals a change in tone, in part caused by Lupin's lycanthropy. Lupin's uncontrolled change allows Pettigrew to escape in the end, leaving Black still accused of betraying the Potters and of being a mass murderer. For the first time, not everything works out for the heroes. Moreover, as Harry learns from Professor Trelawney, Pettigrew's escape, which Harry has to watch twice, eventually allows Voldemort to return to power. This threat signals an important shift in the tone of the series, which becomes progressively darker and begins to involve the demise of well-known characters like Black, Dumbledore, Lupin, Snape, and Moody.

The werewolves are temporarily silent during the fourth installment of the series. Lupin returns to greater prominence during the fifth (where another, unnamed, werewolf also appears), when the major conflict of the series begins in earnest. More important, in *Order of the Phoenix*'s case, a significant transition occurs in which the first of Harry's father figures—Black—dies. This becomes doubly important in *Half-Blood Prince*, thus calling for two werewolves (and a partial one) due to the death of Harry's other father figure (Dumbledore) and Voldemort's complete re-entry to the world. The final installment of the series, in which the threat is finally and utterly ended, includes not only the two full werewolves (Lupin and Greyback) and the partial werewolf (Bill Weasley) but also a half-werewolf (Lupin's and Tonks' son, Ted). As we can see, over the course of the last part of the series, the number of werewolves increases as the significance of the transition moments increase. In the end, though, all save the half-werewolf disappear: Lupin dies, Greyback vanishes, Bill Weasley fades from sight, but Ted Lupin remains in the epilogue.[21]

Monstrosity, Mechanics, and Self-Fashioning

The werewolf changes as it moves into the early modern period, returning to its monstrous roots—as represented in Henri Boguet, Stubbe Peeter, Jean Grenier, Heinrich Kramer and James Sprenger, Jean Bodin, and Thomas Blount. While this change occurred, teratologists and demonologists became concerned with defining the process by which a werewolf changed forms. At the same time, broader European culture turned its interest toward the question of what defined an individual, thus forming an interest in the process of self-fashioning. Each of these points is important to the archetype in that shape-shifters are clearly monstrous and use that trait to enforce social rules, the mechanics and attempts at classification reveal a core mutability to the archetype that reflects the world, and self-fashioning as a form of change and/or disguise is openly represented in the shape-shifter and werewolf. Rowling touches upon all three of these trends in her adaptation of the werewolf archetype. She ignores the English

3. Wolf in Professor's Clothing

lycanthropy-as-madness tradition because it does not fit within the structure of the world she posits — people who simply believe they are werewolves would be as out of place in Rowling's fictional England as "real" werewolves would be in our's.

She deals with the monstrous tradition primarily through the early part of the series, before Lupin's arrival, and with Greyback, once Lupin has been established. Very early in Harry's and readers' introduction to the world, Harry and Draco Malfoy are sent to the Forbidden Forest for detention. On the way, Draco fearfully states, "There's all sorts of things in there — werewolves, I heard,"[22] a threat with which Argus Filch gladly plays along to heighten the students' fears. Later, this sentiment is echoed by Ron Weasley who asks, "Aren't there supposed to be werewolves in the forest?"[23] in an attempt to avoid having to follow the spiders to Aragog. In both cases, werewolves are used to scare children into behaving, in much the same way as a bogeyman or a fairy tale witch might be employed. Through both early introductions, werewolves remain shadowy, an intellectual and emotional threat that the characters, protected as they are at school, are unlikely to ever actually encounter. These moments, however, act in much the same fashion as Marie de France's commentary regarding the *garvulf* in that they usher in Lupin, the tame werewolf.

Even so, that tame werewolf candidly admits that he once was, and can again be, monstrous: "Before the Wolfsbane Potion was discovered, however, I became a fully fledged monster once a month."[24] There is little else directly tying the werewolf to monstrosity, though, until Lupin sets the stage for Greyback's arrival. During this prelude, Lupin tells Harry:

> [Greyback] regards it as his mission in life to bite and to contaminate as many people as possible; he wants to create enough werewolves to overcome the wizards. Voldemort has promised him prey in return for his services. Greyback specializes in children.... Bite them young, he says, and raise them away from their parents, raise them to hate normal wizards. Voldemort has threatened to unleash him upon people's sons and daughters.
> [...]
> At the full moon, he positions himself close to victims, ensuring that he is near enough to strike. He plans it all. And this is the man Voldemort is using to marshal the werewolves.[25]

Based on these tactics alone, Greyback is a clear reappearance of Continental early modern views of werewolves. He meets the criteria in that he changes shape, consorts with wizards and witches (not that this is unusual in Rowling's world), purposely attacks people, and specifically targets children. In fact, in a moment highly reminiscent of Jean Grenier, Greyback practically salivates, saying, "Delicious girl ... What a treat ... I do enjoy the softness of the skin."[26] Grenier told a village girl, "he found [dogs'] flesh less palatable than the flesh of little girls, which he regarded as a supreme delicacy."[27] Placed next to each other, we cannot help but see the similarity of the language and sentiment. Based on the connection, Greyback is in some respect an older Grenier, one who did not get caught early in life, instead managing to remain not only hidden but successful in his own fashion for at least a couple decades.[28] Although a sexualized interpretation could be argued here, a stronger position, based on the text, is that these scenes hint at cannibalism and directly display Voldemort's use of Greyback as an expendable terrorist who strikes at the most vulnerable part of society. This also connects to his bestial nature in that it is a common practice of wolves and similar predators to target young prey as being easier to separate from the herd and catch.

This bestiality is referred to again several times in Greyback's case. The first key moment is when Greyback attacks Harry, who "fell backward, with filthy matted hair in his face, the stench of sweat and blood filling his nose and mouth, hot greedy breath at his throat."[29] Not content with merely biting victims, Greyback always attacks the throat and face, even when he is not transformed. This practice is demonstrated again when he attacks another student during the series' climax and when he attacks Bill Weasley in *Half-Blood Prince*, savaging Bill's face in the process. Harry later described Greyback as having "a face covered in matted grey hair and whiskers, with pointed brown teeth and sores at the corners of his mouth,"[30] adding a monstrous appearance to his monstrous behavior.[31] The lack of hygiene indicates Greyback's place in society, or rather outside it, in that he makes no attempts to take care of his appearance and has no access to any sort of health care. Based on Lupin's descriptions of his time in wolf shape, many of Greyback's wounds are probably self-inflicted. While Lupin is commonly described as greying or shabby, his appearance is generally discussed as being pitiable or pathetic rather than monstrous. The other key moment, one that is connected to appearance, occurs when Harry, faced with Greyback, thinks, "Fenrir Greyback, the werewolf who was permitted to wear Death Eater robes in return for his hired savagery."[32] Yet, as Harry later adds, Greyback's savagery is not allowed to fully enter the society that Voldemort creates. Even the monstrous wizard has his limits. These limits are, of course, part and parcel of his general Hitlerian racial cleansing program; he is happy to harness Greyback's and his shadow's savagery, but neither Greyback nor his fellow werewolves will ever be part of the society they help create. This realization begins to transmute the savage werewolf into a pitiable figure, even if he never comes close to the state Lupin occupies.

Rowling's monsters, like their early modern counterparts, do follow certain rules. As with most of the modifications she made to create her world, Rowling manipulates the mechanics of their existence to meet her literary ends. This is a reappearance, as it is with Pratchett, of the early modern interest in the mechanics of shape-shifting and witchcraft. In some cases, these rules are laid out in a simple format, as is seen in the fictional book Rowling authored under the pseudonym Newt Scamander, *Fantastic Beasts and Where to Find Them* (2001). The inclusion of werewolves in this book places them among non-human creatures, arguing for both monstrosity and a racial interpretation as will be discussed in more detail later. What is more important for the purposes of charting Rowling's early modern influences is that she lays out a few basic mechanics of the werewolf change in this format:

> Humans turn into werewolves only when bitten. There is no known cure, though recent developments in potion-making have to a great extent alleviated the worst symptoms. Once a month, at the full moon, the otherwise sane and normal wizard or Muggle afflicted transforms into a murderous beast. Almost uniquely among fantastic creatures, the werewolf actively seeks humans in preference to any other kind of prey.[33]

While the description answers some mechanical questions, it opens up other questions that will be dealt with later. As the appearances of the werewolves continue, other mechanical rules are revealed through both Harry's discussions with Lupin and physical demonstrations. Interestingly, Rowling presents apparent contradictions to the rules in some cases as well. An example occurs in *Chamber of Secrets* (1999) in which the vain Professor Lockhart claims that while fighting a werewolf, he once "performed the immensely complex Homorphous Charm — [the werewolf] let out a piteous moan [...] The fur vanished — the fangs shrank — and he turned back into a man,"[34] implying that he cured this werewolf, though Rowling later emphatically states that there is no cure for lycanthropy. In this case, she uses the werewolf in an archetypal role as another means of undercutting the authority and self-image of the character through Lockhart's implied claim that he can break the rules that govern the world. Although there is room to argue that the "cure" is temporary, the only other time the charm might have been used in the series is when Black and Lupin force Pettigrew back into his human shape.[35] Moreover, everything else Lockhart claims is shown to be false, so the reader has no reason to trust this particular incident either.

There are other mechanics that Rowling refers to throughout the series, with most appearing in *Azkaban* and later works. Early in *Azkaban*, Rowling refers to the early modern Continental image of werewolves again by having Hermione state that "the werewolf differs from the true wolf in several small ways,"[36] before she is interrupted. The details are later filled in during one of Snape's memories, which Harry manages to see in *Order of the Phoenix*. His father, Black, and Lupin are seen joking over a question about identifying werewolves on the Defense Against the Dark Arts exam[37] when Pettigrew brings up "the snout shape, the pupils of the eyes, and the tufted tail."[38] This example shows the reader that, unlike the cinematic version of *Azkaban*, Rowling intended the werewolves to possess a human and a wolf shape only, in the medieval and early modern traditions, without the hybrid wolf-man of twentieth-century film. It also demonstrates that her werewolves are not identical to real wolves, even if the clues are more subtle than many commonly expressed in early modern sources — including a short or missing tail — yet less subtle or subjective than the behavioral signs that were commonly cited — such as not acting like a wolf.

Most of the information the reader receives about the mechanical aspects of lycanthropy come from Lupin himself, who is like Sergeant Angua in that he is a self-reflective werewolf. He is the one who tells Harry, "My parents tried everything, but in those days there was no cure,"[39] and the Wolfsbane Potion is both a recent discovery and not a cure. As was discussed in the classical and early modern periods, Rowling's transformed werewolves typically lose their access to rational thought. But, Lupin states, "as long as I take [the Wolfsbane Potion] in the week preceding the full moon, I keep my mind when I transform ... I am able to curl up in my office, a harmless wolf, and wait for the moon to wane again."[40] With the potion, he becomes a medieval sympathetic werewolf. Tied in with this statement is the idea that Rowling's werewolves cannot willingly change shape, unlike their early predecessors.

3. Wolf in Professor's Clothing

Throughout the extended narrative, Rowling presents several other insights into the mechanics and rules governing her werewolves. The aforementioned examples serve as a representative sample, save only for the important one that she never truly answers: can the affliction be passed on from parent to child?

The question arises first because of something Voldemort, as Tom Riddle, tells Harry in *Chamber of Secrets*, that Hagrid was "trying to raise werewolf cubs under his bed" when he was a student. Riddle/Voldemort returns to the same question at the end of the series after Lupin marries Tonks. The audience's only authority on the subject, Lupin himself, appears convinced that the condition can be passed on, but does not truly know. The evidence of Ted Lupin seems to prove them both wrong, as do the repeated statements that only those bitten by werewolves acquire the traits, but seeing as the initial information comes from an unreliable source and there is no later evidence, the question still exists and has some bearing on future interpretations of the phenomenon.

The fact that this particular question remains unanswered is important because of its effect on Lupin's brand of self-fashioning, which mimics the early modern concept. Throughout their appearances, both Lupin and Greyback act as representatives of self-definition, a key concept for self-fashioning. Greyback, to reverse their order, gives in to public opinion and his race and affliction. He strives to become the beast that others believe he ought to be as a werewolf. He descends into this concept so far that Harry at one point describes seeing "a grey blur that Harry took for an animal sped four-legged across the hall to sink its teeth into one of the fallen,"[41] referring to Greyback, who is not transformed at the time (we know this, in part, because Lupin is not transformed). He accepts and fully embraces the bestial side that his society believes is his nature. Conversely, Lupin accepts the social view with regard to many of his fellow werewolves, but rejects it for himself. As Baldesar Castiglione and Niccolo Machiavelli recommend their readers do for social gain, Lupin refashions himself for social acceptance. In this way, he displays the potential threat involved in self-fashioning — the monster hiding in society by masquerading as human. He acquires an education, although later in his life he admits to being ashamed of putting other students in potential danger. Not only that, but he eventually becomes a teacher, if only briefly (what he teaches and to whom will be discussed in greater detail below). Throughout his time in the proverbial spotlight, he acts as a peacemaker and as a calm foundation for other characters, notably Black and James Potter. In fact, Lupin states that Dumbledore made him a prefect in his fifth year and says that the headmaster "might have hoped that I would be able to exercise some control over my best friends [...] I need scarsely say that I failed dismally."[42] Even though he failed, the important point is that he made an effort to move beyond his supposed nature and was recognized as a source of civility and socialization rather than a ravening monster.

The words Castiglione uses to describe Duke Guidebaldo apply equally well to Lupin:

> although he was a man of mature deliberation and unconquerable spirit, everything he set his hand to, whether in arms or anything else, great or small, always ended unhappily, as we can see from the many diverse calamities which befell him, and which he always bore with such fortitude that his will was never crushed by fate. On the contrary, with great resilience and spirit, he despised the blows of Fortune, living the life of a healthy and happy man, despite sickness and adversity, and achieving true dignity and universal renown.[43]

While not all of Lupin's endeavors end unhappily, he suffers more than the normal share of calamities. Moreover, he meets nearly all of the criteria that Castiglione sets out for a gentleman: skill at arms (shown in *Order of the Phoenix* and *Deathly Hallows*), loyalty (shown repeatedly), bravery, kindness, modesty, and learning. The only ones potentially missing are noble birth (he is a half-wizard, half–Muggle), music, and painting. Of equal importance is the fact that, like the Harry-Voldemort dynamic and Harry's various friends versus Voldemort's minions, Lupin and Greyback further illustrate Castiglione's statement that "(since evil is the opposite of good and good of evil) the one must always sustain and reinforce the other, and if the one diminishes or increases, the other, as its necessary counter-force, must do the same."[44] Once the good, sympathetic werewolf dies, his monstrous opposite vanishes from the series.

Lupin, Greyback, and Archetype

The sense of balance, or counter-force, discussed by Castiglione and its presence in Rowling's werewolves connects them to a Jungian analysis through the shadow. This entity represents the various personality traits

3. Wolf in Professor's Clothing

that society desires to purge and is clearly present in both Lupin and Greyback, through their animalistic sides, moreso in Greyback's case since he gives himself entirely over to the bestial shadow. Lupin, on the other hand, acknowledges and accepts the shadow, but does not let it control his actions, thereby becoming a psychologically healthy individual in the Jungian sense. Both figures, through their interactions with the shadow, tie themselves to the shape-shifter archetype in several ways. The most obvious of these is that they are capable of changing form and thereby crossing racial and species boundaries. This is only the most cursory connection, though.

When we look beneath the surface and see how the two characters act and respond to their fictional environment, we can see that they fulfill many of the other qualities of the archetype. Both Lupin and Greyback, as with many shape-shifters, act as civilizing figures, as previously discussed. In this capacity, they share a strong symbolic connection with their lycanthropic predecessors. This connection to the past is one key method by which the werewolves fulfill the archetype's promise of stability within mutability, a solid core within the evolving, metamorphic situation. Like Bisclavret or Alphouns, Lupin instructs others in proper behavior. He is considerably more direct in this act, since his first appearance in the narrative is as a teacher, but even after his time as a formal educator is over, he continues to play the part. Throughout the remainder of the series, he commonly takes on a professorial tone in his discussions with Harry. In this, he joins Ron and Hermione as a source of information about the wizarding world, but unlike Ron, at least, Lupin's information is presented in a factual or philosophic manner rather than as common knowledge or rumor. In contrast to Hermione's, Lupin's information also comes from living as a wizard for his whole life and personal experience rather than book knowledge. This provides a third option as a source, one that is neither entirely bookish nor entirely word of mouth. Based on this information and his role as an educator, Lupin manages to subtly and not so subtly guide Harry's moral choices whenever a troubling situation arises. A good example of this occurs when Harry asks about the dementors' soul-sucking kiss and seems convinced that Black deserves that punishment for his alleged crime. Lupin quietly asks if Harry truly believes that anyone deserves that sort of punishment, which causes Harry to reconsider.

Greyback, on the other hand, functions to maintain civility and socialization through fear. He becomes not only a tool that Voldemort uses against those who cross him, but a sort of bogeyman in the wizarding community. The barely restrained violence inherent in his character serves to incite fear of transgression in Voldemort's ideal society, while creating a strong sense of repugnance in his opponents who realize that his actions threaten the fabric of society. That said, even Voldemort himself will not cross the boundary that Greyback passed long before Harry was born. Throughout the series, the only times Voldemort directly attacks or kills another character (except for Harry, for whom there are extenuating circumstances) that individual is an adult. Even Cedric Diggory, while still at school, was technically an adult. The only exceptions occur when Voldemort too was underage. Conversely, Greyback delights in attacking children, an act he routinely salivates over and becomes eager about. In his role as shape-shifter, he frightens both other characters and the audience into a social mold that balks at harming the perceived innocents within society.[45] If the audience acquires this sense of fearing transgression in one aspect of what Greyback does, then they are likely to begin to translate that response to the socio-political entity that he represents and works for, thus enhancing their support for the socio-political entity that opposes his, the social norm. In this respect, the unrestrained werewolf functions as a representation of modern terrorists, working to create fear in service of his socio-political ideals.

Through Greyback's position as an agent of completely unrestrained transgression, juxtaposed against Voldemort's limited transgression, he serves an important function of the archetype. In this role, he commits acts of violence well beyond the norms accepted by society. But through his inherent violence, with its erotic undercurrent and threat of future transgressive violence, he creates a forbidden and vicarious release of the shadow, a place in the imagination where the shadow can act completely unfettered and do as it will.

The socially constructed norm also has a part to play in that Lupin and Greyback represent the archetype's approach to the nature-nurture debate. Through the process of self-fashioning, Lupin manages to master the bestial nature of the werewolf insofar as he is able. I say the latter because the civil, socially acceptable, and calm Lupin does slip away at least once, during which point "he glared at them so fiercely that Harry saw, for the first time ever, the shadow of the wolf upon his human face."[46] The dominance of nurture over nature is a theme that Rowling returns to

3. Wolf in Professor's Clothing

time and time again through Hagrid and Harry, especially through and after *Goblet of Fire* (2000), both in the realm of genetics and that of fate or destiny. Harry also acts to point to nature ascendant thanks to his childhood taken in light of his time at Hogwarts. Likewise, it can be argued that Lupin's pre-lycanthropy nature overshadows his post-lycanthropy nature, but following this line leads to no conclusive evidence since any discussion of his early life is limited or non-existent. The nature dominant option in the aforementioned debate, however, is seen in clearer form with Greyback. That werewolf, as noted previously, embraces the bestial side of his nature and uses it as a form of power to terrorize others. Like the early modern Continental werewolf accounts, he gives in to the basic desires and violence said to be inherent to the form. Because of this reveling in the supposedly bestial, glorifying in his restrained cannibalistic urges (another sometime sign of the shape-shifter archetype), he represents that which is most monstrous about the werewolf and the human — especially so in using the rational human to guide the irrationally violent monster's actions. Tied to their unsettling of the nature-versus-nurture divide is the fact that these figures inherently attack socially imposed categories. The most obvious is that implied above in the fictional Scamander's classification — werewolves are clearly human, but they are discussed in a book about "fantastic beasts." By that very placement, they act to disrupt the categories, as do the centaurs and merfolk also mentioned in the book, but who are clearly sentient and human-like. Beyond that point, Lupin reminds Harry at least twice that the world is not black and white in its morality, usually in reference to Snape — a point upon which Black supports him in *Order of the Phoenix*, referring to Dolores Umbridge.

Neither Lupin nor Greyback function entirely within the older models of werewolf behavior. While they certainly retain most of the aspects of the archetype, they also expand it. The archetype's manifestation has to expand and metamorphose in this case because society and individuals have evolved, and collapsed, several times since the early werewolf films, and even more since the seventeenth-century. As such, the evolution of the archetype into Rowling's representations is a new beginning, another rebirth that the figure undergoes periodically in order to maintain its fluidity, hybridity, and relevance. This expansion occurs not necessarily through the addition of more layers or traits, but through the application of those traits. The role Lupin and Greyback play in discussions of intolerance and racism are clearly an aspect of the shape-shifter archetype's dissolution of artificially constructed boundaries, but they represent a new method of applying that aspect which is not present in the literary werewolf before the modern era. Their use in the discussion of morality and paradox is equally familiar as a form of the boundary aspect, but again is employed using different techniques. To date, Remus Lupin is the first literary werewolf imagined in the role of a school teacher, while he is not the only one, there are very few other examples.[47] Although his figurative ancestors taught lessons, none of them did so in a classroom setting or with the professor-student relationship as such. This particular role also affects his use in instructing others about civility, social compliance, and respect. It is his own nature, or nurtured upbringing, that informs his role as a peacemaker and the discussion of friendship in which he becomes involved.

Like most monsters, Lupin and Greyback are also part of an inversion of the classic hero tale analyzed most notably by Joseph Campbell. According to Crystal L. O'Leary, this inversion begins in that "the monster is born into separation through the father's unnatural act of procreation,"[48] in this case Greyback's biting Lupin to make him a werewolf. Another shift occurs because "the first stage of the monster's journey [is] separation from the human community due to form [and the] second stage of the quest [is] discovery of self in relation to the outer world."[49] In this case, the separation involves Lupin's removal to Hogwarts and the Shrieking Shack as a double separation from the human community, one that he returns from only with the assistance of his friends — Black, Pettigrew, and James Potter. Through this separation, and his later separation into the community of his fellow werewolves, he acquires a greater understanding of the human community, which he endeavors to impart to Harry on several occasions.

Wolves in Education

Monsters, in general and by their very nature, act as educators. Through them, according to Asa Mittman, the "audience is invited to adopt temporarily the perspective of people more marginal than themselves."[50] This is doubly true of the werewolves in Rowling's work. Initially these representatives of the shadow are marginalized as part of a special

3. Wolf in Professor's Clothing

sub-community and world, that of the wizards and witches. Even in that already marginal community, they are further marginalized and pushed to the fringes by both popular fears and legal statutes. The latter is directly seen when Black discusses Umbridge, saying, "She drafted a bit of anti-werewolf legislation two years ago that makes it almost impossible for [Lupin] to get a job."[51] Because of such treatment, the werewolves "have shunned normal society and live on the margins, stealing—and sometimes killing—to eat."[52] Already, the reader begins to learn from these figures, thanks to the self-fulfilling prophecy inherent in these two statements—because of fear that this community will be violent, it is legally marginalized, this in turn causes it to become violent in order to survive.

In Rowling's work, the werewolves—Lupin, Greyback, the unnamed werewolves (Lockhart's and the one in St. Mungo's), and the partial werewolves—all serve to educate key characters, especially Harry, Ron, and Hermione, as well as the audience about a variety of subjects. On one level, the werewolves speak to intolerance, prejudice, and racism. This particular lesson becomes more overt, as will be shown, through Hermione, Ron, and Lupin. The werewolves are only a facet of Rowling's discussion of that issue, but one that is commonly overlooked or dismissed.[53] Connected to this discussion is the use of werewolves to talk about incurable diseases, including HIV/AIDS, some forms of cancer, or multiple sclerosis. The difference between these two issues or lessons is a thin line that Rowling continuously crosses over. Due to Lupin's position, both as a teacher and a friend of Harry's parents, the werewolves, true to the archetype, also present lessons about morality and present apparent moral paradoxes. The latter, Lupin and Black join to explain, are generally discussed through a moral continuum rather than binaries, a fact that has annoyed certain elements of our society, as evidenced by the number of attempts to ban the books on moral grounds. Lessons on morality, at least those coming from Lupin, are inextricably tied to questions of friendship and respect that are of great importance to Rowling and the younger range of her target audience, though they can be a useful reminder for her older audience members as well. The professorial/educator werewolf also functions to educate the characters and audience in civility and socialization. In the former case, Lupin works as a peacemaker and civilizing force. Developing socialization, both Lupin and Greyback work together to both socialize certain characters and to complicate the idea of producing socially normal children or young adults, though Greyback has already been partially discussed in that role.

Monstrosity in all its forms, across every century, has been tied to questions of racial and/or ethnic identity. As Andriano says, "the myth of the beast-monster involves the question — indeed the very definition — of race,"[54] in that many of the monstrous races imagined from the earliest days of writing or storytelling stand in for foreign otherness. Case in point, Rowling's house-elves can be read as pre-abolition African slaves (in the U.S., Caribbean, or Britain) and her goblins can easily be read as standing in for medieval views of Jewish moneylenders.

This is no less true with the case of Rowling's werewolves. Initially, Rowling treats these figures as possibly sentient beings, but not necessarily so. They are discussed as "things" and the students are set to copy "different ways of treating werewolf bites"[55] in class. But they appear to have some capacity for rational thought, thanks to an early mention of the "1637 Werewolf Code of Conduct."[56] Even when Lupin is first introduced, the question of sentience is unresolved, in part by Snape's assigning "an essay [...] on the ways you recognize and kill werewolves."[57] This seemingly innocuous assignment, given that Lupin taught the class about dealing with various "Dark" creatures, takes on a very different tone when the characters and readers discover that Lupin is a werewolf.

The reader quickly becomes aware that Snape's professed view of werewolves is not unique. However, the evidence comes not from his Slytherins, whom the reader comes to expect as his support, but from Ron and Hermione. While Draco responds to Lupin with "Look at the state of his robes [...] He dresses like our old house elf,"[58] in a typical Malfoy statement, he is focused on socio-economic class.[59] As Elaine Ostry notes, it is Ron who acts as "the mouthpiece of common prejudices"[60] and shrinks back from Lupin, a teacher he previously respected. Ron is the one who spits out "Dumbledore hired you when he knew you were a werewolf? ... Is he mad?"[61] This move, switching the roles the reader assumes for her protagonists and antagonists, is characteristic of Rowling's writing, and is rather subtle in this case. The reader's eye easily skims over this passage and accepts it, in part, because Ron and Hermione are Harry's (and the reader's) primary source of information about, and interpretation of, the wizarding world. Since the two of them react strongly, Ron characteristically moreso than Hermione,[62] and they have been trustworthy throughout the series, the reader is led to accept their reactions. Here, the shape-shifter appears in order to cross the boundaries between characters and parts of society in that the otherwise good, positive characters display less positive qualities. The werewolf temporarily withdraws the self-fashioned façade of binary thought to display the grey areas it conceals. Snape, like Draco, remains true to form in his relations with Lupin. As readers tend to do with all of Snape's reactions, we wonder where exactly he falls. Initially, Lupin appears correct in asserting that Snape is holding on to an old childhood grudge. This, of course, paints the Potions Professor as a petty individual. However, Snape later states: "He [Dumbledore] was quite convinced you were harmless, you know, Lupin ... a *tame* werewolf"[63] and "Don't ask me to fathom the way a werewolf's mind works."[64] These two brief statements recall Ron's socialized and nurtured racism, which serves to increase the reader's already well confused perspective on Snape and his motives. Lupin appears resigned to this sort of intolerance as he tells Harry, "This time tomorrow, the owls will start arriving from parents ... They will not want a werewolf teaching their children."[65] To unpack this particular statement, we have to consider both the idea of lycanthropy as a disease that Lupin could easily pass on to any number of children and the terror created by the actions of Greyback and his followers. Since Rowling has established that Greyback targets children as a form of terrorism, and encourages his followers to do the same, the parents of Hogwarts students are likely to think that any werewolf must be the same.

The theme continues throughout the series, with prejudice and intolerance generally using the language of racism. Talking about Hagrid's revelation that he is a half-giant, Hermione says, "It's the same sort of prejudice that people have toward werewolves.... It's just bigotry, isn't it?"[66] Hermione and Kreacher both place the issue firmly within the realm of racism as well. She states "it's the same kind of nonsense as werewolf segregation, isn't it? It all stems from this horrible thing wizards have of thinking they're superior to other creatures."[67] This, of course, has its own racial superiority complex inherent in the use of the term "creatures" instead of "races" or some other less pejorative or bestial terminology. But, the sentiment is the important part, since it ties the anti-werewolf prejudice in Rowling's world to racism. Likewise, Kreacher's statement about "Mudbloods and werewolves"[68] is of the same order in a society where a lack of pure blood is considered by some to be of a different race. Karin Westman has noted from similar statements "that [Ron's] prejudice against werewolves is not isolated but of a piece with other cultural fears against non-wizard species."[69] As if to add subtle insult to injury, we discover in book five that this prejudice came to Ron through another likeable character: his mother. Upon learning that a werewolf is sharing a ward with her injured husband, she asks, "A werewolf? [...] Is he safe in a public ward? Shouldn't he be in a private room?"[70] And her concern comes after years of knowing Lupin, the clearest exception to the prejudicial rule, and at a time far removed from a full moon (seeing as she does not harbor the same fears regarding Lupin at that time).

The source of this prejudiced view, and its racial connotations, is nowhere more evident than in the words of Dolores Umbridge, who tells a class of students that they have been taught by "extremely dangerous half-breeds,"[71] meaning Lupin. The clearest explanation is offered by Black when Hermione asks about Umbridge's racism. He simply states, "Scared of them, I expect [...] Apparently she loathes part-humans."[72] This fear is understandable, to some extent, in the representatives of government. Historically, governments have done their best to "protect" their societies from perceived outsiders, whether these outsiders be Jewish sub-communities, gypsy wanderers, Viking raiders, Irish laborers, or African ex-slaves looking to make a living. The fact that Rowling's werewolves, half-giants, and half–Veela, at least, can blend in with the general populace only makes them a greater threat to the social order because they do not stand out, or at least the werewolves do not most of the time.[73] According to Rowling, and presumably most readers, the fact that the prejudice is understandable does not excuse it. Rather, being understandable only makes it worse because it becomes insidious: the same heroic characters who take a stand against Voldemort and his Hitlerian program against non-pure bloods generally have no problems with the treatment of werewolves and other part-humans. Of the two, this makes Umbridge a much more fearsome and, in some ways, realistic villain than Voldemort could ever hope to be.

As with nearly everything in Rowling's world and involving the proposed archetype, characterizing Lupin's lycanthropy as a race issue is an oversimplification. On the surface, the aforementioned statements from Ron Weasley, Snape, and Umbridge combine with European tradition and common pop cultural thought to create a seemingly clear cut discussion of racism inherent in Rowling's wizarding community. Ostry and Westman point directly to the racism interpretation, stating: "Rowling protests racial intolerance by showing how such creatures as giants [...] werewolves, and elves are treated"[74] and "The tensions [...] among werewolves [...] and wizards echo the fervent tensions between race and class in the 'real' contemporary British politic"[75] respectively. From this perspective, Rowling certainly voices her position against racial intolerance, through the evolving views and general reactions of Harry, Ron, Hermione, Dumbledore, Black, and the Weasleys in their relationships with Lupin. This reading of the character also ties in with issues of socialization.

That said, Rowling's language is far from clear when she brings up the lycanthropy as race issue. When Lupin describes his origins — "I was a very small boy when I received the bite. My parents tried everything, but in those days there was no cure. The potion that Professor Snape has been making for me is a very recent discovery"[76] — he uses the language of illness and disease. Lupin was not born a werewolf. In fact, it appears that none of Rowling's werewolves were born that way.[77] Because of transmission via a bite and the fact that, to quote Katherine Grimes and Lana Whited, "Lupin can be treated but not cured,"[78] the reader is left wondering whether lycanthropy is a sort of retrovirus affecting the genetic code or a disease like HIV/AIDS, as a handful of critics have suggested, or cancer or MS. Among these is Westman, who theorized that "Lupin's status as werewolf [...] could represent contemporary prejudice against homosexuals or those infected with HIV."[79] Giselle Anatol likewise wrestles with the question of race or disease, making the same suggestion of equating lycanthropy with HIV/AIDS.[80]

Rowling herself seems unclear as to whether her lycanthropes are a race or a group of diseased individuals. We should expect this sort of ambivalence regarding categories in reference to the archetype that implicitly resists categorization. At some points she uses the language of racism, as previously noted, and at others she shifts into the language of disease — other children being "exposed" to Lupin, a potion or medication that causes his problem to go into temporary remission, discussions of curing lycanthropy, or Lupin's own statement that "Tonks deserves somebody young and whole"[81] implying that he is not well. At a presentation in 2003, Rowling stated that Lupin was afflicted with a "contagious disease,"[82] but this only works with some of the language she employs when discussing his character, so we can only accept it to a limited extent. In *Order of the*

Phoenix, Rowling primarily uses the language of race relations with Lupin, specifically in references to his social life, Hermione's S.P.E.W., and Umbridge's comments, as noted. But, in *Half-Blood Prince*, the language changes to that of disease, largely in discussing Greyback, the Wolfsbane Potion, and Bill Weasley's bite.[83] *Deathly Hallows* returns to racial language, coming in large part from Voldemort. If lycanthropy is purely a racial issue, one would not expect the Wolfsbane Potion to exist since there is no medication that can, even temporarily, change a person's race. Likewise, if it is purely a disease, then the reader could expect to see more werewolves in St. Mungo's Hospital, especially once Greyback and his followers are set loose upon society.

This ambiguity is typical for Rowling's characters, especially Lupin, and translates itself into the realm of morality as well. Both Lupin and Greyback function to instill morality in both other characters and the audience. In Lupin's case, the morality also carries over into his own actions, since he stands as an example of positive morals. Greyback enforces social morality, on the other hand, through providing a negative example intended to cause fear of transgression as previously discussed. Of the two, Lupin's positive reinforcement is clearly the more effective due in large part to his appearances and positive relationship with the protagonists throughout the series. Lupin's role as an agent of morality is somewhat paradoxical because, as Grimes and Whited note, "as a werewolf, he would be generally perceived as an inappropriate role model"[84] while such characters as Snape and Umbridge are held up as appropriate role models by the same characters, such as Cornelius Fudge and Lucius Malfoy. This is only one potential paradox in his character that is tied to morality.

Readers can see Lupin fulfilling the archetype's role as a moral guide in several ways. The most subtle is during the scenes in which he shares the stage with boggarts — twice in *Prisoner of Azkaban* and once in *Order of the Phoenix*. In all three cases, the boggart, a being that turns into that which the viewer most fears, becomes "a silvery orb hanging in the air in front of Lupin."[85] Just as Harry's dementor-boggart is interpreted, by Lupin, as representing a fear of fear, Lupin's has a subtext beneath the obvious fear of the full moon. Since the transformation becomes less painful with the potion, what the full moon represents for Lupin is the loss of control, the loss of social acceptance, and through that, the possibility of inadvertently harming others, including his friends and their families.

3. Wolf in Professor's Clothing

This, in turn, suggests that what Lupin most fears is amorality and, if we define morality as a social construct, antisocial behavior. If that is the case, then Lupin's attempts to keep his temper and the tempers of others under control make sense as a moral action. His attempts focus on discipline, which Ellen Goldner notes, "appropriates the conspicuous body, redefining it as hideous; it makes of that body a mere (pre)text for the painful production of the private soul,"[86] in the case of monstrous beings. Lupin's private soul then becomes the rock of morality with which he works to guide others. As noted by Green, "The werewolf form liberates Remus from the constraints of propriety"[87] and allows his to shed "any societal constraints and concerns about the outward appearance of propriety."[88] That said, the question remains: does Lupin wish to be liberated? Based on his actions, the answer is very likely: no, he does not desire this liberation, as opposed to Greyback who appears to revel in the relative freedom.

The other, early, key moment in which Lupin establishes himself as a moral guide comes when he and Harry discuss dementors. After Lupin explains that these creatures essentially suck out their victims' souls, Harry quickly states that Black would then be getting what he deserved for betraying the Potters. To this, Lupin simply asks, "Do you really think anyone deserves that?"[89] The question causes Harry to go back and rethink what he knows and what he agreed to. In the process, his mind is changed as he moves toward a more morally positive path, incidentally closer to that which Dumbledore would advise as well. Lupin's place in this role can turn counterproductive, as he later worries, "My kind don't usually breed! It will be like me, I am convinced of it — how can I forgive myself, when I knowingly risked passing on my own condition to an innocent child."[90] Fortunately, Harry has been an apt student of the moral subtext and Lupin's own relationships. He turns the student-teacher dynamic around, making himself the instructor as he deftly turns Lupin's "immoral" act into one that is less immoral than abandoning his wife and unborn child. The scene not only shows that Harry has grown emotionally, but also that he has learned the moral lessons that Lupin and others have subtly taught him, to the point that he can act as a moral guide for them.

Lupin is a problematic moral guide because some of the morals he espouses are not socially positive. Whereas Charles Perrault's Wolf— in his version of "Little Red Riding Hood"— pushes readers toward following rules and maintaining social structures, Lupin advocates violating rules and social restrictions on several occasions. He certainly displays this attitude and moral during his time as a student, roaming the school grounds with James and Black while he is dangerously transformed. Not only does this oft repeated act violate myriad rules, but it also shows a clear disregard for potential consequences that Lupin only recalls after the fact. In spite of finally understanding the possible consequences, he does not learn from this experience, or is eventually convinced to ignore the lesson, as he breaks social conventions during adulthood to marry and have a child. Only later does he fully realize or consider the possible consequences, once it is too late to change anything. This particular disregard for rules, social convention, and consequences is something he implicitly encourages in Harry until the scene noted above in which Harry reverses their positions. This is one of the more subtle morals conveyed both by Lupin and the series: that sometimes, perhaps often, disregarding rules, society, and consequences is a necessity for individual and social development. This requirement seems clear because it is only by breaking the rules and conventions that Lupin can self-fashion and improve his station, and thereby achieve the dream of having a family in which Harry vicariously participates.

The other paradox that arises is the role of the "inherently" violent social outsider as moral guide. Lupin brings this problem to the forefront when he tells Harry, "I'm not a very popular dinner guest with most of the community. [...] It's an occupational hazard of being a werewolf."[91] He is simultaneously a positive and destructive force. Roni Natov addresses this potential issue when she states, "Lupin, who is a werewolf, turns out to be a paradoxical figure: a force of good that can be dangerous as well."[92] The question we have to ask is: is this necessarily a paradox? After all, Dumbledore is both a force of good and rather dangerous (the latter being well known to both Cornelius Fudge and Voldemort). As C. S. Lewis' Mr. Beaver said of Aslan, "Course he isn't safe. But he's good."[93] Being both good (civilized, human?) and dangerous (uncivilized, bestial?) is not necessarily a paradox. Rather, as shown through medieval and early modern werewolf discussions, it is a key component of human nature and one that the shape-shifter archetype is especially apt at discussing. In Lupin's case, this supposed paradox turns into a boon, in that he can use his split nature to spy on Voldemort's allies and attempt to convince other werewolves to support the status quo. In like fashion, Rowling employs this dual nature

3. Wolf in Professor's Clothing

in such a way that she, in Natov's words, "establishes his innocence and evokes compassion for him" while "the potentially destructive part of the werewolf is humanized and offered with understanding."[94] This method causes the audience to subconsciously adopt the underlying morality, positive and potentially negative, inherent in the character.

Lacking humanity to temper him, Greyback is dangerous and harkens back to Perrault's wolf. He represents the unbridled violence and antisocial aspects of the archetype. Because he is presented without redeeming qualities, Greyback is the shape-shifter archetype's representation of the consuming shadow. He espouses violence as the solution to problems, as evidenced by his attempted program to rebel against society. He also stands for a moral code that supports vengeance, terror, and transgressively cannibalistic (and metaphorically sexual) acts. This is clearest in his desire to attack and bite children (the younger, the better) not only in order to indoctrinate them into his own army, but because he has developed a taste for them, especially young girls, as previously discussed. The fact that Greyback apparently survives the series and Lupin does not creates a problematic point. The positive, *bisclavret*, aspect of the archetype, the one that taught the use of reason to master the bestial shadow thus making the civilized stronger, dies, but not at the hands of his opposite (his death occurs off-screen, but seems to be wand-related). The negative, *garwulf*, aspect, the part that teaches violence, transgression, and consumption by the shadow, survives but vanishes from sight. Rowling's sympathetic werewolf does not survive while Perrault's wolf does. In this case, based on Harry's actions, Lupin's demise and Greyback's banishment show that Harry has learned his lesson and made his choice. He has internalized the lessons Lupin taught and thus no longer needs that part of the archetype's guidance, and rejected the Greyback aspect, thus banishing it back into the marginal space at the fringes of the psyche and society. In spite of this marginalization, the fact that Greyback presumably survives while Lupin does not implies that Perrault's wolf, the one that threatens punishment for transgression, is dominant. However, Lupin's instruction method is more effective in that his sacrifices are a core element of the lessons he is meant to teach, ones that Greyback as the negative aspects of the archetype would not understand.

Tied to Lupin's role as a moral guide are the lessons about friendship and respect that he quietly teaches alongside his many other lessons.

The Modern Literary Werewolf

Throughout his appearances in the series, Lupin serves to advance the faith in friendships that Rowling returns to repeatedly. We are told that Lupin took great pains to hide his condition so as not to lose his friendship with Black and James Potter, as he says, "I was terrified they would desert me the moment they found out what I was."[95] Later, he takes pains and makes excuses — "I've been feeling a bit off color [...] this potion is the only thing that helps"[96] — to maintain his friendly mentoring relationship with Harry. Both attempts are undertaken to avoid the fate that met Bisclavret and other earlier werewolves: the loss of their standing, place, and relationships. However, in Lupin's case, the revelation of his condition, which James refers to as Lupin's "furry little problem,"[97] actually strengthens his friendship with the two troublemakers. In order to help him, both Black and Potter undertake a dangerous enchantment, which also happens to be illegal since they were not registered. He states, "Under their influence, I became less dangerous. My body was still wolfish, but my mind seemed to become less so while I was with them [...] Sirius and James transformed into such large animals, they were able to keep a werewolf in check."[98] For Harry, the situation is more complex due to his assumptions about Black, but he does come around. Because of the earlier friendship, Harry's and Lupin's is strengthened after the lycanthropy revelation to the point that Harry unconsciously echoes his father, saying, "But you are normal! [...] You've just got a — a problem."[99] The reciprocal nature of this relationship comes to light at Harry's seventeenth birthday, after Lupin and Tonks leave. When they next meet him, Tonks explains, "The Ministry's being very anti-werewolf at the moment and we thought our presence might not do you any favors."[100] Rowling employs this character as another layer, a fourth perhaps, of her focus on the importance of community, family, and friends.[101]

The question of friendship is inextricably tied to respect in Rowling's work. None of the characters for whom Harry lacks respect — Professors Lockhart, Slughorn, and Snape,[102] for example — ever come particularly close to him. This becomes especially important with Lupin as part of the archetype's role in building and supporting communities and societies. As Terri Doughty notes, from almost the first moment the audience and Harry meet Lupin, "even before he meets Sirius, Harry often seeks reassurance from Remus Lupin."[103] He knows Lupin, initially, as an authority figure thanks to the werewolf's luggage and presence on the Hogwarts Express.

3. Wolf in Professor's Clothing

More importantly, his respect for Lupin as such a figure begins when the professor chases off a dementor. This respect only grows when it becomes clear that Draco Malfoy disapproves of the werewolf. Harry's respect for his mentor reaches its climax at a major turning point, just after Dumbledore's death. After hearing the news, Lupin breaks down, leaving Harry to think that he "had never seen Lupin lose control before,"[104] something that only happens one other time during the series, when the werewolf feels that he has endangered his nascent family. This breakdown becomes important as it shows Harry that three of his mentors — Black, Dumbledore, and Lupin — are in fact merely human.

This respect spreads throughout Harry's third year of school so that by the time Lupin resigns, Harry "wasn't the only one who was sorry to see Professor Lupin go. The whole of Harry's Defense Against the Dark Arts class was miserable about his resignation,"[105] even knowing he was a werewolf. Indeed, at least one quips a hope that their next teacher will be a vampire, clearly showing that he does not mind the "monstrosity" of their ex-teacher. Along with this, as Chantel Lavoie contends, Lupin acquires respect from his friends because his "affliction is seen very much as a handicap, difficult to overcome. It requires a special sort of courage — one in which he must hurt himself to protect others."[106] The others recognize this characteristic and respond to it, pushing themselves to match the courage they respect in him. In this way, Lupin shows that nurture can overcome nature and that this allows for a better, more psychologically complete individual. The other characters come to learn that he is a better person because he demonstrates an identity that lacks rigid, limiting boundaries and is therefore healthier psychologically. The others see this, respect it, and therefore attempt to achieve a similar state. This is especially important for Harry, as the repository of one-eighth of Voldemort's soul, which manifests itself in shadow-like ways that disturb Harry throughout the series. Harry sees the physical strain caused by this particular trait when Lupin comes to help smuggle him away from the Dursleys: "Remus Lupin, who was looking gaunt and grim, his brown hair streaked liberally with grey, his clothes more ragged and patched than ever."[107] This state comes about because of Lupin's work attempting to infiltrate and convince the werewolves around Greyback to rejoin society, in which he again deprives himself in order to help others and work against Greyback.

Lupin's lessons about respect are not limited to acquiring it for himself, though. He also demonstrates a great deal about respecting others, lessons Harry eventually understands. One sign of this aspect of his lessons comes in St. Mungo's when he "strolled away from [Arthur Weasley's] bed and over to the werewolf, who had no visitors"[108] on Christmas Day. Not only does this display a courteous respect for the Weasley family, but also a concerned respect for someone else who suffers from the same "furry little problem" he does. The majority of Lupin's lessons for Harry in this regard, though, focus on Dumbledore and Snape or Harry. He notes that his respect for Dumbledore comes from the latter's belief in giving everyone a chance. Dumbledore, after all, arranged things so Lupin could come to the school. Lupin later states that Dumbledore "gave me a job when I have been shunned all my adult life, unable to find paid work because of what I am."[109] He also reminds Harry that both of them respect Dumbledore, who trusts Snape, therefore not giving Snape at least a chance to be trusted calls that respect in question. Moreover, he states that while he does not like Snape, he respects the man because he "made the Wolfsbane Potion for me every month, made it perfectly, so I did not have to suffer as I usually do at the full moon."[110] While this particular lesson is not absorbed by Harry until near the end of the whole series, it does eventually have its intended effect, once Harry learns why Dumbledore trusted Snape. Green points out that "Remus continues to treat Snape with unerring civility,"[111] also noting that Snape sees the pacific action as weakness. This can be seen as a sign of passivity in Lupin's nature. However, given that Snape is the target of this specific civility, Lupin's past with Snape must be taken into account. Some of his perfect civility in this situation is likely due to remorse about Lupin's failure to rein in Black and James Potter's bullying and some is tied to his gratitude for Snape's production of the aforementioned potion. There is also a reversal in the relationship between Lupin and Harry. In that situation, in which Lupin makes what he thinks is a moral case for abandoning his family, he learns to respect Harry's judgment as well. Not only that, but he indirectly apologizes to Harry for not having that respect: "I'd tell him to follow his instincts, which are good and nearly always right."[112] Once again, the werewolf archetype appears at a turning point, a place of transition. Here the audience sees a moment when the core trio are reunited and the heroic quest is rejuvenated, both by Ron's return and by the exiled trio being able to listen to a radio program produced by some of their friends and relatives.

3. Wolf in Professor's Clothing

Throughout the series, Lupin provides this sort of support to every character he meets, both in aiding his friends and comrades or those he has just met. Part of the support he provides comes in the form of acting as the peacemaker and instructor in civility and correct social behavior. The latter role is clear both from his position as a moral guide and from the fact that he spends most of his time as a teacher, whether in a classroom setting or elsewhere. In situations that threaten to get out of hand or reach a violent level, this werewolf because of his own level of self-control, steps in to defuse the situation before it escalates too far. One of the clearest examples of this occurs when Harry's wish for information initiates an emotionally explosive scene between Mrs. Weasley and Black. Before the situation completely devolves, and while the other characters simply watch, Lupin raises his voice to sharply state, "Molly, you're not the only person at this table who cares about Harry [...] Sirius, sit *down* [...] I think Harry ought to be allowed a say in this [...] He's old enough to decide for himself."[113] Brought back to at least a grudging peace by their ordinarily quiet and calm companion, the others settle down. This role, in part, continues from his place as the civilizing force, much like Bisclavret and others among his predecessors. Another part of his peacemaking role comes from being an educator. Further aspects that certainly inform his pacific place include the self-control he requires to keep from devolving, himself, into a character like Greyback. In this case, the two aspects of the archetype work together as a reminder that a lapse of control and character could easily turn the educator-moral guide into the slavering beast. Greyback, once he finally appears, becomes Lupin's antithesis and that which Lupin could easily become.

That said, Lupin is fallible, a fact of which he is very aware. In the past, when he may have been meant to pacify and civilize certain characters, he failed, though he does not appear too upset about this specific failure. As he tells Harry, after the latter is told his father was not a prefect but Lupin was, Dumbledore "might have hoped that I would be able to exercise some control over my best friends [...] I need scarcely say that I failed dismally."[114] The irony of the werewolf, the perceived poor role model, receiving the position of authority and rule enforcement is quietly ignored during this scene. An even more subtle statement is made in this act since it is neither Black nor James Potter, the pure-blood wizards, who receive this honor, but rather the half-blood and, in fact, "half-breed" (to use Umbridge's term) character. Dumbledore's actions in this presentation work to nudge Lupin further into the realm of socializing other characters, and the audience, by enacting some social construction or modification.

Lupin's role as a socializer and a questioner of socialization is intertwined with his complication of other characters. On the most superficial level, Lupin clearly acts as a socializing force in his position as a teacher, as noted previously. Not only that, but he is a popular teacher whose job is to train his students to defend themselves. On a slightly deeper level, though, Lupin, Giselle Anatol argues, "serves as a racialized Other; he has been 'passing' for human at Hogwarts in order to achieve acceptance."[115] In this position as Other, Lupin works to question socialization and complicate the readers' interpretation of other characters—specifically Draco Malfoy, Snape, and Ron. For example, before his secret is revealed, "no one else [except Draco] cared that Professor Lupin's robes were patched and frayed."[116] Even after the revelation, the reader is told that the entire third year Defense Against the Dark Arts class at the very least, with the possible exception of the Slytherin students, were sorry to see him leave. Through his example, many of the students renounced a common social prejudice. The notable exceptions to this breakthrough are the aforementioned characters. It is notable that Draco Malfoy comes off on good terms in this respect. The only criticism Malfoy has regarding Lupin is the previously mentioned predictable commentary on his appearance: "Look at the state of his robes [...] He dresses like our old house elf."[117] It is Ron and Snape who act as the voices of racial prejudice as has already been discussed. Lupin's role as a moral guide and peacemaker adds to the socialization effect as does the fact that he never really stops being a teacher, even after he loses his job at Hogwarts, his tone with Harry remains partially mentoring and partially didactic. Green states that Lupin's "behavior towards Harry proves [...] baffling,"[118] because he remains in the educator's role, rather than treating Harry as his friend's son. When we look at the relationship through the lens of the shifter archetype, however, Lupin's behavior makes sense: he is an instinctive educator, his role is not to be Harry's "fun loving uncle" (a role already filled by Sirius Black), but rather to prepare Harry for his final confrontation with Voldemort and the sacrifice Harry will have to make in order to finally defeat his nemesis.

This relation of Rowling's work to morality, or moral guides, has been noted by other scholars, as seen above. However, it is an important part of her use of werewolves, which is an aspect of the moral character that other scholars have marginalized in order to focus on Harry, his two closest friends, and perhaps one or two other characters (usually the adult Weasleys or Snape). Moreover, Rowling's use of the werewolf in this role as moral guide speaks to bridging the past and present in that medieval werewolves were put to similar use, though not as obviously and directly as Lupin.

Into the Future

As with Pratchett's, Rowling's werewolves discover new possibilities for uses of the shape-shifter archetype and werewolf. In some cases, these uses are new applications of older themes, adapted to remain relevant and important. The fantastic genres as a whole, and Rowling in particular, not only present updated themes and stories from the past, they move beyond those foundations into unexplored territory, or transformed versions of familiar territory. In this respect, they ask the audience to question and redefine its views and definitions of the world. Rowling's use of the archetype is especially well adapted to this requirement on several levels, from socialization to definitions of race. At the same time, the werewolves provide a link to the past through the various traditions of ancestors from which both Lupin and Greyback are spawned. Not only does this appearance display the archetype's maintenance of stability within mutability, but through the questions they raise and the links they create, both werewolves are truly monstrous in the oldest sense (*monstrum*)[119] in that they both show and reveal various things about ourselves and our world. In the Lupin and Greyback characters, Rowling compares medieval and classical-early modern Continental traditions of the werewolf while demonstrating the thin line between civil humanity and wild bestiality in one of her signature dualities. On the one side, a quiet, civilized, "tame" Lupin, on the other the savage, ravening Greyback, in between a distorting funhouse mirror that shows what each could have become. At the same time, she taps the collective unconscious to retrieve two aspects of an important archetype that she allows to vanish once its work in the series is done.

Rowling moves beyond these roots to present her werewolves as signs of and lessons about issues important to both her target audience and older readers. There are factors, such as disease, friendship, and the socialization inherent in education, that are absent in the earlier sources, whether because they were not important in the same way or did not exist on the scale they do today. Through these issues, Rowling moves the sympathetic werewolf into another aspect of the twenty-first century and approaches an audience younger than Pratchett's. This presentation to a younger audience moves the werewolf and shape-shifter into the future and acts to influence the views of these generations, in many cases before they are exposed to the non-sympathetic renditions that came out of the early and mid-twentieth century or the parodic-slapstick or erotic versions found in the 1980s through today.[120]

4

Southern Wolves

A Plethora of Shifters

Both Terry Pratchett and J. K. Rowling present a variation on the lone wolf figure by taking their werewolves away from the society of other werewolves. They introduce their lone wolves into a broader community for various reasons, as previously discussed. One act that both lone wolves — Angua and Lupin — undertake is the creation of an ad hoc pack made up of members of different races and backgrounds. Both werewolves enter the urban environment in order to find acceptance and resist racial stereotypes. In her Sookie Stackhouse[1] novels, Charlaine Harris also moves the werewolf into an urban environment. This shift in location is not particularly unusual for modern representations of the figure, or shifter archetype. However, most such representations are, as is the case with Pratchett and Rowling, lone wolves or a small family. Harris not only brings one, two, or five werewolves to the city, she brings multiple packs — at least three appear at various times in Shreveport, Louisiana — where at least one pack integrates itself into the normal human society. This is not to say that Harris' wolves remain entirely in the city, they do return to the woods for special occasions, but most of their appearances are in the urban environment.

This environment is a violent one, as demonstrated by a significant body count throughout the series. In this way, there is a further connection between Angua and Harris' werewolves in that they are both part of the mystery genre, although different subgenres since Harris' series is not a police procedural as Pratchett's Watch books typically are. Harris' werewolves, like Angua, do assist in solving several mysteries, including a variety of murders. They are also the cause of quite a few murders and mysteries, mostly the former, as well as considerable violence whether in social rituals or to defend their territory from outsiders. In this way, they deviate from

Angua, but not as much as might be expected. Most of their deviations involve their highly ritualized society, as will be discussed in greater detail near the end of this chapter. Both Pratchett's and Harris' werewolf societies have the potential for impact on the reader's culture. However, despite Pratchett's longevity, Harris' werewolves have, arguably, had a greater cultural impact, at least in the U.S.

The key element in Harris' cultural impact is *True Blood*, the HBO series based on her books. That said, the books and show will be dealt with as independent entities, partially because the books have had their own impact. The most important reason for separating the two is that after the first few episodes, *True Blood* diverges from the novels in myriad significant ways to the point that eventually the only similarities are the core characters — Sookie Stackhouse, Bill Compton, Eric Northman, and Sam Merlotte.[2] *True Blood's* werewolves also appear to be, mostly, minions, fulfilling the same role as *Star Wars'* stormtroopers — everyone talks about how fearsome they are, but they are easily disposed of by all their opponents. Thus, beyond acknowledging that *True Blood* has contributed to Harris' influence, the show will be effectively ignored here in favor of the more canonical novels. The novels do have the disadvantage of being first person narratives, versus the show's multiplicity of perspectives. However, the novels' advantage is a greater depth due to medium, one that lends itself to expressions, and greater explorations, of archetypal figures.

Through her representations of the shifter archetype, Harris creates connections between the classical, medieval, early modern, and modern eras. Her werewolves, especially, reference Ovid and Petronius alongside medieval views of theology, psychology, society, and humanity. They also link the modern to the early modern through conflations of werewolfism and witchcraft. Literary ancestors are then linked to the shifter archetype through confusion, the shadow, and growth. The werewolves create conditions by which certain key characters can find direction, escape problems, and ultimately develop as individuals. In this process, Harris brings early werewolf legend into the modern world not only by way of psychoanalysis, but via science as well, specifically zoology and genetics. The latter informs her discussion of society and her werewolves' social structures, as well as their relationship to normal human, American, society. All of which sets up Harris' use of a modern trend in werewolf fiction: animosity between weres and vampires. Although Pratchett discusses this last point, and uses biology as the basis of his construct, Harris' approach is somewhat different and is not overtly stated as such in the texts, perhaps because the narrative does not come from the perspective of any of her werewolves.

Without her literary ancestors, Harris' werewolves would be unable to achieve the depth of meaning they reach in the novels. Likewise, their role as representatives of the shape-shifter archetype is central in their interpretation and function in the books. The translation of her werewolves to the screen may owe more to film and earlier television predecessors, even though some of the basic elements remain — for example, werewolves changing from man to wolf, not a hybrid form. That particular discussion is beyond the scope of this study, though. The important element is that Harris' werewolves are another link in the chain of archetype continuity, one that owes its composition to many previous links even as far back as Ovid and Petronius.

Alcide's Ancestors

Harris presents a brief reference to both Petronius' *Satyricon* and some Eastern European legends. The Shreveport pack, in an attempt to both aid Sookie and end a threat to themselves, strips and changes forms in the graveyard between Sookie's and Bill's homes. In a similar act, Petronius' Niceros describes a soldier turning into a wolf in a graveyard. Likewise, according to some Eastern European tales, every werewolf either: (a) is created to destroy a particular vampire, thus remaining in the graveyard to hunt, (b) is the result of an improperly "slain" and re-buried vampire, or (c) becomes a vampire upon death. This reference passes as swiftly as Pratchett's remark about "the prophet Ossory,"[3] a nod to Gerald of Wales' *History and Topography of Ireland* in which the writer encounters two werewolves from Ossory. However, Harris' work has a stronger connection to Ovid in terms of the Roman poet's use of mutability.

Ovid's use of mutability in *Metamorphoses* often represented both fertility and vitality, especially for later medieval audiences. These characteristics are applicable to Harris' werewolves, as well as her other shape-shifters. The werewolves are blatantly representative of vitality as they are said to be more alive, more charged with energy, than normal humans, according to Sookie, the narrator. In this way, they also act as a counterpoint to the vampires, as will be detailed in the last section of this chapter. There is some irony in the link between Ovidian mutability and Harris' weres, however, when fertility is discussed. A few characters reiterate the weres' growing infertility, and thus their continually shrinking population, throughout the series. Leonard Barkan does note, in an allusion to Ovid's punishment-reward pattern,[4] that "animal [...] metamorphosis is liable to capture a particularly base element in the formerly human personality,"[5] usually lust, pride, jealousy, or greed. Harris' weres are more complex in their personalities, as honor and loyalty are prized in their society, but there are certainly examples of those who are consumed by their pride, jealousy, and greed as well. Typically, the latter individuals are either members of foreign packs or loners who live outside the pack structure, with the exception of those exemplifying pride.[6]

Montague Summers also points to early sources that link wolves to character traits. His key example is biblical passages that indicate the wolf is a sign of "treachery, savagery, and bloodthirstiness"[7] and heresy.[8] The last trait is not a significant issue in the case of Harris' werewolves, but the first three all find expression through her use of the archetype. Both Sandra Pelt — in her attempts to destroy Sookie — and Patrick Furnan — in his successful bid to become packmaster — employ treachery to further their bloodthirst to the detriment of others. Basim al Saud, who admittedly is only present for part of one book, also falls to treachery against his adopted pack, selling them out to the Fae. Virtually all of the werewolves demonstrate both bloodthirstiness and savagery. However, none surpasses Jannalynn — depicted bashing the skulls of wounded enemies and calling for the execution of packmembers for any serious offense against the pack — who ultimately replaces Basim as Alcide Heveraux's lieutenant and dates Sam Merlotte for a time.

Biblical influence on medieval thought regarding the werewolf is best seen in St. Augustine's *The City of God*. Said influence is also present in a number of other works, including Gerald of Wales' *History and Topography of Ireland* and Albertus Magnus' bestiary. However, both Gerald and Albert were influenced by Augustine's interpretations of the Bible. As previously noted, one of Augustine's core concerns was psychology. Outward appearance did not define humanity in his eyes, rather the conscious mind determined the state of human versus beast. While Augustine was concerned with this form of psychology from a theological perspective — determining

4. Southern Wolves

whether the werewolf could (a) exist and (b) have a soul — the question is equally important to Harris' narrator as she is a telepath. Because she is a telepath, Sookie is able to make decisions about various people almost instantly, due to the feel of their minds. For example, she can read humans' minds with ease, but vampires are a blank spot. The first time she meets any werewolves, Sookie's thought is that "there was a difference about these two, a pulsing sort of heaviness."[9] Then she notices that the "outline of their heads seem subtly different, not exactly human."[10] What is notable here is that she "sees" their minds first — she "sees" with her mind before seeing with her eyes — whether this is because of her abilities or because the Weres' minds stand out as being that significantly different is unclear. A few months later, Sookie notices a similar mind the first time she meets Alcide. She describes the feeling as pulsing, buzzing, and red. The point of these descriptions is to demonstrate that there is something noticeably different about werewolves versus humans, and that it has to do with the mind. When Sookie is eventually asked to try reading a werewolf's mind — at Alcide's request — she thinks, "In his Wereform, these were so primitive they hardly qualified as 'thoughts.'"[11] Part of the problem, Sookie decides is that "the blend of human and dog thought patterns was quite challenging."[12] She later notes that she is "not sure how much of their human consciousness remains when the Weres change."[13] This uncertainty causes problems for determining humanity by way of conscious thought. Because the Augustinian view was predicated on a simple human mind-not human mind dichotomy, Harris' werewolves create an anomaly. The medieval sources — *Bisclavret*, Gerald of Wales, *Arthur and Gorlagon*, *William of Palerne* — all indicate a clear retention of humanity while in wolf shape. Thus, under Augustine's system, they are all human regardless of their outward form. They are also responsible for their actions in wolf form. Harris,' on the other hand, may be neither human nor responsible when changed.

One sign in favor of their bestial nature being dominant is a scene in *Club Dead*. In the eponymous club, a group of animal shifted patrons — both werewolves and other shifters — fight over a human corpse.[14] Because they all wish to eat the body, the case for shifters being non-human in their beast form is strengthened. If they are still human in mind, while animal in body, then they become cannibals, which the text does not indicate. Therefore, they are more animal than man while shifted. On the other hand, there are some strongly human traits in Harris' werewolves that form a bond with the medieval secular sources.

Marie de France's Bisclavret, Gorlagon of *Arthur and Gorlagon*, and *William of Palerne's* Alphouns share a set of common, knightly, characteristics. They are all exceedingly loyal and two — Bisclavret and Alphouns — are helpful and noble in the non-class related sense. Jannalynn and Alcide are the best representations of the loyal werewolf. The former is the epitome of loyalty to her pack and to Alcide, mostly in defending both from outsiders as well as internal threats.[15] Alcide shows both the benefits and problems of loyalty. He demonstrates clear loyalty to his father in his request for Sookie to attend a challenge for the pack leadership — she uses her telepathy to catch the other challenger cheating. Conversely, his blind loyalty keeps him tied to Debbie Pelt, long after he should have ended their relationship and cut his ties to her. Both Alcide and Tray Dawson assume the role of helpful werewolf, or try to. In Alcide's case, Sookie often turns down his assistance in the belief that he is only offering aid in order to acquire favors or a more romantic relationship with her. However, Harris' werewolves are rarely noble, in either sense of the term. All of her werewolves come from working class or military backgrounds, with the exception of Alcide whose family is wealthy, but even they are involved in surveying and construction. The werewolves also tend to be more practical than noble in their treatment of others, including slaying wounded foes rather than trying to help them. Despite this practicality, they do possess some important rituals and others means of tying their society together in an arguably noble fashion.

Barkan has noted that "metamorphosis is an outward sign that the ties that bind [society and individuals] have been loosed."[16] Certain social ties are notably weakened or changed once the werewolves reveal themselves to the general populace, as will be discussed in detail later in this chapter. On an individual level, and within the supernatural community, there are some important connections that start to loosen when the werewolves appear in significant numbers. The three most important are the Sookie-Bill, Bill-Lorena, and Bill-Eric relationships. Sookie and Bill's relationship deteriorates in large part due to the introduction of Lorena, Bill's "maker."[17] Lorena's appearance is also the point where Alcide's presence occurs and takes a major part of the story. His burgeoning relationship with Sookie further strains the Sookie-Bill ties. At the same time, the Bill-Lorena relationship is effectively removed as she works with some werewolves to torture him for information, and to punish him for leaving her. Bill and Eric's ties of fealty are strained when the werewolves kidnap Bill because he is working secretly and directly for Sophie Anne, the vampire queen of Louisiana, around Eric, his effective superior. Because of these actions, Eric essentially severs their relationship by outing Bill as a spy sent by Sophie Anne to seduce and collect information on Sookie. The ties that connect Bill and Eric move beyond the personal into the social as Bill technically owes Eric fealty, support, and loyalty while Eric theoretically owes Bill protection. Such disruptions are echoes of the disturbance that shape-shifters cause for simplistic binary classification, such as Augustine's human-animal division.

The disruption of Augustine's binary classification system is typical of the archetype. At the same time, the system is reinforced to the extent that Augustine and others of his era argued that a human soul cannot be contained in a non-human vessel, thus negating the possibility of true shape-shifting in favor of devilish trickery. Once werecreatures come out to the public, Harris' fundamentalist religious group, the Fellowship of the Sun (FotS), instantly rejects Augustine's theory of humanity and labels the werewolves as monsters. These monsters are made all the more disturbing because they can conceal their monstrosity and walk silently among normal humans, unlike the vampires who hide during the day and often have pasty complexions. In other words, shifters can pass, which has its own racial connotations, especially in Louisiana. The FotS interpretation owes more to early modern teratology and witch hunting than it does to Augustinian theology.

David Gilmore argues that "monsters are sources of identification and awe as well as horror."[18] This was particularly true of the early modern period as the focus of monster stories shifted. In earlier periods, most European monster stories were set at the fringes of the world, beyond civilization, or at least beyond Christendom. By the early modern period, most European monster stories were set in Europe. The focus shifts from the monster far away to the monster close to home. The change in focus makes sense given the Reformation and the political-religious instability that followed. We need only look to Tudor England to find preachers and nobles under Henry VIII and Elizabeth I railing against Catholics hiding amongst the populace, pretending to be good, Protestant subjects; or the same people under Mary Tudor calling for vigilance against Protestants hiding out, pretending to be good, Catholic subjects.[19] The point in both cases being that the enemy undermining society blends in and can easily conceal its monstrosity. Thus, European stories of monstrosity quickly became analogies for Catholics and Protestants. They could be identified with and were a source of horror. Likewise, readers see the mix of identification, awe, and horror in Sookie's relationship with both the vampires and werewolves. The more important of the two for our purposes is her relationship with werewolves. As someone who is quietly ostracized because of her telepathy, even if most claim not to believe in her ability, she instantly identifies with the werewolves and their desire to remain concealed. As a bonus, for her, their minds are difficult to read (but not impossible like vampire minds), so she can relax in their company. There are also demonstrations of awe, which can be both positive and negative, throughout. On one hand, the werewolves are physically strong, heal rapidly, and are a close knit community despite some internal disagreements. On the other, they are not entirely human and do not necessarily think like humans, although they are portrayed as more human than vampires or the fae species. These differences between species lead to a degree of horror as Sookie watches werewolves fight and kill foes, and dispatch wounded enemies. One of the key examples is her relationship with Jannalynn, in which awe regarding the werewolf's power and loyalty and horror at her violence and bloodthirsty nature are equally mixed. When the werewolves' traits and powers are added to other abilities, the awe and horror are enhanced.

Although early modern writers — particularly demonologists, witch hunters, and werewolf hunters — preferred clear categories and delineations of power, there are some things that defy classification. As Jane Davidson explains, "From the late fifteenth through seventeenth centuries, witchcraft authorities debated whether witches could also be werewolves."[20] Harris answers that debate with a definitive yes and a caveat. The answer is provided by Hallow and Mark Stonebrook — werewolf siblings[21] — who attempt to take over Shreveport and curse Eric. A combination of their werewolf nature and their practice of ingesting vampire blood enhances their witchcraft. Most of their followers are also simultaneously werewolves (or other shifters) and witches. Sookie's response to this information is "Werewolves? They were not only witches, but Weres?"[22] The caveat is that while combining werewolfism and witchcraft is possible, most werewolves — notably Colonel Flood (the first Shreveport packmaster readers see) and Alcide — view the combination as problematic at best, repulsive at worst.[23] This conflation of types, and the confusion it breeds, is characteristic of the archetype that blurs the lines of classification even as it reifies them.

Archetypes in Louisiana

The shape-shifter archetype asserts itself in Harris' work by challenging lines of demarcation between various elements of society. One of the most important, and obvious, ways it serves this role is by blurring the line between legend and reality. Initially, the only supernatural creatures that the mundane world knows about are the vampires, who came into the public in a highly orchestrated event. Over time, several characters learn that if one creature of legend exists, the chances are good that others do as well. Of these other species, the shape-shifters and werewolves are among the first to appear and the next to go public.[24] The archetype fulfills its purpose in three ways: sowing confusion, representing the shadow and society, and acting as an agent of growth.

The werewolves first appear, briefly, in the second book of the series, *Living Dead in Dallas* (*Living Dead*; 2009). They are called upon by a group of shape-shifters to act as protection and vanish quickly. When the werewolves return in greater numbers and importance in *Club Dead* (book three; 2003), they cause a problem of classification. Harris, at first, appears confused about how to handle the three classes of shape-shifter she introduces to the series. She notes, initially, that there are shape-shifters (can take any animal form) and there are werewolves (can only turn into wolves). At times, she implies that these are two different types of shifter with different rules governing them. Other times, she implies that werewolves are a subset of shape-shifter who choose to take only one animal form. This confusion may be deliberate, however, because the series is told from the first person perspective of Sookie Stackhouse, who only learns a little at a time. Thus, the confusion may not be Harris' but rather Sookie's. In fact, in *Living Dead*, Sookie thinks, "Sam [a shape-shifter] heard everything, and he was by no means as powerful as a true werewolf. Or at least, that was my evaluation. To tell you the truth, until this moment, I hadn't been sure werewolves actually existed."[25] Given her admission of ignorance, it is odd that Sookie is certain Sam is weaker than the "true werewolf," but the scene also demonstrates that our source of information does not have complete understanding either. Ultimately, in *Definitely Dead* (book six; 2007), Harris and Sookie firmly state that: true shape-shifters can take any animal form (and are very rare), were-animals are shifters who take one animal form, and Weres are exclusively werewolves.[26] The representatives of the archetype, in this case, appear to blend bestial traits and remove the possibility of categorization. However, in the process, they reinforce classification of different elements or representations of the shadow.

The shadow is the animalistic element of the psyche. It contains everything that stands opposite society and social integration. As Ursula K. Le Guin summarizes, "It is all we don't want to, can't, admit into our conscious self, all the qualities and tendencies within us which have been repressed, denied, or not used. [...] It is inferior, primitive, awkward, animal-like [...] powerful, vital, spontaneous."[27] The shadow is, in some ways, the evolutionary root of humanity. Werewolves are a perfect example of the shadow made manifest, as are other human-animal shape-shifters. The best example of the werewolf as shadow, among Harris' werewolves, is Jannalynn through her displays of ruthless, bloodthirsty, violence and relative social awkwardness. She fits neatly into werewolf society, but has trouble dealing with others outside that specialized community. However, in their animal forms the werewolves in general inherently display the animal-like, powerful, spontaneous qualities that make the shadow potentially helpful to the psyche. Likewise, as noted above, Harris' werewolves are described as being more alive, more vital, than normal humans. It is through the werewolves that normal man, e.g., the reader, can vicariously enjoy the bestial or violent tendencies that society frowns upon in a safe manner. Acceptance of the shadow is also an important trait in creating a whole psyche and society.

When Harris' werewolves and other shifters reveal themselves to the rest of the world, they give society a symbolic chance to accept its collective shadow. Reactions to the revelation vary widely. In Bon Temps, where most of the series' action takes place, the locals watched the revelation on the TV at Sam's bar, Merlotte's. While the chosen representative changed shape on air, Sam and Tray Dawson changed shape in the bar. The on air

4. Southern Wolves

transformation was viewed with fear by the newscaster. One of Sam's busboys pointed this fact out and laughed, so "[t]he drinkers in Merlotte's relaxed enough to feel superior. After all, they'd handled this with aplomb."[28] In this way, the drinkers at the bar quietly accept the shadow in their midst, ignoring or ridiculing members of the FotS when they try to lash out at the shifters (and the two vampires—including Bill Compton—that Sam asked to be present in case any problems arose). Even the Vatican is described as accepting the shifters, stating, "They're alive, they're among us, they must have souls. Even some priests are wereanimals."[29] Whether consciously or not, Harris echoes Augustine's requirements for determining humanity and the presence of a soul—if it has a human mind, then it must be a human regardless of outer appearance. On the other hand, others are said to feel deceived and betrayed when their friends and family come out as shifters, e.g., they do not accept the shadow and thus fail to fully integrate all parts of the psyche.

Even though those around them move toward a complete, whole, psyche, the concerns of those who are reticent are not wholly unfounded. They are simply listening to the aspect that Jung called the collective conscious, the source of fads. They have accepted the common misperception of the wolf, and therefore the werewolf. In many of our more popular tales, "[t]he wolf aspect of the werebeast is always consistent with the wolf-phobia of mass culture—wolves are creatures which lust for the kill, are dangerous to any unarmed human being."[30] Those who integrate the shifters, especially the werewolves, into their worldview, therefore, reject the "wolf-phobia of mass culture" and the collective conscious in favor of a more complete mind. Thus, those who accept the shifters among them demonstrate growth as individuals and a society.

The introduction of Harris' werewolves sets individual character growth and development in motion, as well as representing the aforementioned social growth. The two most notable characters in this respect are the Stackhouses: Sookie and her brother Jason. Initially, Sookie is a quiet character who is largely reactive and tries to remain unnoticed. Even though she is the first person narrator, she tries to stay out of sight due to her barely controlled telepathy and the reputation the ability has given her in the small town. During this stage, she reacts to things that happen around her. Others make the plans and tell her where to position herself or others cause problems and she tries to fix them. For example, when Eric requires her service at his bar, Fangtasia, after some resistance, she asks what he wants her to do. Likewise, during the invasion of Shreveport by the Stonebrooks and the following competition for Shreveport packmaster we see Sookie reacting to events around her and people manipulating her in various directions. However, from the point where she first meets Alcide, she starts an evolution into a more proactive personality. By the time we see her in the last four books, she has become the one who often thinks ahead, negotiates between different supernatural species of her own volition, and makes the plans that others execute — for example, she largely plans the death of Victor Madden[31] and brings the conspirators together. For all the, largely subtle, changes Sookie goes through, her brother has more pronounced development.

Jason begins the series as the stereotypical high school jock who aged but never grew up. He flits from relationship to relationship, or rather one night stand to one night stand, and does not think much further into the future than the next morning. He is also incredibly self-centered. Once the werewolves are introduced, however, Jason begins a slow development. In part, this occurs because soon after the werewolves appear, the werepanthers are introduced. Once he is turned into a bitten werepanther,[32] he begins to settle down and become less selfish. His outlook is partially changed by his (failed) marriage to a werepanther and his acceptance into the werepanther community near Bon Temps, which is loosely associated with the Shreveport werewolf pack. Ultimately, although he retains a certain degree of his original personality, Jason does appear to come to a better understanding and relationship with those around him due to his experiences with the shape-shifter archetype's representatives. Both he and Sookie begin to accept their capacity for socially unacceptable attributes — Sookie's acceptance of death and violence around her as more or less normal, Jason's acceptance of his newfound bestial qualities, and both of them accepting their fairy heritage — and become more complete individuals for that acceptance.

From Legend to Science

The Stackhouses' acceptance of their heritage is not only a psychological acceptance, but a genetic one. Genetics are also an important subject for Harris' werewolves. Although she is not the first to bring the shifter archetype from the realm of legend into the sphere of science, Harris does consider her transition of the figure carefully and is one of the more well known writers to do so. The most important science for Harris' werewolves is biology. She employs genetics for their reproductive limitations and methods, various branches of biology for their shape-shifting ability, and germ theory for their ability to create "bitten" werewolves.

As is true of any species, one of the most important concerns for Harris' werewolves is reproduction. This is of even greater concern for the werewolves because, as with Remus Lupin previously, there is their condition to consider as well. In fact, Alcide echoes Lupin when he tells Sookie, "I'm not passing [werewolfism] along. Even a shifter and a werewolf may have a child who has to change at the full moon, though only kids of a pure couple — both Weres or both shifters — can change at will."[33] He unconsciously explains a core element of the medieval theory of reproduction: that like produces like. As in Lupin's case, Alcide does not wish to give his condition to any children he might have. However, he at least, unlike Lupin, knows both exactly what will happen and how to avoid it. That said, he may not be able to do so as every woman he is attracted to, except Sookie, is a shifter or werewolf. Considering this situation, Sookie notes, "Weres and shifters are strongly attracted to each other."[34] The attraction could be a genetic predisposition to finding others with the "condition" attractive, as an unconscious means of propagating the genes. Alcide does note, though, that the werewolves' inherently magical nature has a role to play as well as genetics. This is supported by Calvin Norris — a werepanther — who confirms for Sookie that the first child of any purebreed couple is a wereanimal.[35] The other children do not inherit the ability to change forms.

The principle is also demonstrated in the Hevereaux family as Alcide's sister, Janice, lacks the ability to change shape. It is noted that Janice's "son's recessive Were traits [...] might show as increased vigor and great healing ability. Many professional athletes came from couples whose genetic pool contained a percentage of Were blood."[36] Because only pureblooded couples will produce true werewolves, and even then only one, werewolf couples tend to be fairly open in their relationships and sexuality becomes an important element of their rituals. The increased openness about such things may also be tied to Sookie's statement that "[i]nfertility and a high infant mortality rate plagued the Weres."[37] Due to a low birthrate, the werewolves incorporate sex into many of their rituals, especially the rise of a new packmaster. The marital or relationship status of the new packmaster is irrelevant—as seen with both Patrick Furnan and Alcide Hevereaux when each took on the leadership mantle. The goal is to prove that the new leader can produce pureblood children to help the pack, although there are overtones of demonstrating virility and, thus, strength or power as well. In some ways, the ritual mirrors the medieval and early modern focus on princes producing male heirs, not only for the continuation of their line but also due to beliefs and traditions about the health of the land being linked to the health of the king. Fortunately, for Harris' werewolves, "if Weres can get through the first few months, they live a good long while, barring accidents" or fights.[38] Although they do not possess the practical immortality of vampires, her werewolves can survive for much longer than normal humans, thus producing more offspring, despite the oddity of their genetic inheritance.

Inheriting the ability to shift forms is important for all of Harris' wereanimals, but even more so for her werewolves. Discussion of their shape-shifting ability is often tied to biology, but not necessarily always so. For this study, the werewolves' shape-shifting will be broken down into three areas: manifestation (and benefits), description, and avoidance (and death). The first two have appeared with other authors (Charles de Lint and Pratchett), but not in quite the same manner as Harris' approach. Avoidance of change is not used at all by the authors previously detailed, the closest one comes is Rowling's Lupin who can use a medication to convert his change to a ravening beast into a change to a quiet, passive canine.

As with de Lint's werewolf, the ability to change form manifests itself around puberty for Harris' werewolves. This is confirmed by Alcide in a talk with Sookie.[39] After the first change, the werewolf's ability depends on the purity of their lineage. The less pure-blooded a werewolf is, the more restricted their shape-shifting is in both frequency and speed of the change itself. As noted above, Harris's werewolves can only change at will when they are pure-bloods. Even those lucky individuals have other triggers that affect their transformation. In her first encounter with werewolves, Sookie notes, "she sounded kind of growly. Then I realized it was almost the full moon. Oh, hell. They had to change at the full moon."[40] The

4. Southern Wolves

veracity of this assertion is questionable at the time, because it comes before the narrator knows anything about werewolves beyond normal pop culture depictions. However, in this case, her initial reaction is borne out and confirmed by others. The full moon change is largely a connection to twentieth-century film and some slightly earlier literary sources, as it appears in some nineteenth-century stories. The original source goes back to Gervase of Tilbury during the medieval period, in a theory he proposed that was discounted and ignored by his contemporaries.

There are some other triggers for the change, all related to some form of excitement. Patrick Furnan's wife is the first example as she is described as having round, wide eyes and howling in triumph as her husband fights for the role of packmaster.[41] This scene provides a piece of visual evidence tied to Sookie's earlier assertion, "When werewolves got mad, you could feel it in the air around you."[42] Later, Jannalynn presents more visual evidence as her change is nearly triggered by the stress of combat before Sookie manages to talk her down to a calm state.[43] There are other incidents during which the werewolves, typically as a pack, trigger their change during high stress situations, notably while defending their territory from an outside pack. All of the examples serve to imply that the change is triggered as part of the fight-flight instinct, itself tied to adrenaline surges. Due to the nature of the werewolf response, it is clear that in these cases the shadow side of the psyche — the violent, bestial side — asserts itself. Only rarely, if ever, do the werewolves flee when the change is triggered. More often, a fight of some sort ensues. This certainly creates a means by which the audience can take part in the violence, the fight part of the instinct, in a safe manner whereby the reader risks nothing but still voyeuristically exercises the desire.

One reason that the werewolves can partake in the instinctive drive to fight, rather than to flee, is that their changing ability gives them certain benefits. The most important benefit, in this case, is the ability to recover from injuries quickly. The best example of this ability is Maria-Star Cooper who "had completely recovered from being hit by a car this past January" by early spring.[44] Her injuries were life threatening, to a degree that would likely send a normal human through several surgeries and months of therapy. Other benefits include enhanced senses of smell and hearing, enhanced strength, and excellent tracking abilities. These abilities are balanced by the change itself.

The Modern Literary Werewolf

Many authors who employ the shifter archetype, especially the werewolf, do not describe the transformation from man to beast. Even Terry Pratchett, who gives one of the more complete descriptions, is rather vague, as noted previously. To a certain extent, Harris is vague as well, but less so that Pratchett. For example, when Mark Stonebrook changes, Sookie describes "a sound I knew I'd heard before, though I couldn't trace the memory. It was a sort of gloppy sound. Sticky. Like stirring a stiff spoon through some thick liquid that had hard things in it, maybe peanuts or toffee bits. Or bone chips."[45] She directly attaches the sound to the werewolf transformation some time later as the entire Shreveport pack changes to fight an encroaching pack. Sookie says, "The chill night air was full of the gloppy sound, the sound of hard things moving through thick, sticky liquid, that characterizes the transformation from man to animal. Huge wolves straightened and shook themselves all around me."[46] More detail emerges when Colonel Flood, the first Shreveport packmaster the reader meets, transforms in which "I heard the same gloppy noise again. A haze wrapped around the writhing figure, and when it dispersed, Colonel Flood was curled up in place of the wolf. Of course, he was naked, too."[47] The last description not only presents greater detail, but also provides a connection to a long tradition of werewolf tales stretching back at least to Petronius. All of the classical and medieval werewolves lost their clothing when they changed form. In fact, in some cases their clothing was specifically needed to reassume human form. For earlier audiences, the removal of clothing represented the shedding of social status (at least human social status). But, what do Harris' descriptions mean? On one level, she remains true to the horror genre and certain fantasy genre examples — notably Pratchett — by providing just enough description to tantalize the readers, but not enough that they are truly comfortable with the change. Enough is left unsaid, undescribed, that a certain degree of fear and horror remain due to the unknown. The relatively vague description also underscores the fact that the werewolves, despite being more human than vampires, are still supernatural and inhuman in nature.

An important factor is that the change takes time to occur, time for the "bits" to move around and the haze to dissipate. However, Harris' werewolves can speed the process. Even so, Colonel Flood "had to lie still for at least a minute or two, and it was obviously a great effort for him to sit up. [... he] staggered to his feet, apparently having to deal with some disorientation from his rapid change."[48] This disorientation makes sense, from a biological perspective, as one shifts from having four legs and enhanced senses to two legs and comparatively dull sensory input. Even multiple changes over a fairly short period have their draining effect, as Sookie notes, "The Weres, who seemed to have pulled their clothes on pretty hastily, did look a little ragged. The dark-moon transformation and the rapid change back to two-legged form had taken a toll on all of them."[49] From an archetype perspective, the drain of changing rapidly is a sign that the shadow aspect of the shifter archetype is not to be drawn upon too often. Arguably, doing so could lead to the psyche incorporating the shadow too closely into itself, to the point that the animalistic shadow takes over the self, rather than being a tool to be used as needed by the individual. Harris does, however, offer means by which her werewolves can avoid forced transformations, beyond Sookie's, successful, attempt to talk them down.

The simplest method Harris mentions implies that her werewolves need to actually see the full moon or be touched by its light to trigger a forced change. When he needs to accompany Sookie out on a full moon night, Alcide explains, "I'll try to stay out of the moon, try to avoid stress."[50] This method has also been used to some extent by Rowling as Lupin manages to retain his human shape in *Prisoner of Azkaban*, until the full moon appears from behind a cloud. Then Lupin changes, leading to Peter Pettigrew's escape. In both cases, sighting the moon appears to be a simple plot device to allow for the respective werewolves to remain human until an unfortunate moment — Alcide, like Lupin, is unable to avoid the change, in his case due to unavoidable stress. Linking to Lupin again and other older sources, Harris's narrator explains, "There's a drug you can take, I hear, that can suppress your change; Weres in the military, among others, have to use it. But they all hate to do that, and I understand they're really no fun to be around on those nights."[51] In this case, the drug is introduced because many of Harris' werewolves are active duty military officers, due to Shreveport's air force base. The drug also helps provide some verisimilitude when her werewolves reveal themselves to the public, since many are in high profile positions — the aforementioned military officers as well as priests, for instance — where one would otherwise think someone would notice the person getting sick or going on vacation for three days every lunar month. Finally, Harris has a General Scott Walker

(Army) reiterate, "We change back to human form when we're dead"[52] to argue against a mandatory government shape-shifter registration. The proposal of shape-shifter registration takes on some problematic overtones as Harris' werewolfism has many characteristics of a disease.

Harris presents not only a division between shape-shifters, wereanimals, and werewolves, but also one between those who are born shifters and those who become shifters. In the latter case, her portrayal of the archetypal figure owes much to germ theory and plays with elements added to werewolf lore after germ theory's formulation. This is a necessity as Davidson notes that "there are no cases of persons having been 'infected' with lycanthropy through the bite of, or physical attack of, another werewolf recorded in the period of the fifteenth through the seventeenth centuries."[53] The most important reasons for this lack of cases are first that the concept of germ infection was unknown and second that a bitten werewolf would be transformed against its will, which would circumvent the early modern necessity of a conscious pact with the devil. Such a pact is unnecessary in the case of Harris' born werewolves. With regard to her bitten werewolves, Harris explains, "Weres who were bitten, not born — created Weres, rather than genetic Weres — changed into the half-man, half-beast creatures who populated horror movies."[54] In the werewolf hierarchy, this makes them second-class citizens at best (because they cannot assume a true wolf shape) and pitied individuals who die quickly at worst. Alcide, for instance, explains that bitten werewolves do not usually survive long, nor do they pass on their were traits. He specifically states, "That's when you get your wolf-men. Like the ones in the movies. They die pretty quick, poor people. And that's not passed along" to kids.[55] This is a bit different for some other wereanimals or unusual situations — the prominent example being Jason Stackhouse, who is taken in and taught by the Hotshot werepanthers, whether because they want to increase their gene pool or because of the circumstances of his bitten state is unclear. A better description of a bitten werewolf is "He still had arms, he still had legs, he had a body covered with hair, and he had a wolf's head."[56] Such a creature would be at home in virtually any werewolf movie from Lon Chaney to the recent *Underworld* franchise.

While the genetic werewolves move fluidly between the human and animal worlds, the bitten weres are forced to straddle the division. The true werewolves experience the best of both worlds, they function well in

4. Southern Wolves

human society and can run in the wild, often at will. In fact, they may even be accepted by normal animals while in wolf shape, or they may not. Sookie notes that "[d]ogs [...] reaction to Weres and shifters is [...] unpredictable."[57] One major difference between Harris' bitten werewolves and many seen throughout Hollywood films is that Harris' owe a great debt to germ theory. As Sookie explains, the were state is "harder to catch than almost any communicable disease [...] if you cleaned the wound soon afterward, your chances dropped considerably even from that."[58] Most other modern sources that treat werewolfism as a communicable disease follow a "one bite, it's done" method — for example, the aforementioned *Underworld* franchise and Rowling's werewolves. In those cases, werewolfism becomes a super virus that has no treatment, cure, or means to be avoided. Harris treats the bite-method as any other germ based illness, which lessens the threat and fear response. This method also allows her to play upon the human tendency to fears based on false or little information. When Sookie does get bitten, a few friends in the supernatural community become greatly concerned that she will contract the "disease" because they know little to nothing about werewolves or other shifters. In much the same way, we see hysteria sweep through real world communities in response to myriad diseases from SARS to HIV/AIDS to swine flu. Here, Harris uses the werewolf to tell her audience to acquire information, to conduct research, before coming to conclusions. Thus, she influences society in a fashion.

Coming Out of the Woods

Harris' werewolves, as befits the archetype that can move between human and animal worlds, actively participate in at least three important societies: normal human society, their own werewolf society, and the wider shifter society. They are also involved to varying degrees in the over all supernatural community, but this is somewhat less important for our purposes. Their archetypal effects on society occur in four significant areas: discussions of socio-economic class, their reputation among other shifters, revelation to human society, and their interactions within their own society. Each social area relates back to the shape-shifter archetype's role and the messages that Harris' werewolves send to her audience.

The werewolves function as a vehicle for discussing the complexities of socio-economic class. On one level, "[l]ots of Weres are mechanics, or brick masons, or plumbers, or cooks"[59] and thus face class discrimination from both normal humans and other shifters. Readers must take into account, however, that the preceding statement comes from Alcide Hevereaux, whose family owns a very successful surveying company. The audience may also note that many of the werewolves named in the series are, indeed, mechanics, but that military personnel are prevalent, including officers such as Colonel Flood. On another level, among the shape-shifter community, "[t]he true werewolves scorned such variance in form [as shape-shifters were capable of], and they didn't think much of shifters in general. They, the werewolves, considered themselves the cream of the shape-shifting world."[60] Among the shape-shifting society, the werewolves, at least in their own minds, are the leaders, the upper class, potentially challenged only by werepanthers, weretigers, and other big animals (whose numbers are significantly smaller).[61] This attitude of superiority is best expressed at the challenge between Alcide's father and Patrick Furnan for the title of packmaster. The elder Hevereaux's companion, Christine, displays her contempt for other shifters by commenting that Debbie Pelt, Alcide's ex-girlfriend, "was too much of a diva for someone who isn't even a Were."[62] The disconnect between the werewolves' typical professions and their view of themselves in the shifter community is typical of the shape-shifter archetype. Not only do they straddle the line between human and animal, they also span the gap between working class and virtual nobility. In some respects, this hearkens back to the medieval werewolves, who were all knights (Bisclavret), princes (Alphouns), and kings (Gorlagon).[63] Their divided social standing may also reflect Southern history in the U.S., especially during and before Reconstruction, when even the lowest class Caucasian farmer held a higher social standing than the most well-bred, wealthy, African-American individual. Given that almost the entire series takes place in Louisiana, and only three werewolves are encountered outside the state (two in Texas, one in Michigan although the latter is first met in Louisiana), this connection seems a reasonably strong one.

One of the most important elements determining the werewolves' place in society is their reputation among other shape-shifters. This reputation also introduces a discussion of stereotypes, including ones that most or all of the werewolves support to a degree. In some cases, the were-

4. Southern Wolves

wolves use their reputation to dominate others. However, they also chafe under the yoke of their reputation because they see themselves as better than others around them.

Sookie's first interaction with werewolves sets the tone for future contact. The very first werewolf she meets refers to her as "Food that talks"[64] in a near growl. She partially reads his mind to determine that he was looking for a fight, but notes, "I didn't know if all werewolves were as feisty as this guy, or if it was just his nature."[65] Her shape-shifter companion gets exasperated and asks the world at large why their contact sent for "freakin' werewolves"[66] to help them. The next werewolf Sookie meets is out to kill her. His appearance does not help, as he wears a biker jacket with a wolf head in a white circle as a logo. Just from that information, Sam instantly concludes he is a werewolf, perhaps from some prior knowledge or simply from their reputation.[67] Later, after meeting Alcide, she acknowledges that Sam would be leery of her new friend, because "werewolves had a bad rep."[68] In fact, they are generally considered to be little more than thugs within the supernatural community.[69]

Many of the werewolves use this reputation, as the first one Sookie meets appears to do. Initially, given no other context, the werewolf's reference to Sookie as food conjures many images of the medieval and early modern tales as well as some film depictions. Both Ovid and Petronius tell their readers that werewolves eat men — through Lycaon and an unnamed soldier respectively.[70] Centuries later, Marie de France informs her audience, "A werewolf is a savage beast; / while his fury is on him / he eats men, does much harm" (9–11).[71] Marie then displays a sympathetic werewolf, her *bisclavret*. Early modern sources regale audiences with tales of carnage and cannibalism, especially the trial records of Peeter Stubbe (1590) and Jean Grenier (1603).[72] Like Marie, Harris follows her threatening werewolf introductions with a kind, likeable representation, Alcide Herveaux. Alcide becomes sympathetic partially because of his role in aiding Sookie, but also because of his recently failed relationship with Debbie Pelt. This element of their reputation mirrors some of the archetype's oldest appearances, but Harris demonstrates that her werewolves, although they do exhibit the potential for violent characteristics, are much more complex.

On one hand, Sookie informs the audience, "Werewolves make good bodyguards, according to the common wisdom of the two-natured, because they are ruthless and tenacious. From what I've seen, that's just the bad-boy image Weres have. But it's true that as a rule, they are the roughest element of the two-natured community."[73] Their image may come, in part, from their aforementioned socio-economic status in the non-supernatural community. As they are reputed to be a collection of bar owners, mechanics, and bikers who gather in packs, or gangs, this "bad-boy image" makes sense. The image may also come from their predator side, compared to some of the other wereanimals and shifters. Admittedly, there are other predatory wereanimals — panthers, tigers, owls, and foxes to name a few — but none of the others instinctively gather in packs and have the same size or numbers.[74] On the other hand, the "Weres considered themselves the kings of the two-natured community. They only changed into one animal, and it was the best. The rest of the two-natured community responded by calling the wolves thugs."[75] Therefore, their negative reputation may also be a somewhat false one generated as a response to their arrogance and their views toward others in their society. Several characters state, in one way or another, that the werewolves hold only contempt for other shifters.[76] They do, however, make some exceptions for formidable wereanimals, like panthers (the Hotshot community), tigers (Quinn), and lions (Sam Merlotte, once). Their contempt is likely the result of the fact that they are instinctively pack animals, even with their human side. The other wereanimals that appear in the series are all definitively solitary species — owl, fox, tiger, bear, and panther. Because of their pack instinct, "werewolves are the tough guys of the shape-shifting world. They're shape-shifters by definition, but they're the only ones who have their own separate society."[77] The fact that they have a separate society from other shifters also accounts for their negative reputation, as it is not only a display of instinct but, perhaps, of arrogance. They are seen by others as removing themselves from the larger shifter society, as refusing to interact with other shifters, as if they are too good to do so. This removal causes resentment on the part of other shifters, which in turn creates offense and thus greater separation on the werewolves' part.

Despite the divide between the werewolves and other shifters, the latter still generally follow the werewolves' lead when they reveal themselves to the greater populace. They seek to come out of the shadows of legend and folklore, much as Harris' vampires did just before the series starts. In fact, they use a very similar method, with some werewolves appearing on TV news shows. Before changing on live TV, Patricia, the werewolf chosen for Shreveport's local network, explains that the werewolves are taking the lead because "we're the more numerous of all the two-natured."[78] As she changes, other shifters change in public places, such as Sam Merlotte's bar. Although the method of coming out mirrors that of the vampires, the reactions are more mixed. Sookie notes that TV interviews range from people feeling betrayed and deceived to some fear — specifically that they might accidentally shoot a two-natured neighbor while hunting — to acceptance — as in the Vatican example cited above. One of the most entertaining examples of acceptance comes from a nameless kid in Springfield, Missouri who states, "Our principal is a werewolf [...] How cool is that?"[79] This child echoes Harry's classmates when Lupin's condition is revealed. The government response is to call for legislation regarding a shifter registration requirement.

Such registration mirrors the various incarnations of mutant or superhuman registration acts used as plot arcs by Marvel comics since the mid-1980s. It also serves much the same purpose. The idea of a registration act evokes memories of other registrations based on inherited characteristics, such as race, as well as incarceration based on race — whether the American camps for Asian-Americans during World War II or the Nazis' Jewish ghettos and concentration camps. In this way, the werewolves remind the audience of a very human reaction to the Other. As Brett Hirsh argues, the werewolf is "not only dangerous because it is capable of committing such depraved acts [as cannibalism], but because it is a *hidden* threat."[80] Hirsh's statement is an important one here. Harris' vampires were completely hidden before their revelation. After revealing themselves, they were also easy to spot — pale, pasty complexions, only active after sunset, and the other usual folkloric signs. On the other hand, her werewolves were already integrated into normal human society. They had additional characteristics that others knew nothing about, or, to put it another way, they lied to those around them. Moreover, after revealing themselves, there is no way for the rest of society to identify a werewolf, until (s)he changes shape. Thus, they can hide amongst the rest of the population.

This fact creates a connection between Harris' werewolves and both the early modern period in Europe and the Jim Crow era in the U.S. In the former period, once the Reformation started, the werewolf became symbolic of hidden Catholics, or Protestants depending on the country, trying to destroy society from within. They were concealed, they could be anyone.[81] Likewise, in the Jim Crow period, there were concerns in certain states regarding African-Americans who were pale enough to pass as Caucasian — they could be hidden agents trying to bring down "white society" from the inside. Kate Chopin's "Desiree's Baby" is an excellent example of the reaction that such passing might cause. Again, because Harris' novels take place in Louisiana, seeing the werewolves' concealment in society as akin to passing does not appear to be all that great a leap of logic.

On the other hand, the negative reactions demonstrated by both newscasters and the FotS are understandable. As Lillian Heldreth points out, "The twentieth-century image of the werewolf is largely derived from Hollywood cinema: a man is involuntarily transmogrified into a crazed manbeast, which is consumed by an overwhelming desire to rend that which it loves best."[82] Given such cultural priming, fear becomes a logical response. One might hope, however, that an individual's friends and family would take into account years or decades of good relationships and lack of ravenous murders. In this way, the werewolf asks the audience to question their assumptions and the information they have been fed by pop culture, perhaps even including, in a break of the fourth wall, the novel they are reading at that moment. The audience, therefore, discovers elements of its own society by looking at the werewolf society.

In her study of Tanith Lee's werewolves, Heldreth explains that scientific research finds a complex society among wolves. She points out that they nurture their injured and practice deliberate population control. She also notes that they have a complex social structure similar to humanity's.[83] These traits are also true of Harris' werewolves. Perhaps the most important aspect of their psyche is that they "like to travel in packs"[84] and possess a strong pack mentality.[85] Moreover, when they travel, they can seek guest privileges from other packs.[86] This last point serves to provide them with a home while traveling and lets the local packs know who is moving through their territory, as a sign of respect. Because the pack is so central to their lives and mindset, loyalty is also highly important. In fact, Alcide states, "Weres are nothing if not loyal"[87] even where such loyalty is misplaced and even to non-pack members. Loyalty to the pack requires a sense of honor in dealings within the pack, but even when honor fails, pack loyalty is remembered. This is indeed the case when a new pack member in Shreveport is murdered. His murderer, Ham, "is the murderer of a pack member. Instead of an open challenge, he took the path of

4. Southern Wolves

stealth. That would call for severe punishment, maybe death. We should consider that Basim was a traitor [...] who was willing to deal with someone outside the pack, to plot against the pack interests."[88] Here, Alcide, as packmaster, chides his pack member for taking a dishonorable path. However, at the same time, he notes extenuating circumstances, e.g., that the dishonorable action was taken against a pack traitor in order to protect the pack.

Even though the pack is the core of the werewolf psyche, Harris implies that it is the lowest rung of the werewolf political ladder. She implies that there are powers above the packmaster.[89] Even so, the packmaster carries considerable clout. Alcide explains, "Packmasters [...] have to be really tough. Really, really tough [...] you get elected, but the candidates have to be very strong and clever. There's a sort of — well, you have a test you have to take."[90] The test mixes agility, endurance, combat ability, and mating prowess to determine the best candidate to lead the pack. In many ways, this appears to fit within Darwinian selection as the strongest, cleverest, most agile individual survives the test, in order to propagate the species. The test also fits within normal wolf society as these traits appear in alpha males in every wolf pack. The male part is important here as "the Shreveport pack seemed to be heavily on the patriarchal side."[91] In fact, three of the four packmasters shown in the series are male. The one exception is the head of a pack decimated by Hurricane Katrina, and then wiped out in its bid to take over the Shreveport territory. Oddly, despite his claims that the test is necessary, Alcide is elevated to packmaster without a formal test. That said, the fact that he co-led the pack's defense against an invading pack, and the packmaster died during the fighting, may substitute for the test.

The packmaster test is also a sign of the complexity of the werewolf society as it becomes an important ritual. The one time that the ritual occurs, it is presided over by Quinn — a weretiger who works for a company the officiates important rituals such as marriages and pack rites for the supernatural community — who provides a plethora of equipment and a touch of ceremony. The event is considered so important that everyone in the pack attends as do all the non-werewolf friends of the pack. Moreover, everyone is dressed in their best attire. During the preliminary activities, the importance of rank, hierarchy, and who is associated with whom is discussed. This is noted by Alcide's father arriving with the widow of a former, highly respected, packmaster, indicating that she supported his bid for the position. Such an appearance seems related to the tendency of modern politicians to try to associate themselves with respected, even deceased, members of their party through relatives and spouses. There are other, more common, rituals as well. The most notable is the monthly celebration of the full moon. Harris tells the reader that for this event, the pack assembles to run through the woods together in wolf-shape. The event is important enough that when their usual woods are believed to be unsafe, they seek to relocate to another wooded area, e.g., Sookie's land.

Not all of the pack's nature is positive, though. As noted above, Harris' werewolves are generally seen as arrogant within the shifter community. They also have a certain contempt for non-shifters, whom they refer to as "oneys," a somewhat derogatory term meaning one-natured.[92] On a darker side, and a more shadow or bestial one, although the pack does look out for and nurture its wounded members—see Maria-Star Cooper, hit by a car—the same does not hold for its enemies. In fact, the pack routinely executes its severely wounded enemies. On one level, this is also Darwinian in that, by being beaten, the enemies proved they were not the fittest to survive. On another level, the practice allows Harris to display the inner savagery of some characters, notably Jannalynn who bashes the enemies' heads in with her fists. That said, displays of inner savagery are not limited to Harris' werewolves.

Werewolves and Vampires

Harris' vampires are equally savage, in their own way, and share a mutual animosity with her werewolves, and shifters in general. In this respect, Harris introduces a fairly modern trope that nonetheless does have some roots in folklore. There are some Eastern European tales in which each werewolf exists to hunt a given vampire and return it to the grave. In other tales, a vampire is the result of an improperly buried werewolf. The connection and potential animosity is there, but was uncommon in the medieval and early modern periods. Most modern approaches to the trope have attempted to find some point of disagreement between the species—*Underworld* has the feuding immortal family with one brother a werewolf and the other a vampire, Pratchett explains the species as hunters preying upon the same game (humans) and thus challenging each other for resources, Stephenie Meyer sets up her werewolves as lovers of nature and her vampires as unnatural creatures (White Wolf's World of Darkness line has used a similar reason since the early 1990s).

Harris, on the other hand, never directly explains why the two species dislike each other. Her fairies and vampires have issues because fairy blood is an addictive drug to vampires. But, the shifter-vampire animosity is left to implied reasoning based on several statements that occur over the course of the whole series. Early on, during Sookie's first encounter with werewolves, her driver, Deb, spots Eric and asks if he cross-dates. The other two shifters in the car "both made gagging sounds. 'You can't date a deader!'" one protested.[93] Deb shows that the animosity is not absolute in her reply, "Some [vampires] aren't so bad."[94] The werewolf slang term for vampires — "deader" — implies the major point of contention between the two species. Sookie adds to the implication as she describes the minds of both: vampires' are blank nothings to her telepathy while werewolves and shifters are incredibly vibrant and pulsing, which she associates with excessive life. Or, to use her description, werewolves "run hot."[95] Thus, the major point of contention seems to be that vampires represent lack of, or non-, life while werewolves represent an overabundance of, or hyper-, life.

The differences come to a head in *Definitely Dead*, when a werewolf is turned into a vampire. Jake, the unfortunate werewolf, has no choice in the matter as Sookie's cousin brings him over to save his life, after a fashion. Sookie's response is "A werewolf who'd become a vampire! I'd never heard tell of such a thing. Could he still change?"[96] Why Sookie should or could have heard of a werewolf-vampire is unclear, given that she only found out about vampires a few years before the incident and only discovered that werewolves existed less than a year before Jake was turned. She does, though, run into Jake a few months later and thinks, "Being a combo Vamp-Were had ruined his chances with either crowd."[97] The werewolves will not accept him because he is now a vampire, the vampires will not fully accept him because he bemoans his lost werewolfism. In fact, he later answers Sookie's initial question, saying, "Something's got to make up for not being able to change anymore."[98] He has lost the core element of werewolf, and shifter, identity, and therefore has lost himself. Jake becomes a pitiable figure, for a time. His despondency leads to involvement in a plot against his new species, in which he would apparently commit suicide. So, the animosity between species, while not absolute, does appear strong enough to follow an individual who effectively switches sides, to the point of causing self-loathing and self-destruction, itself akin to the werewolf that exists solely to rebury a single vampire.

South to North and Beyond

Harris manages to successfully create her werewolves from a mixture of classical to modern ancestors and then gives them a southern flair. She remains true to earlier appearances of the shifter archetype whether from Ovid and Petronius, Marie de France and anonymous medieval writers, or Hollywood's legend-making. Each of these diverse sources adds at least one element to her werewolves and their role in both her fictional society and the audience's world. The links between Harris' present and her literary forbearers is clear, if sometimes a little broken. Moreover, she adapts these sources to mystery. In this case, not only the mystery genre and its paranormal mystery sub-genre, but also the mystery of the werewolves and shifters. Harris' genre calls for hidden information, red herrings, and deductive reasoning on the part of both her protagonist and the reader. Her discussion of the shifters and werewolves also creates a sense of mystery as to their nature, initially, and their motives and roles, later.

Adding a degree of mystery, Harris brings the werewolves out of the forest into the city. She is by no means the first to make this transition — *An American Werewolf in London* (or *Paris*), Williamson, Pratchett, and Rowling all predate her work — but she does bring the wolf in without employing the horror genre — as in both *American Werewolf* and Williamson's cases — and without giving them a role of authority — as in Pratchett's and Rowling's examples. Rowling's primary werewolf is a different kind of exception as well, since he only changes form in the wild, never in the city.[99] She also presents the reader with at least four full packs as examples of the archetype, compared to the other sources studied here where typically only one or two werewolves appear. The sheer number of named werewolves, of whom the reader does get at least some personality descriptions, allows her readers to more accurately determine what traits are those of the whole species and what traits are those of the individual without being as polarized as Pratchett's Angua and Wolfgang.

4. Southern Wolves

In drawing from such diverse sources and introducing a variety of other folkloric figures from fairies to shifters to vampires, Harris does create a linkage with Charles de Lint. In the process of shifting between the two, the werecanines move both to another world and to the northern parts of this world. Even so, the two writers begin with the same core material and move in somewhat different directions as Harris brings the werewolf further into the city while de Lint starts to return them to the edges of civilization, in *Wolf Moon* and, arguably, in *Dingo*.

5

Secondary Worlds and Wolf Cousins

De Lint's Canines

Charles de Lint is known for drawing his inspiration from myriad native peoples and pre–Christian European folklore. The latter especially focuses on tales of Faerie and Celtic divinities. Thus, his readers should not be surprised that some of his werecanines are drawn from aboriginal Australian roots, specifically tales of the Dreamtime. De Lint approaches the concept of stories in a manner similar to Pratchett — e.g., they are important and the best stories have a lasting power. His focus on stories and folklore leads his body of work down many paths from the Wild Hunt and Cernunnos to the horn and ivory gates of the *Odyssey*. In many cases, de Lint takes these sources and adapts them to a modern, often urban, fantasy Earth, such that some fae beings appear to exist on the internet's electronic pathways.

In the case of his werecanines, de Lint presents two very different stories set in equally removed worlds. The oldest of his werecanine works is *Wolf Moon* (1988), following a werewolf— Kern — in an imaginary, secondary, world. Here, in addition to the common sources de Lint often returns to, he adds a touch of early film influence that has entered the collective consciousness as being typical of the creatures. On the other hand, *Dingo*, his more recent werecanine novel (2008), is set in an Earth only slightly different from our own. The novel is set in the same Earth as many of his other works that focus on the fictional city, Newford, although it does not take place in the city.[1] Both texts share some traits common to much of de Lint's writing that Pratchett shares as well: the importance of storytelling (especially telling the right story at the right time), folklore, and community.

5. Secondary Worlds and Wolf Cousins

These themes are notably present in de Lint's werecanine works. His werewolf resists the traits that folklore and storytelling claim he embodies. As a result of his resistance, Kern undergoes several psychological changes that mesh well with the shape-shifter archetype. Additionally, he works as an outsider to create that which he never had, a community, in the form of an adopted family — much like Remus Lupin's adopted family of friends and students. In fact, despite inhabiting very different worlds, there are quite a few similarities between Lupin and Kern. Conversely, de Lint's weredingos have to determine when it is best to tell their story to others. They are also stuck in the tail end of a piece of folklore many millennia old, that can be brought to an end — or a new phase — through their actions. In the process, the two weredingos must acquire aid, thus reshaping the community they find themselves in, after their stepfather has spent most of their lives keeping them apart from society for their protection. In this way, they too have some similarities to both Kern and Rowling's Lupin in that they desire and create that which they have lost: the company of others and a society of friends and family, even if the members of that community were previously at odds with each other.

These werecanines serve many purposes in de Lint's work, but they mix medieval, early modern, Australian, and film influences. They fulfill the role of the shape-shifter archetype by approaching humanity's dual nature thereby connecting man and beast, building and shaping communities, acting as agents of change, and connecting the natural to the urban. In de Lint's hands, the werecanines present insight into social interactions. The insight occurs through the weredingos being discussed from the perspective of an outsider in close contact with the shape-shifters. Through these myriad roles and purposes, the werecanines reach de Lint's audiences — adults in the case of *Wolf Moon* and young adults for *Dingo*. They also subvert some of the elements of their genres, as Kern's perspective reverses the traditional fantasy trope of tales following the warrior-monster hunter (there are no warriors and the monster hunter is the villain in this case) while *Dingo* takes the classic young adult fiction trope of avoiding adult supervision but spins it such that the adults have to ultimately choose to give up their supervisory role and most of the adults are not antagonists to be fought.[2]

Winter's First Moon & Influences

De Lint's werewolves, in *Wolf Moon*, as represented by Kern, share a few significant traits with both the medieval tradition and the early modern period. The former appears directly in Kern's actions and role while the latter is more influential in the stories told about werewolves by other characters, notably Tuiloch. Kern has clear origins in the medieval European tradition in that he is a classic sympathetic werewolf, has many similarities to Marie de France's Bisclavret with lesser similarities to Gorlagon and Alphouns,[3] and displays many of the traits that medieval audiences looked for as signs of humanity. Early modern influences are less clear, but focus on Tuiloch the Harper's beliefs and the mechanics of Kern's condition.

Kern is clearly a sympathetic werewolf as his story is told from his perspective and he is never depicted as performing monstrous acts. Throughout his narrative, the werewolf reiterates his desire for companionship, his fear of rejection, and his reactions to the violence commonly directed toward him. As he starts to become accepted by the residents of the Yellow Tinker, an inn he was dragged to in an unconscious state, Kern recalls a woman — Tera — he once tried to make a life with. The memory ends with his thought, "If there hadn't been a storm that night, he would never have escaped the hunters and their dogs."[4] He adds that he never harmed the woman or anyone in the town. Despite this fact, the villagers only saw the monstrous reputation of his kind, feared him because of it, and called upon hunters to drive him away or kill him.[5] That was the last time, he recalls, that he tried to find acceptance for what he was, blaming an instinct for self-preservation for his rejection of further attempts. Even so, Kern finds himself drawn to human habitation and continuously thinking about the possibility of settling down somewhere. Rather than self-preservation, or along with such instincts, the werewolf's fear of rejection and the violence that comes with it play an equal or greater part in his self admonishments to keep his hopes from rising. This fear of rejection is very much akin to that expressed by Marie's Bisclavret over eight centuries earlier.

Like Bisclavret, who tells his wife, "Harm will come to me if I tell you about this, / because I'd lose your love / and even my very self" (54–56)[6] when she asks about the three days he leaves every week, Kern is wary of telling the inn-mistress Ainsy about his condition. As the pair admit to their growing feelings for each other, the werewolf's thoughts parallel Bisclavret's. He assumes that he will lose Ainsy's love, as his predecessor lost his unnamed wife's, if she finds out what he is. However, while Bisclavret based his fear on correctly reading his wife, Kern's concern is based on his previous experience with Tera. Bisclavret ultimately gives in and tells his wife that he is a werewolf, Kern claims cowardice to himself and refuses to tell Ainsy. He has to be forced into his wolf shape by Tuiloch's magic before she knows what he is.

De Lint's werewolf diverges somewhat from his medieval predecessors — Bisclavret and Gorlagon — in that he cannot attack the source of his predicament, because of Tuiloch's status. Kern thinks that because Tuiloch is a harper, attacking the hunter without first demonstrating that he has sufficient cause would violate the sacred place of harpers (something de Lint borrows from the Celts and other related cultures).[7] For Kern's literary ancestors, the act of striking out at their respective wives was considered to have a cause, even though they could not speak to deliver it. Members of their respective courts assumed that, because of their previous behavior, if they attacked someone, there must be a good reason for it. This is not an option for Kern, partially because his opponent is both male and a harper, but also because Kern is known in his human shape. Had Kern been introduced to the Yellow Tinker's residents as a wolf, and lived among them as a wolf, perhaps the situation would have been different. Like Bisclavret's king, Alphouns' companions, and Gorlagon's brother, they might have recognized the humanity in the wolf.

Another significant point of difference is that Kern displays remorse after he accidentally kills two bandits on the road. These were, we are told, his first kills and are justified as the bandits were torturing Tomtim, Ainsy's uncle. In this remorse, he presents an opposition to Bisclavret and Gorlagon, even to Alphouns. Bisclavret seems to see violence, but not death, as necessary to regain his original state, since his wife stole the clothes he needed to assume his human shape. Gorlagon, after his wife transforms him into a wolf, undertakes a guerrilla war against her that ultimately ends in the deaths of her lover, her children, and his wolf-children in the process of regaining his human state. Even tricky Alphouns resorts to violence to bring attention to his stepmother, Braunde, who is responsible for his wolf shape. Perhaps the most important reason for this divergence is one of origins. Bisclavret was a knight, Gorlagon was a king, Alphouns was a prince.

All three were men of war, even though Alphouns is not knighted until after he spends years as a wolf and is restored to his human shape. Kern, on the other hand, came from a rural, likely commoner, family. He refers to his parents' holding and recalls his father taking a silver candlestick into town, presumably to be melted down so Kern himself can be slain. Here we see an important shift in that all the sympathetic werewolves of the medieval period were noblemen, while de Lint's is a commoner.

We know the status of de Lint's werewolf, in medieval terms, due to a few important indicators: clothing, speech, diet, and weaponry. All four were considered necessary indicators of humanity, or lack thereof. For medieval audiences, clothing was the first indicator of social status. The importance of clothing as a sign of one's place in society is clear, historically, with the introduction of sumptuary laws, such as the 1366 Statute of Kilkenny, which legalized distinctions of attire for different social classes — including sleeve length, types of fur trim, shoe type, and other features. John Block Friedman discusses the other three thoroughly, noting that diet was an instinctual indicator of nationality and class, that "[n]early equal in importance to diet as a measure of man was the possession of speech,"[8] and that the last means of determining humanity is the choice of weapons possessed by the individual. Kern passes the clothing test, as even in his wolf shape he carries a small bag filled with clothes (an act that we also see with Pratchett's Angua). He also, mostly, passes the diet test for humanity. Throughout his time at the Yellow Tinker, Kern always eats whatever is cooked in the kitchen. The lone exception that we see is when he goes hunting with the inn's dog, Stram. At that point, the pair chase down a rabbit, which Kern kills but allows Stram to eat first. Kern's first failure is that he cannot speak while in his wolf shape, a trait he shares with all of his medieval ancestors and most of his modern cousins. He also fails the weapons test for humanity. When he heads out to find Tomtim, Kern is offered an old sword that hangs over the Tinker's door. He turns it down, stating that he "wouldn't know how to use it."[9] Because the choice of weaponry determined social status, and humanity, his medieval ancestors would recognize that Kern was a peasant. Moreover, when he does get involved in a fight, he resorts to teeth and claws, the weapons of animals and monstrous beings.

Thus, to some degree at least, Kern succeeds at being human but fails at others, as most werewolves do. However, for modern audiences a couple

5. Secondary Worlds and Wolf Cousins

other factors come into play. First, Kern has long, drawn out, non-wolfish thoughts while in his wolf shape. While he is being chased, he thinks of the creature hunting him as coming from the "realms of myth" and being the "words of a storyteller's tale."[10] The fact that he thinks of myths and storytellers clearly indicates a man beneath the wolf-like exterior. Second, he considers the possibility of vengeance. Given the chance to simply suicide, "[h]e was unwilling to throw away his life. First the harper must be made to pay. That need sustained him more than simple survival."[11] His medieval predecessors would recognize the urge for vengeance as belonging to both man and beast, but modern audiences tend to see the act of vengeance, or vengeance overriding survival instinct, as something more human.

Regardless, he is considered less than human by those around him. This, too, creates a connection with his medieval ancestors as Tuiloch's description of werewolves mirrors the introduction of Marie de France's *Bisclavret*. The harper states, there were "men who were not truly men, who, in darkness and by the light of the moon, shed their human skins to walk the night as beasts, and as such, slay their neighbors, their kith and kin."[12] Likewise, Marie states, "A werewolf is a savage beast; / while his fury is on him / he eats men, does much harm, / goes deep into the forest to live" (9–12). She also says that people used to say, and it happened, that men turned into werewolves. This monstrous depiction disappeared from the literary scene in the medieval period, but returned during the early modern era.

The early modern view of werewolves is largely reflected in de Lint's antagonist. Tuiloch, a harper and wolf hunter, provides a voice for the beliefs commonly held by other people in the valley, when it comes to werewolves. The very first tale that anyone hears the harper tell begins as discussed above. This tale, he calls "Tascar, the Wehr wulf" and fills it with betrayal, bloodshed, and cannibalism. He also tells Kern that, so far as he is concerned, werewolves do not have friends.[13] He later states that he hunts true wolves quickly, because they are beasts, "but you [Kern] ... your kind. You are somewhere in between [man and beast]. Pain should be yours and torment, before the kill. How else can you pay for the crime of being what you are?"[14] In the past, he claims to have destroyed families, entire villages in order to slay one werewolf. His tactics are straightforward: he tells tales of monstrosity, secretly causes a couple grisly murders, whips the locals into a fevered pitch, then exposes his prey. Although there is no overtly demonic connection in this position, the tactics and general view regarding the bloodthirsty, man-eating werewolf have much in common with Henri Boguet ("Of the Metamorphosis of Men into Beasts"; 1590) and the trial of Jean Grenier (1603). In each trial case from the sixteenth and seventeenth centuries, there is a transformation causing chaos, at least one murder, a court supposedly attempting to protect young children and women, torture, and an execution. Most of these elements are also present in Tuiloch's methodology, although he replaces the court and the execution is reversed in this case — the werewolf survives and the judge is executed. Kern falls for the beliefs, initially, after he is exposed. He notes that he was already condemned based on the evidence of both fear and legend.[15]

The very legends that de Lint uses to cause Kern's troubles are the ones that inform his capabilities. Throughout early modern sources, we see a keen interest in the mechanics for shape-shifting; from Boguet to the trials of Peeter Stubbe (1590) and Jean Grenier, Jean Bodin (1580) to the (in)famous Heinrich Kramer and James Sprenger (*Malleus Maleficarum*; 1486) discussions of how, exactly, a man might change into a beast — or at least believe he had done so — were key elements. De Lint's work is no different. In his depictions of Kern, de Lint uses various situations to demonstrate his werewolf's abilities and limitations. Like Pratchett's Angua, Kern has access to his lupine senses in "manshape" (as he calls it).[16] This sense is so acute that he memorizes scents to differentiate people, much like a typical canine. His senses are such that, being a creature of magic, he is even able to sense magical auras. In a more modern, clinical moment, the werewolf explains that "his metabolism was such that wounds healed quickly — far more quickly than they might with someone not like him. A shapechanger. His tissues were highly regenerative. His bones were much more pliable than theirs — for flexibility was important when one changed from man to wolf."[17] Kern further demonstrates that the fact he is part wolf, which would normally send livestock into a frenzy, has no effect on cattle. He states that he is able to charm them, a sort of eye contact hypnosis that dampens their fears. However, there are limits to this ability. Kern points out that dogs were too closely related to wolves, and therefore to werewolves, for his ability to charm animals to work.[18] Thus, he must establish dominance with the inn's dog via other means, as will be discussed in depth below. His only significant limitation, aside from the fear engen-

5. Secondary Worlds and Wolf Cousins

dered in others, is "the silver that was poison to his kind."[19] This modern addition to the werewolf lore was likely added for two reasons: first, de Lint ties his werewolves to a moon goddess and silver is traditionally associated with the moon in Western folklore; second, de Lint gives his werewolves regenerative abilities that also come from modern sources. Typically, in the latter case, werewolves that possess recuperative powers have some weakness that negates said powers (for example, Pratchett's werewolves). Otherwise, when they appear as monsters, there would be no way to permanently get rid of them. The final mechanical aspect is the change itself.

Unlike earlier writers, and even to some degree his contemporaries discussed in previous chapters, de Lint does show Kern's change from man to wolf almost every time it happens. In a point of similarity with Rowling's Remus Lupin, Kern's first change came fairly young, around the age of thirteen (a bit older than Lupin). He describes the first change as being very painful, full moon triggered, and difficult.[20] After that first change, however, Kern is able, like Angua, to shift form at will. When he sets off to find Tomtim, "a moment he stood, neither man nor beast but some terrible hybrid of the two, upright but furred, with a wolf's jaw but a man's brow, then he was loping along the road [as a wolf]."[21] Unlike both Lupin and Angua, de Lint's werewolf is capable of taking a hybrid form, although the one time he does in *Wolf Moon* appears to be the first and only time he has done so. The hybrid form seems an easy one to achieve as Kern's entire description is that he stood up, decided to change, and stopped it half completed. Likewise, his shifts between forms appear fluid and fast as he changes form in mid-leap so that he can use the wolf-shape's superior jaws to tear the bandit's throat, all in the process of saving Tomtim from said bandits.[22] This ability to fluidly shift between man and beast with no discernable pause is also a perfect example of the shape-shifter archetype's dual nature.

Kern and Archetype

A few key elements of the shape-shifter archetype are its doubled dual nature (man-beast; shadow-civilized), its role in building and shaping communities, and its role as an agent or representative of change. De Lint's Kern fulfills all three roles. His antagonist also demonstrates the dual nature of humanity, while opposing the werewolf's community building and resisting change. As in the medieval works and Rowling's, the juxtaposition of the sympathetic werewolf and the unsympathetic human antagonist underscores the points that the archetype is employed to demonstrate.

Without discussing archetypes, Nicole Jacque-Lefevre notes, "the figure of the lycanthrope is [...] a reflection of the definition of nature, being, and man."[23] The archetype presents this reflection as its dual nature, both man and beast. In many cases, the werewolf doubles the display of dual natures by not only representing the man-beast nature but also the civilized-shadow duality.

Kern demonstrates his dual nature before we learn his name, or even that he has a human side. *Wolf Moon* begins with a nameless wolf being hunted through the woods. During the chase, the wolf displays some human tendencies, such as looking back due to his human need to catch sight of who, or what, pursued him, for revenge (as previously noted).[24] Later, Kern is startled by Ainsy's maid, Fion, who describes him as warily watching her, seeming like a trapped animal, then "[h]e seemed to shimmer before Fion's widening eyes, from man to beast to man."[25] The initial description occurs while Kern is in his "manshape," yet he still reacts like the wolf. Both incidents display the crossover that occurs between the werewolf's shapes — he retains human characteristics in wolf shape and wolfish characteristics in manshape. Thus, one of the dual natures of the archetype is shown. This nature is emphasized when Kern thinks, "his lupine senses sometimes fed too much data for him to concentrate overly much on mannish affairs. It was always easier to assimilate a situation and make decisions without the wolf thoughts clouding his judgement. Just as the wolf was superior in certain situations [...] so too was the man. It was often too easy to distract the wolf."[26] This duality is key to both the archetype and humanity. In the latter case, the high functions of the mind help us process information and make rational decisions. However, the more bestial elements of our psyche are those that keep us safe in other situations — for example: dangerous situations when the fight-flight instinct kicks in or something as everyday as driving where, if we let the rational parts of our mind take control, our reaction time would diminish considerably. Kern later fondly recalls running in the woods as a wolf in the winter and actually runs in order to burn off his anger. The wolfshape acts as a shadow-like release for his pent up anti-civilized impulses, it

5. Secondary Worlds and Wolf Cousins

allows him to work out the issues in a comparatively safe fashion — e.g., by running harmlessly through the woods or hunting rabbits. Despite his problems, Kern does finally accept his shadow, noting that while his shifting ability may often appear to be a curse, "to be trapped always in one shape — that was indeed a greater curse."[27]

Due to his relationship with the werewolf, the hunter — Tuiloch — also reflects the dual nature of the archetype. Once he locates Kern — perhaps the first werewolf to elude him — the harper-hunter begins a savage "game" to dishearten and discredit the werewolf. The so-called game costs the lives of a farmer near the inn as well as one of the inn staff, Tolly. In both cases, the harper calls up a beast out of legend to rip his victims apart, in the most stereotypically bestial fashion he can imagine. He displays, in his thoughts, the savagery he claims is inherent in the werewolf, but is in fact the province of man. The hunter's plan is, ultimately, to have every person at the inn, an adoptive family, at each other's throats, for his own entertainment. These thoughts and actions place Tuiloch firmly in the role of the monster that he claims werewolves, not men, are. Part of the harper's problem is that, unlike Kern, he has no shadow release as such. Instead, he has the feragh, a beast out of legend that he creates through his harp music-magic. This beast is, in many ways, Tuiloch's shadow made manifest. He never comes to terms with his shadow. He lets the shadow consume him, to the point that the shadow's manifestation cannot exist without him and vice versa. When the feragh is destroyed, the harper's end follows swiftly. He has invested so much of his being into the shadow, creating an unbalanced personality, that his demise must come almost immediately after his shadow's.

Through the feragh's and harper's demise, the inn community reforms in a different configuration than at the start of the action. However, Kern started shaping the community and, in some ways, building it much earlier. Soon after his arrival at the inn, the werewolf considers his past and notes, through his dual nature, both his loneliness and his desire for company, a community. He acknowledges that one reason he lives as a nomad is to stave off the loneliness, as well as being chased off when his secret is discovered. Thus, his nature simultaneously craves and distances him from the sense of belonging to a given place or group of people. He notes earlier that "the wolf packs shunned him for his strangeness — for the very humanity that men could not see once they learned his secret."[28] Here, we see a

The Modern Literary Werewolf

werewolf akin to Pratchett's Angua. Unlike, for instance, Gorlagon — who creates his own pack of wolves — neither Angua nor Kern can move between the two species whose appearances they share. Avoided by the wolves, the best they can hope for is to pass among humans. Unless, that is, they construct a community of their own. As previously discussed, Angua's solution is the specialized community of law enforcement. Kern's is the ragtag collection of people who inhabit the inn that is located a few hours from the nearest town. In its own way, the inn straddles the line between the civilized and the wild, existing as it does on the border between the two. This makes it the perfect place for Kern's community as he can interact with humans while still being able to run the woods at will during the nights without significant fear of running across other people.

However, humans are not the only component of this community, nor are the humans necessarily easy to win over. Another important element is the dog, Stram. His initial reaction to Kern is fear and aggression. This, of course, affects how the humans who witness their first meeting respond to the werewolf. During one of his first evenings, though, Kern employs the wolf side of his nature to establish dominance and respect with Stram, in a very canine-like way. He, gently, pins the mongrel to the ground until Stram submits, then leads the dog on a hunt for rabbits, offering Stram the first bites after their prey is caught. While the others initially find the dog's change of heart odd, they quickly accept it. On the other hand, Fion, who resists the harper's spell, eventually seeks out Kern for his help in freeing the others. Even as she tries to find him, however, she thinks, "[s]he couldn't forget what he was now. Could she ever forget? Or would the fear always be there, hidden, but tainting their relationship?"[29] Despite the fact that her need is there, it does not immediately override the instinctive fear reaction, something Kern eventually has to help Fion and the others get past before he can truly build a community for himself, and possibly others of his kind. This contrasts with William and Melior in *William of Palerne*, who state, "now sertes, for soþe, / þis best has mannes kynde • it may be non oþer / se what sorwe he suffres • to saue vs tweine!"[30] (2505–2507).[31]

Just before the final climax with Tuiloch, the werewolf vows to find other werewolves and create a safe place for them to live a positive life. In this way, Kern seeks to build a second community for a second family. Although the narrative ends soon after Tuiloch's defeat, the possibility of

5. Secondary Worlds and Wolf Cousins

Kern using the inn as a base to find and help other werewolves is there. This goal would fit with his work to rebuild the inn community and defend it. Moreover, it ties in neatly with his arrangement — very similar to Bisclavret's — in which he is "normal" for the most part, but changes to run in the woods from time to time. This arrangement denotes acceptance of his capabilities, one that echoes the court's acceptance of Bisclavret's change.[32] In order for these communities to exist, a change had to occur, one that the werewolf effected, heralded, or both.

There are a few layers of change that follow de Lint's werewolf. On the most surface level, Kern is an agent of change in that his very presence at the Yellow Tinker modifies the social dynamic amongst the residents. As with any small, close knit group of people, the addition of a new person causes shifts and changes within the group. On a slightly deeper level, Kern is the herald of change in that his appearance leads to Tuiloch's arrival and the murders that the harper-hunter commits. The deaths shake up one family, the entire valley, and the inn's family. The deaths that Kern directly causes also create a change in the social dynamic in that they save Tomtim's life. Without the deaths of the two brigands and the third's flight, the tinker would very likely have died on the road, which would have profoundly affected his niece and her surrogate family. On one level, the brigands' deaths maintain the status quo — the residents of the inn can go on as normal with all of their members — but on another, the fight gives Tomtim enough clues as to Kern's true nature that the tinker holds back from his family. He keeps the secret to allow Kern a chance to fit in. This leads to the third layer of change that Kern affects. He causes others to modify their way of thinking about himself and werewolves. For example, upon seeing Kern after he fled, Fion thinks that she saw resignation in his eyes and appearance, which causes her to consider the possibility that he had concealed his ability precisely because of the negative, violent, reactions of others.[33] Just a few weeks before, such thoughts would never occur to her regarding werewolves. She would have considered them monsters out of legend, as she told Tomtim after one of Tuiloch's songs.

On the other hand, the harper-hunter stands as a representative of the status quo. He is the embodiment of the legends that cause fear in both human and werewolf, a sort of self-loathing in the latter case. If his claims can be believed, Tuiloch represents the static ways of the past because he is practically immortal and has hunted werewolves and wolves for several centuries. However, he is shown to be a consummate liar throughout his appearances, so this claim may also be false. Regardless, it is no coincidence that the harper-hunter's death is required for the old, fear inducing beliefs to melt away. Once Tuiloch — as the old prejudices — is defeated, the werewolf finds complete acceptance among the Tinker's family. That is four minds changed, not counting Kern's own views of himself. The number may be small, but it is a start. The werewolf's own view of himself is modified during his trials as well and comes out stronger and decided upon a positive, constructive course of action, rather than continuing his nomadic life of running. Through the defeat of the agent of the hidebound status quo, the rest are given the opportunity to adapt and evolve into the present and look toward the future.

Modern Cousins

De Lint's werewolf also has a significant amount in common with his modern cousins, even as he is used in somewhat different ways. The most notable parallels occur with Pratchett's Angua and Rowling's Lupin. Kern shares a few questions that Angua tries to answer as well, he also has some similar views about his existence. Likewise, he pre-dates several attitudes that appear with Remus Lupin in terms of his desires, concerns, and issues.

Both Angua and Kern wrestle with some questions inherent in their species. One of the key questions is why people fear wolves, specifically because humans often commit the atrocities they blame on wolves. Angua, perhaps a bit more cynical or worldly, has similar questions. Her's, however, are answered using the voice of Gaspode, the talking dog. As noted previously, Gaspode explains that canines do not like canines that think like men, and men do not like men who can perform like canines. In effect, Angua, through Gaspode, comes to the same conclusion as Kern: that they are somewhere between man and wolf and are, therefore, going to be accepted by neither species. Or, as Kern puts it, "too much the wolf to live among men. Too much the man to live among wolves."[34] Angua comes to this conclusion partially through her family and partially because of her interactions with both wolves and humans outside her family's sphere of influence. All three communities, even her acceptance in the Watch com-

5. Secondary Worlds and Wolf Cousins

munity, inform her idea. Kern, on the other hand, comes to the same conclusion through his socially enforced nomadic lifestyle.

De Lint's werewolf has some stronger connections to his descendant, Remus Lupin. On one hand, they share desires. Both desire a family, normalcy, and learning. His desire for acceptance in the Tinker's family clearly demonstrates his wish to have both a new family to replace the one he lost and to have some sort of normal, sedentary life. Kern, like Lupin, also focuses on learning for learning's sake. He notes that he wishes to experience the world, not for any particular gain, but rather simply to experience it. With their desires also come their concerns. As shown previously, Lupin worries about his relationship and getting close to others. Part of his concerns manifest as worries that he will not be able to provide a normal life for his potential wife (Tonks) and that he will pass his condition on to his child. In Kern's case, these concerns appear in his worry about what the Tinker's residents will do when they discover what he is. Kern is particularly concerned with Ainsy's response, simply because of his simultaneous desire and fear both for and of a close relationship with her. His fears for the relationship are those he shares with Lupin when either werewolf comes close to making friends. In Kern's words, "when they discovered his secret [...] all earned friendship would die."[35] The same concern fills Lupin's potential relationships with Potter and Black, and continues to do so even into adulthood well after the closeness of their friendship has been amply demonstrated. However, Lupin's friends were drawn closer to him almost immediately upon learning of his condition — they were inveterate troublemakers and risk-takers. Kern's potential friends, on the other hand, are innkeepers and farmhands, relatively cautious people who generally avoid trouble — with the exception of Tomtim. The source of both werewolves' concerns is the fact that they are "locked in the lies of legend and false histories that told them they were evil, that the change could not be controlled, that when they changed they must strike out at those who did not have the curse."[36] Admittedly, in Lupin's case the change is not controllable, but his childhood at the school demonstrates that, even without a recently developed medication, he did not need to harm others. Perhaps more importantly, Lupin, like Kern, is clearly not evil despite their shared condition. However, both characters face prejudices and persecution based on the commonly held beliefs of others that are based in legend and misinformation. In a similar vein, legend and history are wrapped around de Lint's other werecanines.

Wolf's Antipodal Cousins

In some ways, de Lint's other werecanines can be said to have their origins in another world, like Kern. As weredingos, they come from Australia but their story takes place in North America, somewhere in the general vicinity of de Lint's fictional city Newford. On another level, much of their existence is tied to the Dreaming, the source or setting of many traditional Australian aboriginal stories. De Lint plays with traditional Western expectations of the were-animal tale by presenting twin weredingos in *Dingo*. The sisters, Lainey and Em, are very different in personality, although they are virtually identical in appearance. Early in the narrative, they have to appear in public as a girl and a dog in order to conceal themselves. They swap times of day as human and dingo in order to be fair about the restrictions on their lives. Initially, before the supernatural elements become known, this appears as a personality change for both dingo and girl.[37]

Like Lupin, their story is told from someone else's perspective. This has some effect on their role as representatives of the shape-shifter archetype. Even so, they work to build and shape communities, connect the natural to the urban, and connect man and beast, all necessary attributes of the archetype. Despite being inspired largely by Australian influences, there are still some connections between Lainey-Em and the Western werewolf tradition. De Lint moves beyond the Western tradition, though, first by incorporating the aforementioned Australian elements. He also adds an outsider's perspective that differs from Harry Potter's contact with Lupin. In a related vein, de Lint focuses on social interactions, specifically those of the weredingos and teenagers in general. The latter are quite different from both Rowling's and Pratchett's approaches, even though the other authors involve their werewolves' social connections with others.

Archetypal Dingos

The weredingos, like all shape-shifters, fit within the archetype in a variety of ways. The most important three in this case are community building, connection between the wild and urban, and connection between man and beasts. To a lesser extent, they serve to create a connection

5. Secondary Worlds and Wolf Cousins

between the past and present, both for themselves and for the two people closest to them. De Lint's weredingos bridge the gap between opposing pairs in each case.

Community building occurs on at least two levels in *Dingo*. First, it appears within the scope of the town as represented by Miguel (the first person narrator) and his opposite, Johnny. The two are initially antagonistic toward each other for various reasons, not least of which is an incident in which Miguel's father threw Johnny out of his record-comics store. Even without this incident, their personalities ensure that they would not get along with each other. However, a request for help from Lainey and Em brings the high school adversaries together on the same side — Miguel for Lainey, Johnny for Em. While Johnny and Miguel never become close, or friends, a certain sort of respect does develop between them by the end of this part of their story. The other major form of community building that the weredingos are involved in crosses generations. Lainey and Em are being hunted by the oldest known weredingo, supposedly the first of their kind, Warrigal (another word for dingo). Due to various stories and warnings from their mother and step-father, they fear that Warrigal means to kill them in order to cause his release from an ancient curse. By the end, due in part to Johnny's actions, the twins both free Warrigal with no injury to themselves and come to an amiable relationship with him, in which he also causes their father to stop chasing them. At the same time, there is a generational community built around Miguel. He discovers, via Lainey and Em's step-father, that he is also descended from werebeasts, in this case crows-ravens and a bit of indeterminate canine. Due to this knowledge and his challenging Warrigal in the name of both lineages, Miguel finds himself followed and protected by flocks of black birds. In the future beyond this part of the story, de Lint leaves open the possibility of Miguel finding shapeshifting relatives and becoming a fuller part of their community. Given the species involved, his lineages likely cross the rural-urban divide as well.

The bridge between wild and urban is linked in many ways to that between beast and man, to the point that they are virtually inextricable. Lainey and Em draw Miguel and Johnny from their urban town, where most of *Dingo* is set, into the wild Dreaming, where Warrigal is trapped. They demonstrate that the border between the worlds, and thus between the wild and urban, is a thin one. Likewise, the line between beast and man is narrow. To underscore these points, the four shift between worlds on a beach, the slim border between land and sea. Moreover, they make the transition around dusk, the border between day and night. In each case, the transitional time and place make the transfer between worlds easier, according to the weredingos' step-father. The man-beast binary breaking is one that all human-animal shape-shifters very clearly demonstrate. The twins go a step further with their alternating roles — first, Lainey is human and Em is canine when they meet Miguel; they swap the next time he sees them, but they met Johnny, off stage, in the same roles; the third time Miguel meets them, Lainey is human again. Every change is accompanied by a personality shift in both the human girl and the canine, which Miguel originally interprets as a sign of mental illness. Eventually, the explanation of the twins' fair time sharing is accepted, however, once they give up the need to swap roles.

Time is an important element in the last connection that the weredingos affect. They forge connections between the past and present, or act as the impetus for such connections. In their own case, they come to terms with their own past and their ancestors — namely Tallyman (their father) and Warrigal. They also cause Johnny to reconnect somewhat with his own past. Through his being temporarily allied with Miguel, he discusses his absent mother and his grandparents as well as his early desire to produce art. However, he feels trapped by his family's past due to their reputation. Because of their history in the town, everyone expects Johnny to be an uncultured bully, like his father and, probably, most of his other male ancestors. In this way, he is like the twins who are, for a time, trapped by their past, lineage, and certain expectations. However, the twins break out of these assumed roles and set the stage for Johnny to do the same, if he truly desires to change. In Miguel's case, the connection to the past works in two ways. First, the aforementioned discussion of his hidden lineage ties him to an unclear past that he may look into at some point (assuming de Lint writes more about these characters). Second, he agrees to do a favor for the spirits of some aboriginals the group meets in the Dreaming. The task is a simple one — burying a small bone in sacred ground — but it has a significant impact for the ancient spirits. The act also has some significance for Miguel as the ground he chooses is the cemetery in which his mother is buried — as he notes, it is the most sacred ground he can think of. Thus, in the process of helping spirits from the past, he reminisces on his own familial past through his relationship with his mother.

5. Secondary Worlds and Wolf Cousins

Working Within Tradition

Despite predominantly tapping an Australian tradition, *Dingo* also has a few characteristics in common with the European werewolf tradition. Following from the medieval period, there is a definite connection via consciousness while in animal form and a creed of non-violence similar to Bisclavret and Alphouns as well as an inversion in which the audience sees the change. De Lint also displays a very early modern concern with the mechanics and rules of transformation. Through Miguel, he completes his European influences by incorporating the early modern English view of lycanthropy as insanity.

One of the important tests for humanity, according to medieval authors, was the question of human consciousness. Albertus Magnus (Albert the Great) states that "[o]ne of the properties peculiar to human nature is the feeling of shame engendered by committing an evil deed."[38] Augustine goes a bit further to state, "Whoever is anywhere born a man, that is, a rational mortal animal, no matter what unusual appearance he presents [...] no Christian can doubt that he springs from [Noah]" and is thus human.[39] By this standard, de Lint's weredingos show themselves to be entirely human. They clearly retain their rational minds in dingo form, as Miguel notes personality changes in both the girl and the dingo that perfectly mirror Lainey's and Em's minds. Moreover, the twins appear to communicate on some non-verbal, perhaps telepathic level, implying that even as canines, their minds are human. However, they lack verbal speech, as is true of all the medieval werewolves, except Gerald of Wales.' Miguel notes, "I know it's ridiculous, but because I have this paranoia that Em understands everything we're saying, I feel the need to get Lainey away from her dog for a moment."[40] Em does indeed understand everything Miguel and Lainey say, because she retains her human mind in canine form. Miguel acquires his "paranoia" from seeing her react to everything that he says and all of Lainey's responses in a manner beyond the norm for a dog.

The twins are beyond the norm for dingoes due to their creed of non-violence, at least toward other shape-changers, as well. However, this creed places them in company with medieval antecedents such as Bisclavret and Alphouns. Both medieval werewolves avoid true violence throughout their tales, until confronted with their villainous wife and stepmother respectively. I say true violence here because Alphouns does resort to a threat of violence — screaming and leaping at various people but not making contact — in order to feed and disguise his charges (the eponymous William of Palerne and his love, Melior). In Bisclavret's case, we never see any violence on his part until he needs to display his wife's deception, despite the fact that he is a knight (and therefore presumably a warrior) and must be using some violence (hunting) in the woods while he is stuck in wolf shape, if only to eat.

De Lint diverges from medieval sources in much the same way that Pratchett and Rowling do: he shows us the transformations of his werecanines. This will be covered in more detail below, with regard to the twins, but Miguel and his father also see Tallyman change shape. Miguel describes the process simply as seeing Tallyman "[stand] there as a dingo for a long moment, and then he shifts into his manshape."[41] Given that the twins' father is used for the purpose of evoking fear in the characters, and potentially the audience, the decision to leave his transformation so bland might be an unusual one. However, by the time Tallyman appears, Miguel has already seen Em change shape — from dingo to human — in front of him and described it in some detail. He has also been touching Lainey while she changed shape — from dingo to human. Therefore, the change itself holds no fright factor for him. Tallyman, on the other hand, may still be fearsome, but not because of his ability to change.

The process of change, the mechanics, is also a tie to the early modern period. Various religious and secular sources on the continent were very interested in lycanthropy, specifically how one effected the transformation from man to beast. Many modern fantasy writers are similarly interested in the mechanics, more from a world-building perspective. De Lint is no exception here. Miguel describes the first shape-shift he witnesses — Em transforming from dingo to human — as follows:

> Because a shimmer like a shivering mirage runs from the end of Em's muzzle all the way to the end of her tail. Every inch of her quivers, then she starts to rise up onto her hind legs, *changing* as she does, gold-red dingo into pretty young woman with red-gold hair, who's a twin to Lainey. Except it's not Lainey.[42]

The change appears to be smooth and is obviously not painful, as some shape-shifts in modern sources are.[43] Thus, Miguel's later description of Tallyman's transformation is brief, matter of fact, and simple. Miguel also touches Lainey as she changes shape, noting that he felt "the fur recede [...] the shape of her bones and muscles changing until it's Lainey facing me."[44] While the description is not clinical, it is definitely not coming from a disconcerted or fearful source.

Unlike most early modern accounts, there is no external device necessary to cause or trigger the change. Perhaps more importantly, unlike Pratchett's Angua or de Lint's Kern, the twins' clothing changes with them. This is an important difference, as it is specifically noted. The same presumably happens with Rowling's Lupin, but no one comments on it one way or the other. De Lint's narrator does not initially consider the question, but his temporary partner, Johnny, does. This makes sense for de Lint's characters — both high school aged boys — especially Johnny, given his family.

There are a few other rules that these weredingos follow. At the same time that he holds Lainey through a change, Miguel discovers that even in human shape, she is stronger than she looks — perhaps implying that she retains some of the dingo's muscle strength. He also learns that "cousins" (as the weredingos call all shape-shifters and those related to them) have a sort of psychic link between parent and child. Due to this link, parents have some paranormal control over their child. This, we are told, is an evolutionary trait that helps the cousins remain hidden. The link dissolves when the child reaches adulthood — signified by finding a mate. Thus, when the twins tell their father that they are engaged to Miguel and Johnny, the link is severed. All of these mechanics are essentially the natural laws under which the werecreatures operate. As was believed by the early modern writers, every monster, every paranormal being had to operate under some set of rules that could be understood. On one hand, this insistence upon natural (or supernatural) laws was likely a psychological means of making the writer feel more in control, assuming the writer and reader believed such beings existed.

There were some early modern sources, mostly English and Scots, who held that all cases of shape-shifting were the manifestation of mental illness. They claimed that lycanthropy was caused by excessive melancholy, or sometimes choler.[45] Regardless, it was seen as a psychological problem that could be potentially fixed by rebalancing the humors or causing the person's mental state to shift back toward a non-melancholy focus. De Lint employs a similar position with his weredingos through Miguel's perspective. When he first discovers the Lainey-Em switch, his first thought is "This smacks an awful lot of some kind of bipolar disorder, or multiple personalities."[46] He even extends this view beyond the human half of the pair, to include the canine. When the dingo's reaction to him changes — from borderline hostile to loving — Miguel thinks, "What do I know about dogs? Who knows what goes on inside their heads."[47] Even after Lainey's explanation of the twins' entire situation, Miguel holds to the psychological disorder position, and even Lainey cannot blame him. Given a post–Freudian world, in which armchair psychologists are virtually everywhere, who can blame Miguel for assuming bipolar disorder or multiple personality disorder are the culprits? Ultimately, however, the "real" nature of the transformation is demonstrated, moving de Lint's weredingos beyond the early modern conception and into something notably different.

Werecanines from Down Under

De Lint builds upon a few traditions with his werecanines, but ultimately produces something significantly different. He first incorporates some, mild, Australian influence that tweaks the western werewolf story. He also presents the perspective of an outsider in close contact with the werecanines, in a method rather different from Rowling's. Finally, he employs some focus on teenage social interactions in a fashion that diverges from both Rowling and Pratchett in important ways.

The use of Australian influences in *Dingo* appears to be minor at first. After all, de Lint is merely swapping out one canine species for another with his werebeasts. However, because he chooses a very continent-specific canine, he also brings along the culture that exists around the species. He does not simply use a, for example, were-doberman instead of a werewolf. The former is ubiquitous enough in the western world to be effectively non-cultural specific. On the other hand, the dingo is unique to Australia and has its own body of folklore, legend, and other tales. One of the most important additions is the Australian concept of the Dreamtime that is pervasive in the narrative. As Basil Sansom has noted, there is a strong connection between the Dreamtime and shape-shifting figures. He explains, "Metamorphosis makes the [Dreamtime] stories politically subversive because, in each of them, an original Dreaming Power seems to turn the conditions of existence topsy-turvy as it reasserts its dominance in the face of whitefella occupation of the land."[48] His statement specifically refers to some aboriginal stories, but is applicable to *Dingo* as well. Throughout the course of the story, Warrigal seeks to reassert his position and activity — thus a Dreaming Power returns. He does this in an area that is a mixture of Canada and the U.S.[49] both of which have their fairly recent experiences with indigenous peoples who seek to preserve their traditions in the face of European colonization. The choice to make his point of view protagonist an individual of Hispanic descent — Miguel — and two of the other three protagonists Australian underscores the colonial people asserting themselves in "whitefella" occupation. This seems especially apt given that only Miguel is said to be a "cousin," not Johnny, whose family is obviously Caucasian, or Miguel's best friend, who is described as looking like a stereotypical California surfer.

The "cousin" status is another important part of Australian lore that de Lint employs. Lainey explains the connections between three types of beings: cousins (shape-shifters), guests (indigenous Australians), and spirits. She claims that the cousins were in the land first, thus why they refer to the indigenous Australians as "guests." These cousins are bound by honor, regardless of animal species, age, or strength of bloodline. According to Stephen — Lainey and Em's stepfather — the bounds of honor even transcend how long the person has known about their lineage. He brings this up because Miguel's chief complaint about a plan to challenge Warrigal is that Miguel only found out about his cousin lineage a few minutes earlier and, therefore, had no contacts among the crow or canine lines.

Miguel's knowledge of his lineage is an important point because of his perspective as narrator. Even after Stephen explains his lineage, Miguel is an outsider looking in. He has no shape-shifting ability and knows nothing of their culture. In these ways, he is somewhat akin to Rowling's Harry Potter, the story is told from his perspective rather than that of the werebeast, regardless of the were's importance to the story. However, Miguel differs from Rowling's eponymous protagonist in three significant ways: first, he is closer to the werecanine in question; second, he spends more time with the werecanine; and third, he turns out to be related to the werebeasts, although not of the same species.

While both Harry and Miguel are close to their respective werecanines, Harry's relationship with Lupin is a very different one. He has a teacher-student relationship, even when Lupin is no longer officially a teacher. Even without that relationship, they would retain a generational gap and the fact that Lupin was Harry's father's friend for many years. On the other hand, Miguel and Lainey are the same age and become involved in a romantic relationship, rather than a professional one. Although Lainey teaches Miguel about her world, their relationship is never quite a teacher-student one. They are more equal in standing within the relationship. Additionally, Miguel is initially concerned about Lainey's sanity, while Harry just finds Lupin's periodic disappearances — explained as illnesses — vaguely mysterious. What is telling is that the reactions of everyone in *Dingo* to the shape-shifters is either curiosity or stunned acceptance, not fear. In this way, they are similar to Harry's reaction rather than Ron Weasley's. This is a potentially unusual reaction in Miguel, Johnny, and Miguel's father, though, because, unlike Harry, they have not had the advantage of nearly three years' experience with magic before discovering werecanines. On the other hand, this means they also lack any social prejudices that clearly flow through Harry's magical community.[50] Then Miguel discovers that he also has cousin lineage, as noted above, and is therefore also, technically, a supernatural being even if he lacks powers.[51] Ultimately, Miguel reacts with acceptance of Lainey's reticence, asking himself, "When do you start to tell your potential boyfriend that you can change into a dingo?"[52] Put in those terms, it is indeed difficult to blame the weredingos or see them as particularly threatening.

The romantic relationship that removes the weredingos' potentially threatening aspect is also an important element that de Lint employs with the archetype. While both Pratchett and Rowling explore the social relationships surrounding their werecanines, de Lint's approach is rather different. Remus Lupin's relationship with Harry involves a hierarchy. Regardless of the situation, the characters and readers are always reminded that Lupin is one of Harry's teachers (or was) and is a surrogate parental figure, as he was one of James Potter's closest friends. Likewise, Sergeant Angua's relationships are largely hierarchy based — with Commander Vimes, Captain Carrot (a romantic relationship, but their ranks are still there), Corporal Nobbs, or any of the other Watch officers whom she either outranks or is outranked by. Even her relationship with Sgt. Colon, despite their equal rank, has a certain hierarchy as Colon is a native to the city and is a more experienced member of the Watch. Miguel and Lainey's

5. Secondary Worlds and Wolf Cousins

relationship, as well as Johnny and Em's, lacks these social hierarchies — they are all high school aged young adults with no positions of authority. Additionally, there is more constant contact between Miguel and the weredingos than is generally seen between Lupin or Angua and any other single character in their respective narratives. In part, this contact comes from the weredingos being main characters in a small ensemble narrative (as opposed to Angua, who is a major character, but is part of a very large cast).

As part of the relationship, Lainey and Em do undertake some fairly typical teenage behavior and attitudes, or deliver some veiled messages. In the latter case, Lainey tells Miguel, "When we're in human shape [...] We're just like anybody else — except we can change into dingos."[53] This statement both makes sense in the story's context, but its wider interpretation covers any potential oddity in the "normal" young adult audience. She does not explain that there appears to be a telepathic connection between the twins.[54] Later, the twins explain that their stepfather is also a "cousin" but cannot change shape, because his bloodline is too diluted. This gives the teens capabilities that their elders lack, somewhat akin to Rowling's Harry who has abilities (and, thus, responsibilities) that older wizards do not. Those powers can be empowering, but they come with drawbacks — such as the attention the twins get from Tallyman, who wishes to sacrifice them in order to gain favor with Warrigal. Demonstrating the pros and cons also shows up in their social interactions because Johnny and Miguel get drawn into the cons. In the process, both males learn that nothing comes without a price, whether that be a sacrifice or some sort of drawback — Johnny gets to be the hero, but temporarily loses Em; Miguel gets Lainey, but also gets Tallyman's redirected attention. However, the interactions are not entirely serious, as seen when Miguel refers to the twins as weredingos. Em is clearly not happy with the name (presumably, she prefers "cousins," perhaps as more respectful), but Lainey is equally clearly amused.

Myriad Iterations

Through both *Wolf Moon* and *Dingo*, de Lint merges traditional werewolf lore with more modern additions and a few twists that keep the archetype evolving. In the former case, his twists are minimal and he keeps to the more traditional with modern lore incorporated in such a way that it helps separate his narrative from more traditional secondary world fantasies. With *Dingo*, he steps away from the more common narratives, but does so by remaining true to his style as he focuses on indigenous peoples and their tales. This method is a theme that runs throughout his Newford stories, whether the indigenous peoples be the Celts (who, admittedly, are not entirely indigenous), what the Canadians refer to as the First Nations, or Australian Aborigines. His work, thus, seems to be an appropriate way to introduce a sample of the myriad ways that the werewolf has been reimagined by modern (twentieth- and twenty-first century) authors through diverse short works.

6

Variety...

Myriad Werewolves

The preceding chapters have shown the shape-shifter archetype, as represented by the werewolf, in a variety of roles from monster to police officer, teacher to rover. They only reflect a small portion of the variety of uses that the archetype was adopted for over the last century. To touch upon the greater range of possible roles, a look at several shorter works is in order. This shift in direction is also in keeping with earlier traditions as most of the classical, medieval, and early modern werewolf tales were brief and relatively to the point.[1] Modern short story writers have continued the werewolf's role as both monster and police officer (with variations, including SPCA officer and night watchman). They have also added the figure to introduce historical periods and mindsets to younger, and older, audiences. Some have expanded the professional roles to include doctors and other fields. A few have brought the werewolf into the realm of science fiction (SF) to discuss issues of extinction and conservation. The latter uses have involved both genetic experimentation and time and dimensional travel.

Throughout the following examples, a common thread of the shape-shifter's survival and adaptability is clear. Regardless of what time period it is placed in or role it assumes, the figure fits and proves useful to present a wide range of discussions. Harry Turtledove sets his piece in twelfth-century Cologne, roughly the time Marie de France wrote her werewolf *lai*. He uses the shape-shifter to explore period socio-religious tensions, while mixing in modern views of the werewolf. Robert Randisi, Robert Weinberg, A.C. Crispin, and Kathleen O'Malley bring the werewolf into the twentieth-century with their own takes on the werewolf as officer of the law. All three werewolves share some traits with Pratchett's Angua, but differ in significant ways — including the fact that two are a SPCA officer and a store night watchman. Crispin and O'Malley use their werewolf to right the world's wrongs while Randisi and Weinberg demonstrate how their werewolves adapt to the modern world and use their peculiar abilities to make a living among normal humans. Philip José Farmer shifts direction to show one werewolf doctor, in the process touching on an entire hidden culture, before passing the gift-curse on to a sheriff. Barbara Paul demonstrates a complex and public werewolf culture infused with support groups. Jane Yolen and Larry Niven take the werewolf into the future, after a fashion. Both bring the shape-shifter to bear on issues of conservation, genetics, and evolution by very different roads. On the other hand, Brad Strickland takes the futuristic werewolf and prepares to launch him into space as, perhaps, the ultimate interplanetary colonist, with a bit of an homage to Golden Age SF.

In every case, the werewolf figure is fluidly adapted to the setting, as it is in other, more convoluted, tales presented in anthologies alongside those discussed in this chapter.[2] Throughout the works, the werewolf is updated in order to bring the archetype into the modern world, beyond the monster movies of the 1930s.[3] All of the werewolves presented in this chapter, as well as those not chosen, represent various aspects of the shape-shifter archetype and fulfill the archetype's role, morphed for a new audience. Most repeat the same or similar messages that shape-shifters, as werewolves, have given readers for centuries. Not only do they present these messages in different ways, but they also bring new issues and debates for a new audience, one that has problems the earliest writers of werewolves might consider fantastic in and of themselves.

Historical Werewolves

A well known writer of alternate histories, Harry Turtledove has tried his hand at werewolf tales a few times, most notably in his *Fox* series.[4] However, even in that series, the werewolves are only present briefly and vanish soon after their appearance, except in the title character's memories. Turtledove uses the figure more fully in his short story "Not All Wolves" (1988). In this piece, he remains fairly close to historical views while making some additions and creating a strong connection to the shape-shifter archetype.

6. Variety...

One of the first striking elements of the story is that Turtledove sets it in Cologne, France, 1176. The twelfth-century French setting is likely no coincidence as it connects to Marie de France, who wrote "Bisclavret" in the twelfth-century (although she may have done so in England). His werewolf, like Marie's, is a sympathetic figure and lacks the capacity for speech. We know he is a sympathetic figure because he thinks, "*I do no harm*" as he runs from a mob.[5] He does discover some means to communicate, after a fashion, much like Marie's knight. Dieter, the boy turned werewolf, attempts to find secluded places to change form. This is perfectly in keeping with medieval werewolf narratives, where the werewolf never changes shape in sight of others.[6] Likewise, Dieter fits well within both St. Augustine's and Gerald of Wales' conception that the rational mind is kept during transformation — thereby indicating that no real change has occurred as the individual is still human. The reader sees Dieter's thoughts as he flees as well as being told: "Inside the fleshy envelope of a wolf, though, he kept the wits he had as a boy."[7] Thus far, the werewolf is a match for every tale from the medieval period as well as many of the ecclesiastical conceptions of the werewolf. Turtledove even brings in more fringe medieval authors, noting that the werewolf transformation is brought upon by the full moon — a nod to Gervase of Tilbury (the only extant medieval writer to consider a connection between transformation and moon phase).[8]

Despite his connections to the medieval conceptions, Dieter does demonstrate a few modern additions to the werewolf. He is described as having supernatural healing abilities that are cancelled out by fire. He also notes that his first change occurred at the onset of puberty.[9] Turtledove then adds the silver vulnerability that is familiar from Hollywood films, but lacking in earlier sources — although it makes sense when the moon phase is tied to the transformation, due to the linkages between silver and the moon in folklore. A last change, and possibly the most significant, is that Dieter is being hunted through a city. Most of the medieval period's werewolves were hunted in the wild, so this shift is notable. On one hand, the choice moves the werewolf from a place where his animal form would be helpful to one where it hinders him. The decision also works for the boy, a beggar (and therefore marginalized individual). Unlike Bisclavret or Gorlagon, Dieter is not a noble and lacks a support system or family. He has never been hunting, thus he stays with the place he knows best, the city. Perhaps more important than these modifications are the uses that

Turtledove makes of the figure that demonstrate the shape-shifter archetype at work.

Given his space limitations, Turtledove does not have room to enter into heavily nuanced or long term discussions of issues with his werewolf character. Nor does he have the space to employ a variety of subjects. Instead, he focuses on two aspects of basically the same topic: prejudice. While he is running, Dieter reflects that his pursuers' "excited shouts reminded him of the baying of wolves."[10] On the surface, this description may not have a clear tie to prejudice. However, it does demonstrate that the pursuers have become that which they supposedly hate. The choice in description also connects the pursuers to the wolf pack and brings to mind mob mentality, the loss of individuality to the mob. This idea is directly connected to prejudice in that Dieter eventually gains refuge in the Jewish section of the city with an old man, Avram. When the mob catches up with Dieter, Avram hides him. When asked the next morning why he helped, Avram replies, "One thing you should remember always — you are not the only one ever hunted down Cologne's streets."[11] The revelation causes Dieter to consider anti-Jewish mobs in a different light. The story and werewolf, then, bring an understanding regarding Judeo-Christian relations in twelfth-century France that is both historical and potentially useful today. As is typical of the archetype, Turtledove's werewolf simultaneously reaffirms and denies the lines of division in society.

Police Wolves II

As discussed in the previous chapter on Pratchett's Angua, the werewolf as law enforcement officer is an excellent example of the archetype's role in preserving society. The similarities between Angua (introduced in 1993) and her short story predecessors (all 1991) bear some note alongside their roots in older traditions and the archetype. To that end, we will begin with Robert Randisi's Lisa Bain — who is closest to Angua in some ways — before moving to Robert Weinberg's Otto Stark — who, like Angua, is on the night watch — and A.C. Crispin and Kathleen O'Malley's Therese.

Notable as a detective writer, Randisi slips into the paranormal with his story "Partners." In many ways, his protagonist and werewolf — Lisa Bain — has notable similarities to Pratchett's Angua. Both work on police forces where they believe everyone knows about their shape-shifting ability, but no one talks about it, at least not directly. Bain's partner notes, "He always covered for her, always managed to make it believable. He often suspected that the others knew."[12] Likewise, both appear to be forced to change form with the coming of the full moon. In Angua's case, the change can occur at will any other time, which does not seem to be the case for Bain. Additionally, Bain appears to need to see the moon to change, as "[Lisa] looked up and saw that the moon had broken through the clouds."[13] Obviously, the moon was full before it was visible, but this does not seem to have forced a change. In this way, Randisi draws upon Gervase of Tilbury and modern pop culture renditions of the werewolf. Another difference is that Angua becomes a wolf, while Bain turns into a hybrid man-wolf form.

Randisi also draws upon a few medieval ideas, complicating them to some degree. Augustine argued that if a being retained the human mind, rationality, then it was human regardless of its outer form. Bain appears to remain rational. However, "[t]he beast heard the sound of the shot. It penetrated through layers and years of bestiality."[14] From an Augustinian perspective, then, Bain is human, but just barely. Her partner adds to the borderline position of her changed nature as "[Frank] looked at the beast, who was standing still, head cocked, studying him. / He extended his hand to the beast. This part always frightened him the most, because he always feared that one of these days recognition would not dawn in those feral eyes — and at the same time, he always knew it would."[15] Thus, Bain appears to remain rational, but the human mind is buried beneath layers of wolf-mind. The hybrid body, then, houses a hybrid mind. The hybrid mind calls the Augustinian definition of humanity into question, something none of the medieval sources do. But, Randisi is not writing for a medieval audience. His modern audience is familiar with the monstrous werewolf as well as the sympathetic werewolf. Both elements of the archetype are viewed by the audience through the lens of modern pop culture, especially movies.

Seeing the werewolf aspect of the archetype in its wolf-man form is, perhaps, one of the most familiar appearances for modern audiences. Ever since Lon Chaney, Jr., the hybrid man-wolf has been the most popular film expression of the werewolf. Bain takes this form as "Jerry turned and saw a huge, hulking form lift the two-hundred-pound Stupid completely off his feet."[16] The figure "looked like a wolf, but it was standing upright."[17] This appearance of the archetype clearly evokes a fear response in the audience, or is meant to do so. It uses this fear, generated in other characters in this case, to uphold the law. Bain, as a police officer, enforces the rules of society by assaulting the ad hoc gang that she and her partner caught in the act of robbery. The werewolf, here, acts as judge, jury, and executioner and is, perhaps, a bit harsh in the punishment she delivers (none of the would-be-thieves survives, admittedly one shot at her partner and shot her twice). Her actions reaffirm society's values regarding property and represent an older method of dealing with violations before incarceration was an option (due to resources). In this way, Bain does operate in a manner somewhat similar to the wolf in *Little Red Riding Hood*, especially Charles Perrault's version.[18] At the same time, the werewolf reinforces social bonds as she saves her partner's life, and in turn he covers for her. This bond is reminiscent of the bond between vassal and lord witnessed with Bisclavret, Gorlagon, and Alphouns. In all three cases, the vassal — a partner in the social contract — performs, in some cases life saving, service for the lord, who in turn protects the vassal.

The roles of lord and vassal also come into play with Robert Weinberg's "Wolf Watch." In Weinberg's story, the werewolf— Otto Stark — is a night watchman at a department store. After discovering that one thief is a former employee of the store, Otto thinks, "Traitors deserved no better death."[19] Since this thought occurred to him while in wolf-shape, Otto clearly retains his human mind while changed. There is considerable evidence of both the lord-vassal relationship and Otto's retention of humanity throughout the story. For example, after eviscerating one burglar, "Mentally, Otto grimaced in annoyance. Claw wounds always left a mess. It took hours to clean blood stains off furniture."[20] He later pretends to be cowed by a crucifix in order to draw a burglar away from a display of fragile Christmas ornaments. After dispatching that thief, Otto congratulates himself because "he had protected the fragile ornaments from damage. His quick thinking had saved the store a good deal of money."[21] This thought not only demonstrates his capacity of human rationality, but also his loyalty to the company — the modern equivalent of a feudal lord. While chasing one thief, Otto also notes that "he knew better than to try the grooved metal stairs [of the escalator] with his claws. Wolves were not constructed for escalators."[22] As noted previously, he is, then, wholly

6. Variety...

human according to the dominant medieval traditions, despite lacking speech.

However, Otto falls short of full humanity in a couple other areas. The most obvious is his choice of weaponry. According to the traditional sources, a person's choice of armament determined their status as human. John Block Friedman explains that the upper classes (the civilized people) during the medieval period bore swords, maces, and other chivalric or mounted weapons. The lower classes, just above animals and monsters, wielded whatever was close at hand: pruning hooks, pitchforks, or spears. Those who used a club or no weapons — relying instead on claws, teeth, and fists — were non-human or sub-human.[23] Otto, upon hearing an odd noise, notes, "[t]he nightstick he left on the table, preferring not to carry it when trouble threatened. The heavy club only got in the way."[24] This may seem a bit unusual to modern readers, but works perfectly with medieval views as both the nightclub and being unarmed were signs of non-humanity. To underscore this point regarding social status and weaponry, Otto earlier thinks, "Some night watchmen carried guns, but not Otto. He disliked weapons of all types. The billyclub was only for show. He never used it."[25] Just based on the lord-vassal relationship and the choice of weaponry, Weinberg draws upon older conceptions of the werewolf. These are not the only elements that float up through the centuries, though.

Like the medieval, and classical, werewolves, Otto strips before he changes shape. Some later werewolves have clothes that apparently change shape with them — Remus Lupin, seemingly, has this ability, for instance. Perhaps more important is Otto's diet. As Friedman notes, food is an important indicator of nationality and social class. In Otto's case, it also indicates humanity, or lack thereof. He ultimately eats the intruders (humans), but cleans up afterwards — using the store's cleaning supplies — and calls upon some ghouls (who work for the city sanitation department) to dispose of the rest of the corpses. The fact that Otto partially eats the burglars places him in the realm of cannibalism, and thus monstrosity. The act also brings up some important questions regarding Otto's status, though. Eating the intruders is technically, after all, only cannibalism if Otto is also human. If Otto is something else, another species, then he is simply a predator and the thieves are prey. This was an equally thorny question for medieval audiences: if the werewolf was a wolf, then eating

The Modern Literary Werewolf

humans would not make it a cannibal; if the werewolf was a human, then eating humans would make it a cannibal. But, the werewolf is neither human nor wolf, it is something in between. It violates the binary thought by presenting a third option. Classifying the new option may not be possible, but this is not necessarily a problem. The important point is not the classification, but the effect of rupturing the simple either-or categories. In this way, Otto firmly holds his position as a representative of the shape-shifter archetype, since one of the archetype's core purposes is to question categories and binary structures.

As a representative of the shape-shifter archetype, Otto's primary role is to police society and reaffirm social bonds. In his own small way, he ensures that certain boundaries are observed and those who violate them are punished. He notes that people break into the store all the time, but he always catches them because of his special abilities. Therefore, the store keeps an outdated, effectively non-functioning alarm system that people are constantly avoiding. That said, Otto himself disables the alarm and elevators before he investigates strange noises, to keep the police from showing up. He also reaffirms the social structure by remaining loyal to his employer, or lord, while punishing (and executing) those who not only break with their "lord" but return to harm the "lord" as a form of revenge. His shape-changing abilities help in both roles as he can assume the form of an aging, somewhat slow, watchman who does not carry a gun, which serves to draw in those who would violate society's mores. Once they are effectively trapped inside, the werewolf punishes them, somewhat akin to Perrault's wolf, once again. Weinberg does make a few modernizations to the archetype's presentation and the werewolf, as should be expected.

Diverging from earlier sources, but keeping with many modern tales, he does leave his werewolf vulnerable to silver while capable of regenerating other injuries. He also mixes sorcery (to use Otto's term) and willpower to create the change as both will and a spell are necessary to shift forms. This, Otto claims, is linked to his family line, traced to Transylvania. The link between the werewolf and eastern Europe is a fairly strong and old one, even if Transylvania has become more synonymous with the vampire for modern audiences. Weinberg delves beyond the supernatural into the pseudo-scientific as well, relating that a fellow werewolf who was also a molecular biologist once explained the transformation to Otto in scientific terms, including how much energy was burned. Finally, Otto is said to watch no television, except werewolf movies. The latter, we are told, he watches for entertainment and amusement, because the writers get most things wrong — his transformation is not gradual or metamorphic, but rather replacement (he also takes a wolf, not wolfman, form, which is more in keeping with earlier sources).

In some ways, Weinberg's story is less than serious. He incorporates some moments that draw, at least, a smirk or smile. This choice reminds us of the close ties between the shape-shifter archetype and the trickster. A.C. Crispin and Kathleen O'Malley, however, present a decidedly more serious approach to the werewolf in their story "Pure Silver." Their narrator, and eventually werewolf, is an officer for the Society for the Prevention of Cruelty to Animals (SPCA). She is, thus, a police officer — or watchman — without being a police officer, at least in Washington, D.C., in 1991. Despite being a completely normal human, Therese is able to identify the story's primary werewolf on sight. This ability is explained as something she does with everyone, associating an animal with them instinctively. She thinks, "I didn't believe in monsters [...] but when I thought of that old man, all I saw was a werewolf. A kindly Jewish werewolf ... right. Sure."[26] The why is not explained.

Crispin and O'Malley draw little from classical, medieval, or early modern sources except for the existence of werewolves themselves and Gervase's connection of change to the moon. However, Joshua Tobeck, the werewolf, has a great deal in common with Pratchett's Angua. Most of these traits are passed on to Therese, adding to some similarities she already possesses. Like Angua, and some later "traditional" werewolves, Tobeck's presence causes anxiety in other animals. This was seen with de Lint's Kern and Williamson's Barbee as well to different degrees. In this case, a police dog "lunged and whirled, frantically barking" and appeared high strung when the werewolf was nearby.[27] Angua notes that wolves and dogs do not generally like werewolves, Kern has his issues with the Yellow Tinker's livestock and dog, Barbee has similar problems with other canines. The tradition of animals reacting violently to werewolves is not new, nor is it as old as the early modern period. But, it has become a fairly common trait of the archetype's appearance. A probable reason is that the werewolf is neither fully human nor fully wolf, especially if it retains the human consciousness in wolf shape. Because the werewolf does not fit into either category, it is strange, it stands out, attention needs to be drawn to it as it may be a threat. The werewolf is, indeed, a threat, but not necessarily in the way that many animals would perceive it. Rather, it is a threat to binary thought and conceptions of the world. It introduces grey areas, a continuum rather than a simple either-or.

The continuum concept is very important for Crispin and O'Malley's werewolves. On one hand, Tobeck is a murderer. However, he specifically targets Nazis who escaped to the U.S. to bear the brunt of his shape-shifted violence. He acts as judge and executioner, but is also a protector. Tobeck implies that he only changes on nights with a full moon and that he, and his family, terrorized concentration camp guards on those nights.[28] He also implies that his entire family were werewolves, or "special ... very old. Blest."[29] The roles as judge, executioner, and protector are exactly what should be expected from a representative of the shape-shifter archetype. The roles represent both positive and potentially negative aspects of the archetype in that the protector defends its charges, even if they do not realize they are being protected. However, the judge and executioner are more problematic roles. In both cases, the werewolf is policing society and culling the herd of dangerous members, thus saving the greater herd. On the other hand, the werewolf does this in a very final way, without resort to trial, evidence, or complete assurance that the individual deserves punishment. In Tobeck's case, he claims he can smell the ex–Nazis, this is his only evidence, but even he admits that in D.C. his sense of smell is not entirely reliable. Regardless, he executes whoever he thinks should be removed from society — an act that would otherwise be considered that of a deranged individual. This is not the first time that madness and lycanthropy have been connected, as discussed with Williamson. Tobeck is clearly also used to invoke fear, as his changed description indicates: "His clawed paws/hands were soaked with blood. He must've been six feet four, and weighed at least two hundred pounds. And his face! A wide-muzzled animal glared [...] The teeth were huge, impossibly long and sharp."[30] The description is immediately followed by a scene in which Tobeck attacks Therese, during which she acquires his family heirloom and kills him, thus taking on his self-appointed mission and abilities.

Crispin and O'Malley do make some changes to the archetype, though. One of the more interesting modifications is that Tobeck carries an heirloom that triggered his first change. This heirloom is a silver knife. The knife is passed on to Therese, triggering her ability to change form as well. However, Crispin and O'Malley's werewolves are also vulnerable to silver, as the knife is used to kill Tobeck. The silver knife becomes interesting precisely because it both starts the shape-changing ability and ends it. In a way, the knife becomes a representation of the social place of the werewolf himself—without it, the werewolf cannot exist; with it, the werewolf dies meanwhile without the werewolf, society rots from the inside; with the werewolf, the crime rate increases through the murders (s)he commits. Presumably the werewolf can change shape without the knife after the first time because Tobeck says he hid it just before he was taken into the concentration camp so the Nazis would not get it, but he changed shape several times while he was imprisoned. Like Lupin and Greyback, though, the werewolf is uncontrolled while (s)he is changed. Thus, Tobeck (and later Therese, presumably) positions himself near a target before the change occurs. Unlike Lupin and some of the others, Tobeck can heal at a very rapid rate — wounds are gone within hours. These abilities are, obviously, useful for the archetype's role as protector. Other werewolf protectors have different means of aiding those around them.

Werewolf, M.D.

Philip José Farmer presents a take on the werewolf that begins with a doctor, ends with a sheriff, and briefly touches on an entire hidden society in the middle. His short story "Wolf, Iron, and Moth" is set in a small town and begins from the wolf's perspective. The wolf is quickly shown to be the town's doctor and the archetype evolves from there, building out of its historical roots.

Perhaps the two most notable elements of Farmer's story in connection to medieval roots are the werewolf's change and the werewolf's mind. In the former case, the change to wolf is connected to the moon phase, another nod to Gervase of Tilbury. This werewolf, Varglik, is completely controlled by the moon phase. He cannot change form any other time, nor can he resist the full moon. Varglik does, like Rowling's Lupin, attempt to control himself while changed, by locking himself in a cage. The result is that, like Lupin, he badly injures himself. The difference is that Lupin continued to lock himself away, accepting the self-injury; Varglik simply moves out of the city to a town surrounded by woods. When he changes, Varglik becomes entirely non-human, even by Augustinian standards. He notes that he had "no memory of being Man any more than he would remember being Wolf when he again became Man."[31] Thus, his human mind vanishes when he becomes a wolf, making Varglik not human for Augustine. This is a bit of a change from most medieval roots, that show werewolves who are still human in mind, if not in body. However, it does fit with some of the early modern accounts.

Another key early modern connection is Varglik's wolf-form diet. He is described as having eaten cattle, sheep, and dogs. Two children are also added to his tally of deaths, and presumably meals. In fact, in wolf shape, Varglik thinks, "being a werewolf, it desired human flesh above all flesh."[32] The death list is very similar to that recounted in Jean Grenier's trial (1603), at which a girl said Grenier told her that in his wolf form he killed and ate many dogs, but preferred "the flesh of little girls."[33] Also like Varglik, Grenier was taught to strip and wear a wolf skin in order to change his form. In Varglik's case, the wolf skin only works for certain people, and glows in such a way that only those who can use it see the light. Farmer's werewolf is thus quite similar to Grenier, aside from the werewolf's age (Grenier was thirteen).

From this historical base, Farmer begins to modify the archetype. He reaffirms one common element of the archetype. After a brief affirmation, one of Farmer's more interesting additions is a hidden society of werecreatures. This society leads to Farmer's scientific take on the figure. These changes come after Farmer asks, "But werewolves ... what are they? A plus not-A makes B?"[34] The philosophical question is at the heart of the shape-shifter archetype, and is meant to be rhetorical. This is the question writers of both fiction and non-fiction have been asking for millennia regarding human-animal shape-shifters: where exactly do they fit in standard classification systems? The best answer is that they do not fit anywhere, their role is not to fit, but precisely to not fit, to question classification.

The shape-shifters themselves ask questions about where they fit in, to some degree, in Farmer's story. He alludes to a hidden society that spans the world. The most overt appearance of this society is an organization calling itself the "Werewolf Association of the World" (WAW) that produces a magazine every four months. This association also notes the existence of weretigers, werecrocodiles, werejaguars, werebears, and were-mountain lions as well as extinct werefoxes. As is typical of special interest magazines, the WAW magazine includes a personals section and an article detailing the results of a mail survey of werewolf sex habits. The magazine also carries a reminder that the reader must shred it after reading (to preserve the secret).

The WAW magazine is also where Farmer introduces his pseudo-scientific approach to werewolves. One of the articles is said to link werewolfism to a recessive gene that requires a bite or a werewolf skin to activate. Additionally, the local sheriff comments on the fact that Varglik steadily gains weight throughout the month, only to completely lose it during the week surrounding a full moon. Scientifically, this is a method of building up body mass to fuel the transformation. The change itself is fully, graphically, described over the course of three pages, during which Varglik dissolves into a jelly-like mass and re-solidifies as a wolf. The wolf is ultimately killed, not by silver, but by a .30-caliber lead bullet. This is both a premodern take on the werewolf and a nod to science. As the sheriff who shoots Varglik thinks, the same laws of physics and chemistry that apply to all beings also apply to Farmer's werewolves. When the werewolf is killed, it does not revert back to human form, as is common in other modern and some earlier tales. The reason is simply given that there is no transformation because the cells are dead, therefore they cannot be active. Taking the pseudo-scientific approach works well for Farmer as it modernizes the werewolf and archetype, while also being true to Varglik, as a doctor (thus, a man of science).

Werewolves Anonymous

Barbara Paul approaches the werewolf, like Farmer, from the perspective of its own society or sub-culture in her short story "Never Moon a Werewolf." However, she expands on the idea of a hidden shape-shifter culture — via Farmer's magazine — to an open social organization of werewolves. Unlike Farmer, Paul's werewolves are publicly known and acknowledged by human society. Although Paul does not say how long her werewolves have been in the public eye, we discover that they have been out long enough to be accepted and exploited, but not long enough for overt prejudices to fade.

Unlike many of the other pieces discussed in this chapter, Paul avoids

Gervase and modern film with regard to forced change during the full moon. However, she does retain many ties to the medieval werewolf. Perhaps the most important point of retention is that her werewolves are, like Bisclavret and Alphouns, sympathetic yet feared. The readers' sympathy is aroused from the start as the story opens on a meeting of a werewolf support group. The second speaker of the night, Norman, acknowledges that he has a problem changing shape from time to time and needs help from the group. The same anecdote demonstrates the fear produced by the werewolf as, once he is able to take wolf form, Norman instantly scares off his knife and pipe wielding assailants (of whom, he admits, he is scared). Likewise, as with Bisclavret, they have a reputation as man-eaters, one that proves to be undeserved. The recounted scene also tells readers that Paul's werewolves, like their medieval ancestors, can only take the form of humans and wolves, with no hybrid shape. Also like their medieval ancestors, these werewolves remove their clothes to change form[35] and do not use man-made weapons, relying only on their teeth and claws to intimidate opponents. Throughout the story, however, they are much like Alphouns in that they attempt to deal with threats in a peaceful fashion. Paul's werewolves also meet the Augustinian standard for humanity as they possess their human minds while in wolf form. Moreover, they hold full conversations with each other—presumably in "wolf speech"; for example, a werewolf called Fergus says, "**But we don't kill humans ... except in self-defense**"[36]—while in their wolf shapes.

The archetype manifests as Paul's werewolves in that they serve to question boundaries and demonstrate a more animalistic side of humanity, unconcerned about the restrictions of society. They also highlight issues of prejudice and discrimination. Perhaps the best example of their removal of boundaries and restrictions of society comes in the discussion of "Full Moon." Although Paul's werewolves do not have to change during the full moon, they choose to do so. As the narrator, Gordy, explains, "Full Moon was the night to abandon oneself utterly to the glories of werewolfdom. [...] It was werewolf party night."[37] He later notes that all the non-werewolves in the city stayed inside on that night every month, even the police. During the celebration, there is hunting—although Gordy notes that "they left the dogs alone, as a sort of courtesy to disadvantaged cousins,"[38] so even without the social restrictions, there are unspoken rules—and competitions such as length and volume of howling. The werewolves also focus

6. Variety...

attention on two elements of prejudice and discrimination. Once the first help group meeting breaks up, Gordy and his friend head to a bar only to find it "had a new sign in the window: *No Werewolves.*"[39] The sign and the impetus behind it are a clear reference to the days of segregation in the U.S., approached from a different angle. Because the werewolves can pass (as discussed with Harris), Gordy's friend suggests going in anyway, since no one will know. Gordy, however, states that they should go somewhere else rather than give money to bigots. The other incident that evokes the issue of prejudice is one of Gordy's clients, who benefits from Gordy's medical donation but still brings a group of rifle bearing men to the Full Moon celebration to hunt the werewolves as they leave the park. As Gordy notes, the hypocrisy here is evident. The pack does work together to drive the "hunters" away, as will be discussed in greater detail below.

The city pack is, in many ways, akin to the werewolf societies envisioned by Charlaine Harris (but less violent) and Farmer (but not concealed). Additionally, as with Harris, Paul's werewolves have a monthly "party night" and can transmit their condition via bites. The latter is also a connection with Rowling's werewolves. However, Paul's note that they are careful about who they bite — or at least who they allow to live after being bitten — due to concerns that only the right people be given the gift of lycanthropy. This view opposes those of Rowling's and Harris' werewolves, who generally see lycanthropy (or bitten lycanthropy; respectively) as a curse, although many of Rowling's are questionably discriminate about who they bite. For instance, Lupin avoids biting anyone, Greyback targets children, and the others are presumably indiscriminate. Moreover, like Williamson, Paul's werewolves employ a focal object to aid their change, something they call an emoticon,[40] like the hair pin Will Barbee focuses on for his first change.

Paul's werewolves also represent a range of socio-economic classes and professions. The only four whose roles she defines are a counselor (the nameless group leader), an office department head (Zelda), a hair transplant donor (Gordy), and a TV personality (Maxine). Fergus' job is undefined, but he describes some discrimination in hiring practices when Gordy asks about possibly working with him.[41] In many respects, they are more varied in backgrounds than Harris' werewolves. Their jobs are also used not only to introduce discussions of discrimination (Fergus) and control (in Zelda's case), but for a bit of humor as well. Gordy's job is a prime example. He works as a donor at a hair transplant clinic because "one [hair] was all it took. A week after the implant, the client needed a haircut. He also had to shave twice and sometimes three times a day."[42] This entertainment value is layered on top of the amusement regarding the werewolves' method of dealing with Wexford — the man who tried to have them hunted.

Through an Alphouns-like leap-scream routine, the pack frightens off Wexford's guards. While he is vulnerable, he literally offers the pack the shirt he wears, ripping it off and throwing it at them. The werewolves, gaining inspiration from this act, cause him to strip, then herd him toward the city docks. There, they force him onto a ship as a stowaway (without his wallet, credit cards, or identification) which ships out early, possibly for China or "[t]o somewhere, at any rate."[43] Which leaves the pack and its organization as a help group, a sort of Werewolves Anonymous.

Officially, the organization is called Lycanthropes Anonymous and is designed to assist werewolves in any way possible. The goal is not to "cure" their condition, but to help with any issues related to the condition that they come across. Most seem to involve problems with changing form — as is the case with all three speakers: Norman, Zelda, and Maxine. That said, members are all introduced basically the same way: "'Hi, my name is Norman and I'm a werewolf.' / 'Hi, Norman!' everyone called out."[44] Zelda and Maxine follow the same formula,[45] a nod to various Twelve Step programs, including Alcoholics Anonymous. In some respects, this reads as a parody or subversion as the organization does not attempt to remove the condition. On another hand, L.A. could be an homage to A.A. as both groups attempt to control the condition.

Once and Future Werewolves

Within the last few decades, some authors have started moving the werewolf into the future. They have adapted the shape-shifter archetype, in the form of the werewolf, for science fiction (SF). The shape-shifter in SF is certainly not unusual,[46] but including the werewolf is different as most SF shape-shifters are humanoid-humanoid.[47] Human-animal representatives of the archetype are fairly rare in SF. The shift from the fantasy and horror genres to SF opens some new opportunities for the archetype, as exploited by Jane Yolen, Larry Niven, and Brad Strickland. Two of the three use the werewolf, at least partially, for environmental conservation purposes, in addition to others. Strickland takes a different route, viewing the werewolf as the ultimate interplanetary colonist in a bit of an homage to Golden Age SF writers.

Yolen's "Green Messiah" (1988) is very explicit in its use of the werewolf for environmental purposes. Like Farmer's story and Williamson's novel, hers is somewhat loose in its scientific explanations, but does use the trappings of science to explain the effect. Even so, her werewolf retains some tenuous links with the past. Lupe, the werewolf, is supposed to be a scientific experiment, the goal of which is to turn some humans into wolves so they can take over and lead wolf packs in order to save the dying animal species. The scientists involved assume, like Augustine, that Lupe will retain her human mind — which will supposedly give her an edge over other members of the pack and gain her control of them. However, after the transformation is complete, it is unclear whether Lupe is mentally human, wolf, or something else. Ultimately, for the reader the answer may not matter, although for the fictional scientists it is a measure of success or failure. That may be one of the binaries that Lupe is there to call into question — perhaps she is meant to turn the succeed-fail duality into a continuum whereby the scientists succeed, but not necessarily to the degree they'd like (or failed, but not as badly as they could have). Although the scientists only consider their measurable, quantifiable methods, Lupe does not completely trust in them. She recites a spell, first in Spanish then in English, then in "Wolf" to ensure the transformation happens. The use of spells as part of the change is an old tradition seen in the early modern court documents — including Jean Grenier's — medieval tales —*Arthur and Gorlagon*— and classical sources —*Satyricon*. The retention of the spell is representative of exactly what the scientists claim they were trying to do: work with legendary traits.

The head scientist on the project takes Yolen's werewolf entirely into the realm of SF. He claims that the old traits associated with werewolves — hairy palms, unibrows, and the like — are "a real genetic link with humanity's past [... thus] some [humans] are descended from *Canis lupus*, the wolf."[48] With this supposed line of descent established, the scientists claim they can attempt to turn a person into a wolf to save the wolves. To ensure that this creates a true werewolf, Yolen notes that the subjects will theoretically be able to change back and forth between forms. Underscoring the move to SF, the scientists work at the Asimov Institute. However, Yolen is very sparing on details when the actual change occurs. She simply states, "when the full Change came over her [Lupe]."[49] It happens and it is over, there is no fanfare, no gory details (as we see above with Farmer). Ultimately, for Yolen's use of the archetype, the change itself does not really matter; everything else around the change, especially the reasons, are the important parts.

Yolen's story adapts the shape-shifter for use in the environmental movement. The werewolf is employed as a warning, and a means of reversing damage. In effect, the archetype is still protecting, judging, and teaching others. Yolen is not the first to use the archetype in this way, but she is one of the first to use the werewolf form of the archetype for the green movement.[50] In this way, she is different from the other writers in this chapter, even though Niven touches on the subject.

Niven's "There's a Wolf in My Time Machine" explores the werewolf— after a fashion — with regard to environmentalism, but in a roundabout manner. The narrator, Svetz, travels through time and across dimensions (although he thinks he is only traveling through time) to recover extinct species for a futuristic exhibition. In the process, he slips into an alternate Earth due to a malfunctioning part. On the Earth he discovers, simian life never advanced beyond the Neanderthal stage, if that. However, lupine life became humanoid. Niven's nod to modern tradition has the wolf-men living in homes lit to the level of a full moon. He does note that their technological development is rather advanced, but skipped over environmentally damaging technology like fossil fuels, because of the smell. Svetz eventually realizes that the wolf he captured in his world's past turned into a wolf-man to adapt to the parallel world. Likewise, the wolf-woman he takes with him, Wrona, becomes a dog when he returns to his Earth — the werewolf transformation, after a fashion.

Svetz recalls that the initial damage that effected his side trip was caused by a horse that used its horn to damage a panel. Given that he describes a unicorn, Svetz apparently crosses dimensions occasionally without necessarily realizing it. Like Yolen, Niven plays with the idea of parallel evolution, just in a different way. He describes Wrona as large with pointed ears, eyes far apart, a grin that "stretched *way* back,"[51] and long, sharp fingernails. This matches his description of the transformed wolf in his machine: "he saw the intruder towering over him, the coarse thick hair, the yellow eyes glaring, the taloned hands spread wide."[52] The reader is given an idea of exactly how "towering" the creatures are when Wrona's home is described, as the ceilings are built for a twelve foot tall person.

Why are these large wolf-men the focus of the story? Niven uses the pseudo-werewolves (a term we might use because they do not appear to change shapes) for two important purposes. As touched on above, they provide an environmentalist message. The environmental element is clear in Svetz's mission to recover samples of extinct species, that have to be kept in captivity in specially constructed environments because Svetz's Earth would kill them via pollutants. The message presented regarding industrial damage and species extinction is blatant. Niven's werewolves also present a clear environmentalist position when he discusses the technological developments of the parallel Earth. The werewolves developed without the environmentally destructive effects, due to their possession of more acute senses, specifically smell. The fear response is the next notable usage. Svetz's reaction to finding a large man-wolf sharing a confined space is understandable. The unconscious predator-prey relationship, often used with the more animalistic representatives of the archetype, is clear in this case. Likewise, Niven presents Svetz's fear that he will regress, de-evolve, to become one of the primitive simians that the werewolves keep as slaves, pets, and food sources is easy to comprehend. The regression potential, the opposite of what Svetz's wolf does, can also be tied to the environmental issues, as environmental destruction can lead to social and technological regression in myriad ways. In these ways, Niven uses the archetype to send a warning about our own society and to explore some ideas of parallel evolution. The latter meshes with the archetype's binary questioning aspect. In this case, the binary is the human-animal, or human versus not-human, divide that the werewolf is so commonly used to question.

There are some ways in which Niven's explorations can be tied to Strickland's werewolf. On one level, Strickland is also discussing environmental issues, although his Earth environment is carefully balanced and controlled. However, the colonial environments are still wild and unregulated, thus a perfect place for his werewolf. Sending the werewolf out as a colonist, to spread his "condition" among the general populace of colonists, ties Yolen's and Niven's evolution ideas together and produces something that is different.

Brad Strickland's "And the Moon Shines Full and Bright" builds from some medieval principles. One of the most notable is the retention of the human mind while in wolf form. Strickland's werewolf, Kazak, initially appears to lose his humanity when he changes shape.[53] However, the scientists working with him run several tests, including a mock escape, to determine if this is indeed true. They conclude that he does retain some humanity, and is thus human.[54] He is also said to remember his time as a wolf.[55] After his escape, Kazak needs to be returned to his human form before he can be sentenced. This is also a lingering element of the medieval and early modern eras. If the werewolf is a beast, or mostly beast, then it cannot be held accountable for its actions, at least not in the same way a human is. If the werewolf is a human, then it can be held accountable. Therefore, sentencing Kazak in his wolf shape would be meaningless, he has to be in his human form. In his human form, Kazak fulfills another medieval requirement for humanity—clothing. He desires clothing in human shape, as a sign of his humanity. This is despite the fact that he is told that Earth's future society is clothing optional due to shifts in social views and the technological ability to control the weather. The lead scientist thinks the connection between humanity and clothing is archaic and amusing, which also says something about his level of humanity in the werewolf's medieval roots. Finally, as with all the pieces in *The Ultimate Werewolf* anthology, Gervase's moon-linked change is present with Kazak as well.

Kazak is also a strong representative of the shape-shifter archetype. He fulfills four of the major roles of the archetype, although some are only implicit. As a werewolf, a wild creature in a heavily structured and controlled Earth, Kazak crosses boundaries between the past and present, uncontrollable and controlled. The end of the story—Kazak's choice to remain in captivity on Earth or be shipped to the off-world colonies—crosses another boundary: that between the "civilized" colonizer and the "uncivilized" colony. Likewise, his potential for mutability causes problems in Earth's rigid society. However, the scientists suggest that his abilities may be used to form stability in the colonial populace by strengthening the gene pool and giving them a better chance of survival. When Kazak implicitly takes the choice to be transported to the Venus colony, he effec-

6. Variety...

tively escapes to the unclassified, proto-terraformed, margins of Earth's interplanetary society. This creates a new beginning, the birth of a new populace with Kazak's potential abilities, and a form of rebirth for Kazak himself. Each trait further solidifies his place within the scope of the shape-shifter archetype. But, Strickland moves beyond the characteristics reader expect from the werewolf and shape-shifter in general.

Some of Strickland's modifications to the werewolf, we have seen before in the work of other writers in this chapter, others are his own take on approaching the figure from a semi-scientific perspective. Many modern writers have created scientific or pseudo-scientific explanations for the relatively modern werewolf-silver interaction. Strickland is no exception. His scientist's explanation is that silver disrupts the hormones that allow a werewolf to regenerate, an echo of Williamson's discussion of silver and werewolves.[56] He also brings up the modern accounting of a wolf's, or werewolf's, ravenous nature — that they are unnaturally hungry in order to make up for the lost biomass used to fuel the transformation. As with Williamson and others, both explanations serve to inject contemporary understandings of physics and biology into the archetype's body of appearances. These are fairly minor, but widespread, modifications to the archetype that reflect earlier transformations as well. Perhaps the earliest attempts to discover a scientific means of describing shape-shifter changing comes in the early modern period, as various continental writers seek to determine the limits of the werewolves they put on trial, or instructed others about. For example, G. Haver's translation of *A General Discourse of the Virtuosi of France, Upon Questions of all Sorts of Philosophy, and Other Natural Knowledge* (1664), states that transformations must be illusion "[f]or otherwise, how should the Sorcerer reduce his Body into so small a volumn as the form of a Rat, Mouse, Toad, and other such Animal into which it sometimes is turn'd."[57] Clearly, the "Virtuosi" are arguing based on what would later be called the Law of Conservation of Mass. In both the historical and modern cases, the writers move to the limits of current knowledge of the sciences, then extrapolate a little further.

This extrapolation gives Strickland the basis for his homage to the Golden Age SF writers. Once Kazak has been prodded, probed, allowed to escape, and otherwise tested, he is told that he will be sent to the colony on Venus. By 1991, scientists and SF writers knew that Venus was uninhabitable, and the chances of making it even vaguely habitable are remote.

However, the SF writers of the 1930s through 1950s, as well as the pulp era writers that they followed, set numerous stories on Venus, often depicting the world as covered in giant rainforests. It is here that Strickland's scientists plan to relocate "the world's last werewolf."[58] He is told that this will be a boon to him as well because he will retain his enhanced abilities but, since Venus lacks a moon, he will not have to change shape. Whether the removal of his shape-shifting ability is a pro or con to Kazak is left unanswered.

Changing to Survive

The shape-shifter archetype and its representative, the werewolf, have adapted to survive and remain meaningful in the modern world. As society evolves, so has the archetype, while retaining its core traits, roles, and meanings. Even as the werewolf changed to incorporate new issues, new dualities, and new boundaries, it never relinquished its roots in the classical, medieval, and early modern traditions. The preceding authors and their interpretations of the figure have demonstrated some of the variety that came out of this adapting. Even so, they are only a small percentage representing a far greater collection of stories, roles, and modifications to the central elements of the shape-shifter and werewolf. Despite ranging from the historical to the futuristic, there is still considerable territory that the stories leave unexplored, some of which has been penned in on the figurative map by other writers and some of which simply says, "Here be Monsters" as a warning, or invitation, to those who follow.

In the process, these werewolves have gone beyond the problems of their ancestors, most of which involved marital or social relationships, often with a dose of justice or vengeance. The modern werewolf begins to discuss issues as diverse as conservation, time travel, hidden societies, adaptation of one's skills, and teaching history. Many of these topics were foreign, possibly even unthinkable, to their literary ancestors, such as conservation and time travel; others were commonly known or seen, but not necessarily discussed in the same context, such as hidden societies. The werewolf's adjustment to other subjects keeps the archetype alive, vigorous, and an active part of our literary and social world. The sheer ubiquitous nature of the beast, as it were, amply demonstrates that there

6. Variety...

is still something evocative about the werewolf and shape-shifter in the modern world, despite the fact that we no longer fear the wolf from direct experience, but rather by reputation. Not only has the werewolf adapted and survived, it has thrived as a figure of horror, sympathy, understanding, monstrosity, education, justice, and revenge (whether violent or non-violent[59]).

Final Thoughts

Our Story Thus Far

The werewolf, and shape-shifter archetype in general, clearly plays a complex role in the Western literary and cultural traditions from our earliest Graeco-Roman roots to modern genre fiction. The latter often uses the archetype in neomedieval and neoclassical forms, drawing earlier traditions, appearances, and tones into the modern era. While the werewolf generally appears as a side figure, both the shape-shifter and the werewolf command attention as important mentors or social police and as marginal figures. Certainly the core characters present in *William of Palerne*, Pratchett's Discworld,[1] Harris' fictionalized Louisiana, and Rowling's fictionalized England are important both as an impetus for the story and in themselves. Likewise, Williamson's central werewolves are the story, without them there is no antagonist and therefore no plot or exploration of the psyche. However, the marginal characters — at least those who continuously reappear and have speaking parts such as Alphouns (supposedly marginal), Lupin, Angua (as part of an ensemble cast), Jake, Jannalynn, and Basim — are no less important in what they show the audience or say on behalf of the author. In the case of *William of Palerne*, the story would end prematurely without the marginal character, who shows himself to actually be the central character, despite the romance being named for William.

Because of its traits and role, the shape-shifter archetype is divorced from Jung's trickster archetype. Especially in the form of the werewolf, the shape-shifter removes itself far enough to be considered an archetype unto itself, independent of, or perhaps interdependent with, the trickster. While there are numerous werewolves and shape-shifters that clearly represent Jung's trickster — Alphouns with his leap-scream-run routine, for instance, or Lupin in his relationship with Black and James Potter — there are many for whom the trickster is merely one of many aspects to their character, or in whom the trickster is effectively non-existent. For instance, Pratchett's Angua presents no notable connection with the trickster, yet serves an archetypal function as a guardian of social mores. This is true of Williamson's Barbee and Bell, who share few, if any, trickster traits but clearly represent the shadow and have other archetypal roles regarding the psyche. The shifter sometimes employs the trickster's traits, and often the trickster changes shape, but the shifter's use of trickster elements is merely one facet of its role and effect. Another important facet is the shape-shifter's role in bridging gaps, such as those between time periods, as expressed in discussions of neomedievalism. Thus, the shifter stands on its own, as has been demonstrated through its representation in the werewolf.

Charting the werewolf as a representative of the archetype requires us to also consider the tradition of literary and cultural werewolves stretching back to at least the Romans and ancient Hellenes, perhaps even back to Babylon. Modern scholars, and general readers, can look back and see recognizable elements of Rowling's Lupin, Pratchett's Angua, Williamson's Barbee, Harris' Hevereauxes, and other modern werewolves in Petronius' soldier, Ovid's Lycaon, Pausanias' Demarchus,[2] and Virgil's Moeris.[3] Likewise, the influence of Marie de France, Gerald of Wales, and other medieval writers can clearly be seen in their modern descendants as the traditions and the archetype are exhumed, dusted off, and polished to be presented to the modern audience. We also see that while the figure went into a remission, of sorts, during the early modern period it remained present in the literary-cultural landscape by being concealed in the form of theatrically presented madness — through John Webster's *The Duchess of Malfi*— and popular trial and demonological literature — such as Jean Bodin, Henri Boguet, Heinrich Kramer and James Sprenger, and the trials of Peeter Stubbe and Jean Grenier. The archetype manifests with a related purpose in later fairy tales presented to younger audiences, in which the werewolf and shifter lurk just beneath the surface — for example, Charles Perrault's version of "Little Red Riding Hood." When the time once again became ripe, during the transition into the modern era, the werewolf returned openly through the horror genre, initially, eventually to be adopted within the fantasy genre, in children's, young adult, and adult formats. The morphological indeterminacy of the figure enhanced its evolution during this transition. I use the term evolution in this context in its biological sense, involving adaptation to a changing environment, rather than in a neces-

Final Thoughts

sarily improvement focused form. That is to say, rather than implying that Pratchett's werewolves, for example, are in some way better than Ovid's, or that Pratchett is a better writer, I intend the sense that Pratchett's werewolves are adapted to a modern audience. In that respect, we can safely say that a first century B.C.E. Roman audience would respond better to Ovid's Lycaon than to Pratchett's Wolfgang, although they would probably recognize the similarities between the two. However, the figure could not remain unchanged, unevolved, after passing through a period in which it was considered in a sympathetic light (secular writers from the twelfth to fourteenth-centuries), another in which associations with witchcraft and madness effected their own changes (roughly the late-fourteenth through early nineteenth-centuries), and its acquaintance with horror film and fiction (the early twentieth-century). And the evolution has not always been especially positive, as evidenced by 1980s parodic-slapstick movies such as *Full Moon High* (1981), *Teen Wolf* (1985), *A Canadian Werewolf in Hollywood* (1987), *Teen Wolf Too* (1987), and *The Monster Squad* (1987).

The sheer pervasiveness of the werewolf and shape-shifter archetype in the modern era speaks to their continued popularity and psychological importance. Due to this widespread popularity and psychological role, academics ought to be investigating the werewolf and shape-shifter, as they would with Shakespeare or the trickster, in attempts to determine how they work and why they have remained popular over the course of more than twenty-one centuries.[4] This work has demonstrated that the figure remains popular not only for the reasons that most monsters are popular — transgressions of social conventions or being simultaneously fear inspiring and intriguing, among others — but also because of its connection with the wild, animal world that is, despite our technological and social advances, still a part of our psyche and genetic being. This connection, combined with a long tradition, maintains the shape-shifter archetype. Because of the tradition, one with which most people are at least subconsciously familiar, readers, moviegoers, and other audiences recognize certain elements of the archetype and respond to them. This same familiarity breeds a sense of interest and puzzlement in the audience when we see a writer subvert or build upon the tradition, adding something that we were not expecting, or reversing our expectations. The werewolf has proven exceptionally useful in this regard, as Marie de France demonstrated nearly nine centuries ago when she subverted her audience's expectations about

Final Thoughts

a ravening werewolf by displaying a sympathetic figure. Modern generations fed a diet of werewolf lore from horror movies, novels, and folklore respond in much the same way when confronted with a sympathetic werewolf or non-horror action werewolf, or any shape-shifter for that matter. This particular study represents the smallest tip of the iceberg that is modern manifestations of the archetype in the literary and cultural studies fields. Hundreds of modern authors have been necessarily passed over in favor of the small sample chosen for this work.

Genre fiction is, arguably, the best place to see the archetype's representation. Fantasy and supernatural fiction are the perfect genres to look at in this respect. As the heirs to folklore, fairy tale, and legend, they are the modern genres in which archetypes most often appear. Because archetypes are never directly perceived by the conscious mind, they must be seen through imperfect representations, much like Platonic Forms. Moreover, they must speak to the collective unconscious. In other words, they must tell the viewer or reader something important about the human experience. This accounts, in part, for the continued popularity of the shape-shifter archetype. The fact that such figures also actively engage the viewers' emotions — whether fear, envy, excitement, or sympathy, for instance — adds to their popularity and their strength as expressions of an archetype. One of the last important reasons that werewolves, and human-animal shifters in general, remain popular as an archetype is that they are given a pass, a means by which they can choose not to follow normal social expectations. Through the animal shifter, the reader and viewer can vicariously violate social norms without directly threatening society or their own safety. This role simultaneously acts as a sort of emotional release valve and questions social norms, creating a tension that is common to all appearances of the shape-shifter archetype.

As with any such study, or sense of cross-fertilizations over stretches of time and differences in cultures, the lessons that can be acquired often involve tension, contortion, and defensive or camouflaging comedy. Moreover, when we see clear moral preaching, we need to look beneath the surface, first to evaluate the overt message and second to determine what covert messages wait to be discovered. While the bridging effect is certainly an important focus of this study, we should not forget or dismiss modern adaptations and expansions, since that is where the application of literary studies to the primary (physical) world occur. Modern adaptations and expressions are also the primary interest of much of the audience and readership, thus giving scholars a point of contact with the broader public that is, arguably, much needed. One way in which such studies can be important is in illuminating the adaptation of the old to the new — showing how writers and artists have grounded themselves in previous traditions and methods that they have reshaped to fit within the modern world. For example, Rowling's use of terminology. Many of her first readers believed that she made up the term "muggle," but a quick search of the Oxford English Dictionary shows that the term was first used in 1275 in the *Brut* manuscript, with a different definition.[5] In many cases, both aspects speak to the creative processes that are an integral part of human nature as represented in the shape-shifter archetype, that also link us to certain species of animals.[6]

Future Work

While I have endeavored to be fairly representative in this particular survey and analysis, there is still much that can and should be done with the shape-shifter archetype and the werewolf. Because the figure is incredibly pervasive — with shape-shifter tales appearing in virtually every known human culture and werewolves appearing in many different cultures — any study is necessarily limited, thus leaving room for further work in several different fields. Investigations can be expanded into directions as diverse as other modern novels, television, music, and film. Future studies can, and ought to, test the theory and archetype by including non-werewolf subjects such as human-to-human transformations (including Malory's Merlyn, Spenser's Archimago, and technological metamorphoses in modern science fiction), the wide variety of other human-animal transformations (such as Rowling's animagi or Tolkien's Beornings), or other modern authors (Jim Butcher or Tanith Lee, for example).

The study of these figures should be expanded into the realms of television and film due in part to the resurgence of werewolves and shape-shifting in both areas. Excellent television examples include the metamorphic security chief Odo in *Star Trek: Deep Space 9*, technological means of shapechanging displayed in the *Babylon 5* telefilms, and the various shape-shifters present in *Buffy*. The BBC's *Being Human* (also being run

Final Thoughts

in a heavily adapted form by the Syfy Channel), Syfy's *Sanctuary*, and MTV's re-imagining of *Teen Wolf* as a TV series are also prime candidates for further research on this subject. The *Star Trek* franchise, as a long standing focus of academic research, is, perhaps, a good starting point while the current spate of research on the *Buffy/Angel* series lends itself to such a survey. We can see similar examples in the movie industry from the interest in werewolves displayed by the *Underworld* franchise and *Van Helsing* to the amorphous shapechanging villains in the *Terminator* franchise. The werewolf and shape-shifter have even insinuated themselves into late-twentieth century music, such as Warren Zevon's "Werewolves of London" and Metallica's "Of Wolf and Man"—the latter of which musically and lyrically explores the human-animal divide, or lack thereof.

This pervasiveness is one reason I contend that the shape-shifter is an archetype unto itself, most commonly represented by the werewolf. The fact that this figure has insinuated itself into so many aspects of our entertainment and instructional media calls for greater academic study in its modern iterations. Earlier appearances are being and have been discussed in fair to great detail, notably the medieval werewolf.[7] Later forms have largely been ignored or relegated to brief references in larger works covering a particular author, such as Rowling, with a few exceptions including Lillian Heldreth's "Tanith Lee's Werewolves Within: Reversals of Gothic Traditions" (1989) and Charlotte Otten's *The Literary Werewolf: An Anthology* and *A Lycanthropy Reader: Werewolves in Western Culture*. Both of Otten's works, though, only provide primary sources, which are helpful, but do not include secondary criticism. Much of the critical work currently published on modern manifestations of the archetype and werewolf are non-academic in nature and take the form of semi-researched encyclopedias (such as Brad Steiger's *The Werewolf Book: The Encyclopedia of Shape-Shifting Beings*)[8] or mere lists of books with brief plot summaries (such as Frost's *The Essential Guide to Werewolf Literature*).[9] Even these focus almost entirely on the werewolf, leaving other manifestations as either afterthoughts or non-existent. Since these figures are so pervasive that they appear throughout our society and since they continue to fascinate us after anywhere from 2,100 to 77,000 years, they clearly have great psychological importance to us as a species and a culture. Because of this implied importance, we need to explore their roots, current manifestations, and functions in greater detail.

Chapter Notes

Introduction

1. Malcolm South, "Introduction," *Mythical and Fabulous Creatures: A Source Book and Research Guide,* ed. Malcolm South (New York: Greenwood Press, 1987), xx.
2. Joyce E. Salisbury, *The Beast Within: Animals in the Middle Ages* (New York: Routledge, 1994), 5.
3. See Cynthia Whitney Hallet's *Scholarly Studies in Harry Potter* (Lewiston, NY: Edwin Mellen Press, 2006) and Heather Arden and Kathryn Lorenz's "The Harry Potter Stories and French Arthurian Romance," *Arthuriana* 13.2 (2003): 54–68, among others.
4. Saint Augustine, *The City of God,* trans. Marcus Dods (New York: The Modern Library, 1993).
5. Jeffry A. Massey, "*Corpus Lupi*: The Medieval Werewolf and Popular Theology" (Ph.D. diss., Emory, 2003), 60.
6. Caroline Walker Bynum, "Metamorphosis, or Gerald and the Werewolf," *Metamorphosis and Identity,* ed. Caroline Bynum (New York: Zone, 2005), 82.
7. Ibid.
8. Caroline Walker Bynum, "Introduction," *Metamorphosis and Identity,* ed. Caroline Walker Bynum (New York: Zone, 2005), 20.
9. In S. J. Wiseman, "Hairy on the Inside: Metamorphosis and Civility in English Werewolf Texts," *Renaissance Beasts,* ed. Erica Fudge (Urbana: University of Illinois Press, 2004) 70–86, and Catherine Karkov, "Tales of the Ancients: Colonial Werewolves and the Mapping of Postcolonial Ireland," *Postcolonial Moves: Medieval Through Modern,* eds. Patricia Clare Ingham and Michelle R. Warren (New York: Macmillan, 2003), 93–109.
10. Sigmund Freud, *The Wolf-Man and Other Cases,* trans. Louise Adey Huish (New York: Penguin Classics, 2003).
11. Sabine Baring-Gould, *The Book of Were-Wolves: Being an Account of a Terrible Superstition* (New York: Causeway Books, 1973), 7.
12. Carl G. Jung, *Four Archetypes: Mother/Rebirth/Spirit/Trickster* (Princeton: Princeton University Press, 1992), 4.
13. Amy Green, "Interior/Exterior in the *Harry Potter* Series: Duality Expressed in Sirius Black and Remus Lupin," *Papers on Language & Literature* 44.1 (Winter 2008): 88.
14. For example, Sharon P. Johnson, "The Toleration and Erotization of Rape: Interpreting Charles Perrault's 'Le Petit Chaperon Rouge' within Seventeenth- and Eighteen-Century French Jurisprudence," *Women's Studies* 32 (2003): 325–352; Lynn Enterline, "'Hairy on the In-side': *The Duchess of Malfi* and the Body of Lycanthropy," *The Yale Journal of Criticism* 7.2 (1994): 85–129; and Joseph Pappa, "The Bewildering Bounded/Bounding Bisclavret, or Lycanthropy, Lieges, and a Lotta Leeway in Marie de France," *Crossings* 4 (2000): 117–143.
15. Jung, *Four Archetypes,* 135.
16. Kirby Smith, "An Historical Study of the Werwolf in Literature," *PMLA* 9 (1894): 4.

Notes — Chapter 1

17. Ibid., 5.
18. Archbishop Wulfstan of York may have been the first to use the term in 1008. Although he did not coin the term, as he drew upon oral Saxon and Celtic traditions, he certainly made the term popular.
19. Two notable non-horror examples are Thomas Malory's Merlin (who adopts several guises ranging from appearing as a young child to an aged man) and Edmund Spenser's Archimago (who also adopts several human guises through magic).
20. Green, "Interior/Exterior in the *Harry Potter* Series," 87.
21. Ibid.
22. Jeffrey Jerome Cohen, "Monster Culture (Seven Theses)," *Monster Theory: Reading Culture*, ed. Jeffrey Jerome Cohen (Minneapolis: University of Minnesota Press, 1996), 6.
23. Hal Clement, *Cycle of Fire* (New York: Ballantine, 1981).
24. David D. Gilmore, *Monsters: Evil Beings, Mythical Beasts, and All Manner of Imaginary Terrors* (Philadelphia: University of Pennsylvania Press, 2003), 19.
25. Michael Cheilik, "The Werewolf," *Mythical and Fabulous Creatures: A Source Book and Research Guide*, ed. Malcolm South (New York: Greenwood Press, 1987), 275.
26. Irving Massey, *The Gaping Pig: Literature and Metamorphosis* (Berkeley: University of California Press, 1976), 195.
27. Quoted in Chapter Two.
28. As related by Sabine Baring-Gould.
29. Werewolves, and other shapeshifters, arguably go back much further, perhaps even as early as Catal Hüyük (ca. 6000 B.C.E.) according to some researchers, such as Adam Douglas.
30. Notably Caroline Walker Bynum, Leslie Sconduto, Jeffry Massey, S.J. Wiseman, Catherine Karkov, Kirby Smith, Irving Massey, Sabine Baring-Gould, Frank Hamel, Montague Summers, and many of the other scholars cited at the end of this work.

Chapter 1

1. The Operation intended to create a uniformed commando force to conduct a guerilla war behind Allied lines as Germany fell toward the end of the war. Ultimately, the unit was never combat effective and was dismantled.
2. Alan C. Elms, "Darker Than He Thought: Jack Williamson's Fictionalization of His Psychoanalysis," *Extrapolation* 30, no. 2 (1989): 211
3. See Elms, "Darker Than He Thought."
4. Caroline Walker Bynum, *Metamorphosis and Identity* (New York: Zone, 2001), 94.
5. Including Boguet, Kramer & Sprenger, Bayfield, Brinley, Deacon & Walker, and Havers. See note 16.
6. John Carey, "Werewolves in Medieval Ireland," *Cambrian Celtic Medieval Studies* 44 (Winter 2002): 56.
7. Jack Williamson, *Darker Than You Think* (New York: Berkley Medallion, 1969), 97–100.
8. Saint Augustine, *The City of God*, trans. Marcus Dods (New York: Modern Library, 1993), 16.8.
9. Ibid., 18.18.
10. Jeffry A. Massey, "*Corpus Lupi*: The Medieval Werewolf and Popular Theology" (Ph.D. diss., Emory, 2003), 60.
11. Williamson, *Darker*, 116.
12. Ibid., 12.
13. Ibid., 117.
14. Marie de France, *William of Palerne*, and *Arthur and Gorlagon*, respectively.
15. Williamson, *Darker*, 38.
16. *A True Discourse. Declaring the Damnable Life and Death of One Stubbe Peeter, a Most Wicked Sorcerer* (1590); Robert Bayfield, *Της Ιατρικης Καρτος or A Treatise De Morborum Capitis Essentiis & Prognosticis* (1663); John Brinley, *A Discovery of the Impostures of Witches and Astrologers* (1680); John Deacon & John Walker, *Dialogicall Discourses of Spirits and Divels* (1601); G. Havers, trans., *A General Collec-*

tion of Discourses of the Virtuosi of France Upon Questions of all Sorts of Philosophy, and Other Natural Knowledge (1664); Reginald Scot, *The Discoverie of Witchcraft* (1584).

17. Jane P. Davidson, "Wolves, Witches, and Werewolves: Lycanthropy and Witchcraft from 1423–1700," *The Journal of the Fantastic in the Arts* 2.4/8 (1990): 57.

18. Williamson, *Darker*, 81.

19. Ibid., 95.

20. Norman R. Smith, "Portentous Births and the Monstrous Imagination in Renaissance Culture," *Marvels, Monsters, and Miracles: Studies in the Medieval and Early Modern Imagination*, eds. Timothy S. Jones and David A Sprunger (Kalamazoo, MI: Medieval Institute Publications, 2002), 268.

21. Simon Goulart, "Admirable Histories," *A Lycanthropy Reader: Werewolves in Western Culture*, ed. Charlotte Otten. (Syracuse: Syracuse University Press, 1986), 44.

22. Williamson, *Darker*, 96.

23. Ibid., 149.

24. Ibid., 189 and 199.

25. Ibid., 105.

26. Ibid., 102.

27. Full title: *Glossographia: or a Dictionary, Interpreting all Such Hard Words of Whatsoever Language, now used in our Refined English Tongue; With Etymologies, Definitions, and Historical Observations on the Same. Also the Terms of Divinity, Law, Physick, Mathematicks, and Other Arts and Sciences Explicated* (London, 1661).

28. Goulart, "Admirable Histories," 41.

29. Sabine Baring-Gould, *The Book of Werewolves* (New York: Causeway, 1973), 90.

30. Williamson, *Darker*, 124–5.

31. Ibid., 235.

32. Ibid., 246–7.

33. Ibid., 278.

34. Edith Benkov, "The Naked Beast: Clothing and Humanity in Bisclavret," *Chimeres* 19.2 (1998): 27.

35. Williamson, *Darker*, 238.

36. Elms, "Darker Than He Thought," 41.

37. Williamson, *Darker*, 232–8.

38. Ibid., 107.

39. Ibid., 110.

40. Elms, "Darker Than He Thought," 205–218.

41. Williamson, *Darker*, 153.

42. S.J. Wiseman, "Hairy on the Inside: Metamorphosis and Civility in English Werewolf Texts," *Renaissance Beasts*, ed. Erica Fudge (Urbana: University of Illinois Press, 2004), 57.

43. Leonard Barkan, *The Gods Made Flesh: Metamorphosis & the Pursuit of Paganism* (New Haven: Yale University Press, 1986) 66.

44. Williamson, *Darker*, 19–20.

45. David Gilmore, *Monsters: Evil Beings, Mythical Beasts, and All Manner of Imaginary Terrors* (Philadelphia: University of Pennsylvania Press, 2003) 191.

46. Dennis Kratz, "Fictus Lupus: The Werewolf in Christian Thought," *Classical Folia* 30.1 (1976): 58.

47. Williamson, *Darker*, 96–7.

Chapter 2

1. In this case, Samuel Vimes' reading the story *Where's My Cow?* to his son at the same time every night. The novel itself can be likened to the timely productions of *Lysistrata* that occurred from 2001 to 2007.

2. All produced since 1983, though his non–Discworld publications go back to 1963. Lspace: Discworld & Pratchett Wiki, "Bibliography," accessed 27 March 2012, http://wiki.lspace.org/wiki/Bibliography#Novels.

3. These latter two characters clearly mimic Messers Croup and Vandemar in Gaiman's *Neverwhere* as well as Croup and Vandemar's predecessors in Fleming's *Diamonds are Forever* (at least in the film version).

4. Caroline Walker Bynum, "Introduction," *Metamorphosis and Identity*, ed. Caroline Walker Bynum (New York: Zone, 2001), 30.

Notes — Chapter 2

5. Terry Pratchett, "Imaginary Worlds, Real Stories," *Folklore* 111 (2000): 159.
6. Ibid., 160.
7. For instance, his primary city, Ankh-Morpork, is very obviously London while Klatch is substituted for a mix of France — as in "pardon my Klatchian" or the Klatchian Foreign Legion — and North Africa — geographically, in that it is a large desert against the sea — confusingly, Quirm stands in for France geographically, and even the conception of the world — a flat planet resting on the backs of four elephants standing on a turtle — comes from numerous mythologies.
8. Jeffrey Jerome Cohen, "Monster Theory (Seven Theses)," *Monster Theory: Reading Culture,* ed. Jeffrey Jerome Cohen (Minneapolis: University of Minnesota Press, 1996), 18.
9. Amanda Cockrell, "Where the Falling Angel Meets the Rising Ape: Terry Pratchett's Discworld," *The Hollins Critic* 43.1 (February 2006), 3.
10. Ibid., 12.
11. "Because of the nature of race relations in the 1960s, the publishing industry was unprepared for a Black futurist-fiction author who forced readers to address the lingering legacy of racism. Thus Delany used legerdemain to make his stories socially relevant, yet acceptable to publishers." (Gregory E. Routledge, "Science Fiction and the Black Power/Arts Movements: The Transpositional Cosmology of Samuel R. Delany, Jr." *Extrapolation* 41.2 [Summer 2000]: 129).
12. The Norman French term for werewolf, used by Marie de France in her *lai* "Bisclavret" to denote monstrous, man-eating werewolves.
13. The term used by Marie de France to denote her noble, sympathetic werewolf (see note 12 above). H. W. Bailey has translated "bisclavret" as: rational wolf, speaking wolf, or clothed wolf. William Sayers has translated the term as leprous wolf.
14. Terry Pratchett, *Thud!* (New York: HarperCollins, 2005), 165–6.
15. Terry Pratchett, *The Fifth Elephant* (New York: HarperTorch, 2001), 47.
16. Cannibalism, in the case of the werewolf, is a problematic term and issue. If the werewolf is still human, then eating humans might be cannibalism. If the werewolf is a wolf or something else entirely, then eating humans is not cannibalism.
17. Pratchett, *Elephant,* 257.
18. Ibid., 262.
19. Pronounced Be-yonk.
20. Pratchett, *Elephant,* 88.
21. The Prophet Ossory appears a number of other times — in *Hogfather* and *Jingo,* for instance — as Washpot, a.k.a. Visit, is quite fond of quoting him.
22. Pratchett, *Elephant,* 47.
23. Ibid., 147.
24. Ibid., 262.
25. Ibid., 265.
26. Ibid., 268–9.
27. Ibid., 275.
28. Ibid., 301–3.
29. Ibid., 337.
30. Pratchett, *Thud!,* 167.
31. Bynum, "Introduction."
32. John Aberth, *The Black Death: The Great Mortality of 1348–1350: A Brief History with Documents* (New York: Bedford, 2005).
33. Pratchett, *Elephant,* 291.
34. Ibid., 123.
35. Ibid., 274.
36. Caroline Walker Bynum, "Shape and Story," *Metamorphosis and Identity,* ed. Caroline Walker Bynum (New York: Zone, 2001), 188.
37. Some of the texts state that Ankh-Morpork has never been successfully invaded by foreigners, for example, because the natives absorb the invaders and take their money regardless of the newcomers' species, gender, or ethnicity.
38. Pratchett, *Elephant,* 262.
39. In fact, in later books such as *Making Money,* Pratchett notes that most of Ankh-Morpork thinks Corporal Nobbs is the werewolf on the Watch.

Notes — Chapter 2

40. Pratchett, *Elephant*, 138.
41. See John Carey's work regarding Irish werewolves.
42. Malcolm South, "Introduction," *Mythical and Fabulous Creatures: A Source Book and Research Guide,* ed. Malcolm South (New York: Greenwood Press, 1987), xxi.
43. Pratchett, *Elephant*, 102.
44. Ibid., 336.
45. Pratchett, *Thud!*, 63.
46. See *Thud!*: "Angua normally avoided Igor's laboratory, because the smells that emanated therefrom were either painfully chemical or, horribly, suggestively organic" (14) and "that was the problem with the wolf times; the nose took charge" (165).
47. Pratchett, *Elephant*, 308.
48. Ibid., 64.
49. Similar to Rowling's non-magical wizards being referred to as Squibs, which could be tied to the yennork concept.
50. Pratchett, *Elephant*, 157.
51. Ibid., 62.
52. Ibid., 265.
53. Ibid., 234.
54. Ibid., 264–5.
55. Ibid., 76.
56. Ibid., 256–7.
57. Ibid., 109.
58. Ibid., 147.
59. Ibid., 135.
60. Ibid., 197.
61. Ibid., 199.
62. Ibid., 201.
63. Ibid., 212.
64. Who began his life as a street kid and Watch constable. He was eventually elevated to the ranks of nobility against his will and nature.
65. Pratchett, *Elephant*, 344.
66. Ibid., 345.
67. Cockrell, "Where the Falling Angel," 10.
68. David Buchbinder, "The Orangutan in the Library: The Comfort of Strangeness in Terry Pratchett's Discworld Novels," *Youth Cultures: Texts, Images, and Identities,* eds. Kerry Mallan and Sharyn Pearce (Westport, CT: Praeger, 2003), 181 n 8.
69. Pratchett, *Elephant*, 31.
70. Ibid., 115.
71. Jane Yolen, *Touch Magic* (Little Rock: August House, 2000).
72. Pratchett, *Elephant*, 115.
73. Ibid., 156–7.
74. Ibid., 359.
75. To some extent the same can be said of sexism as well, since all members of the Watch are referred to as watchmen. Only Nobby and Carrot ever treat Angua as female, until *The Fifth Elephant* and late in *Thud!* at least when Vimes begins to as well, and a large percentage of the Watch is made up of dwarfs who generally appear physically and psychologically sexless anyway, at least until the later novels in which female Ankh-Morpork dwarfs start being openly female.
76. Pratchett, *Elephant*, 139.
77. Ibid., 157.
78. Ibid., 296.
79. Ibid., 355.
80. Ibid., 159.
81. Or partial week, since the Discworld's weeks have eight days.
82. Pratchett, *Thud!*, 131.
83. Pratchett, *Elephant*, 84.
84. In some of these legends, wolves guard graveyards to keep the deceased in their graves. Alternately werewolves have been associated with tracking and hunting vampires in related legends. Most are associated with Greece, the Baltic region, and Romania. See Adam Douglas' *The Beast Within* and Ankarloo and Henningsen's *Early Modern European Witchcraft*.
85. Such as the *Underworld* franchise, among others.
86. Pratchett, *Thud!*, 13.
87. Pratchett, *Elephant*, 346.
88. Pratchett, *Thud!* 127.
89. Ibid., 136.
90. Ibid., 134.
91. Ibid., 241.
92. Pratchett, *Elephant*, 347.

93. Pratchett, *Thud!*, 239.
94. Ibid., 240.
95. Ibid., 134.
96. Pratchett, *Elephant*, 20.
97. Pratchett, *Thud!*, 337.
98. Edith Benkov, "The Naked Beast: Clothing and Humanity in Bisclavret," *Chimeres* 19.2 (1998): 28.
99. Pratchett, *Elephant*, 15.
100. While Corporal Nobbs is technically considered a human, he is said to have to carry around a piece of parchment to prove this fact.
101. Pratchett, *Elephant*, 359.
102. Pratchett, "Imaginary Worlds," 160.

Chapter 3

1. Examples of the special traits appear in numerous modern forms, including the Underworld franchise, White Wolf's World of Darkness franchise, Pratchett's Discworld, and Lon Chaney Jr.'s wolf-man movies.
2. Such as the humor surrounding the Society for the Promotion of Elfish Welfare—S.P.E.W.—started by Hermione in *Goblet of Fire* or Harry recalling "Dumbledore's idea of a few words, 'nitwit,' 'oddment,' 'blubber,' and 'tweak'" during Dumbledore's funeral (*Half-Blood* 644).
3. Joseph Andriano, *Immortal Monster: The Mythological Evolution of the Fantastic Beast in Modern Fiction and Film* (Westport, CT: Greenwood, 1999), xi.
4. Dennis Kratz, "*Fictus Lupus*: The Werewolf in Christian Thought," *Classical Folia* 30.1 (1976): 58.
5. Heather Arden and Kathryn Lorenz, "The Harry Potter Stories and French Arthurian Romance," *Arthuriana* 13.2 (2003): 58–9.
6. Andriano, *Immortal Monster*, xi.
7. Adam Douglas, *The Beast Within: A History of the Werewolf* (New York: Avon, 1992), 111.
8. Hereafter referred to as *Prisoner of Azkaban* (*Azkaban*). The rest will be referred to as *Sorcerer's Stone*, *Chamber of Secrets* (*Chamber*), *Goblet of Fire* (*Goblet*), *Order of the Phoenix* (*Phoenix*), *Half-Blood Prince*, and *Deathly Hallows*.
9. Since this aspect of Greyback's character comes late in the books, he could be read as her take on real world terrorism. He could also be taken as a commentary on abused children also becoming abusers, although this claim would require a greater knowledge of his background than Rowling provides.
10. Save only at the initial discussion of Hogwarts uniforms, Quidditch uniforms (also quite vague), and the dress robes used during both *Goblet of Fire*'s Yule Ball and Bill and Fleur's wedding in *Deathly Hallows*.
11. Even compared to other authors writing for the target age range with similarly aged characters such as Judy Blume, her later books are exceptionally tame in this regard. Admittedly, this is not terribly important to her focal plot, although that does not stop her on other aspects and issues.
12. Amy M. Green, "Interior/Exterior in the Harry Potter Series: Duality Expressed in Sirius Black and Remus Lupin," *Papers on Language & Literature* 44.1 (Winter 2008): 100.
13. Arden and Lorenz, "The Harry Potter Stories," 58.
14. See Matilda Tomaryn Bruckner, "Of Men and Beasts in *Bisclavret*," *Romantic Review* 82.3 (1991): 251–269; Joseph Pappa, "The Bewildering Bounded/Bounding Bisclavret, or Lycanthropy, Lieges, and a Lotta Leeway in Marie de France," *Crossings* 4 (2000): 117–143; Brent Stypczynski, "Evolution of the Werewolf Archetype from Ovid to J.K. Rowling" (Ph.D. diss., Kent State University, 2008); Kerry Shea, "Male Bonding, Female Body: The Absenting of Woman in Bisclaretz," *Cold Counsel: Women in Old Norse Literature and Mythology*, ed. Sarah M. Anderson (New York: Routledge, 2000), 245–259; Michelle Freeman,

Notes — Chapter 3

"Dual Natures and Subverted Glosses: Marie de France's 'Bisclavret,'" *Romance Notes* 25 (Spring 1985): 288–301.

15. J. K. Rowling, *Harry Potter and the Half-Blood Prince* (New York: Scholastic, 2005), 334–5.

16. Interestingly, as with his transformations, this final transformation from life to death happens off-screen for both Lupin and Tonks. The reader only knows that their deaths have happened when Harry recognizes their bodies laid out with the other dead and injured characters.

17. J. K. Rowling, *Harry Potter and the Prisoner of Azkaban* (New York: Scholastic, 1999), 350.

18. I use the phrase "target readers" or "target audience" to refer specifically to the children's/YA audience that Rowling wrote the books for, as opposed to the older readers who have also become significant fans of the series.

19. Caroline Walker Bynum, *Metamorphosis and Identity* (New York: Zone, 2001), 188.

20. These are two different things: Black being an animagus capable of turning into a dog of his own free will and whenever he chooses versus Lupin who is forced to turn into a wolf and had the ability/curse thrust upon him. Rowling treats them as two very different beings.

21. The epilogue is also a point of transition in which most of Harry and Ginny's children (along with Ron and Hermione's and Draco's) are getting on the train to Hogwarts, some of them for the first time.

22. J. K. Rowling, *Harry Potter and the Sorcerer's Stone* (New York: Scholastic, 1998), 249.

23. J. K. Rowling, *Harry Potter and the Chamber of Secrets* (New York: Scholastic, 1999), 269.

24. Rowling, *Prisoner of Azkaban*, 353.

25. Rowling, *Half-Blood Prince*, 334–5.

26. J. K. Rowling, *Harry Potter and the Deathly Hallows* (New York: Scholastic, 2007), 447.

27. Sabine Baring-Gould, *The Book of Werewolves* (New York: Causeway, 1973), 89.

28. Given that Lupin was born circa 1960, since he was in James Potter's class and Potter was born in 1960, and Greyback first appears in 1997, Greyback must have been living as a werewolf for at least twenty-seven years — since 1970, the year before Lupin would have arrived at Hogwarts.

29. Rowling, *Half-Blood Prince*, 598.

30. Rowling, *Deathly Hallows*, 450.

31. This appearance can be juxtaposed to the equally monstrous Voldemort in his younger, dapper, appearance and the well groomed Malfoy family, though the latter merely play at being monstrous.

32. Rowling, *Deathly Hallows*, 447.

33. Newt Scamander, *Fantastic Beasts and Where to Find Them* (New York: Levine-Scholastic, 2001), 41–2.

34. Rowling, *Chamber of Secrets*, 162.

35. Assuming that the point of the spell is to force shape-changers of any type back into their human shape, thus "homorphous."

36. Rowling, *Prisoner of Azkaban*, 172.

37. To which Lupin's laughing response is "One: He's sitting on my chair. Two: He's wearing my clothes. Three: His name's Remus Lupin …" (643).

38. J. K. Rowling, *Harry Potter and the Order of the Phoenix* (New York: Scholastic, 2003), 643.

39. Rowling, *Prisoner of Azkaban*, 352.

40. Ibid., 352–3.

41. Rowling, *Deathly Hallows*, 646.

42. Rowling, *Order of the Phoenix*, 170.

43. Baldesar Castiglione, *The Book of the Courtier*, trans. George Bull (New York: Penguin, 1976), 42.

44. Ibid., 109.

45. Clearly, though, the examples of Dudley Dursley and Draco Malfoy are intended to remind us that children are not entirely innocent.

46. Rowling, *Deathly Hallows*, 213.

47. The most notable of which occurs in Laurell K. Hamilton's work.

Notes — Chapter 3

48. Crystal L. O'Leary, "Transcending Monstrous Flesh: A Revision of the Hero's Mythic Quest," *Journal of the Fantastic in the Arts* 13.3 (2003): 240.
49. Ibid., 241.
50. Asa Simon Mittman, "The Other Close at Hand: Gerald of Wales and the 'Marvels of the West,'" *The Monstrous Middle Ages*, eds. Bettina Bildhauer and Robert Mills (Toronto: University of Toronto Press, 2003), 107–8.
51. Rowling, *Order of the Phoenix*, 302.
52. Rowling, *Half-Blood Prince*, 334.
53. Notably Sarah E. Maier and Steve Barfield in Cynthia Hallet's *Scholarly Studies in Harry Potter*, both of whom touch on issues of race in the series, but only with regard to Muggle-borns, house elves, and giants. Julia Eccleshare is equally brief in *A Guide to the Harry Potter Novels*, discussing the issue, but only with Muggle-wizard relations. The same is true of Suman Gupta, who is interested in class and slavery issues, but only in relation to house-elves and the wizard-Muggle dynamic.
54. Andriano, *Immortal Monster*, xv.
55. Rowling, *Sorcerer's Stone*, 220.
56. Ibid., 263.
57. Rowling, *Prisoner of Azkaban*, 173.
58. Ibid., 141.
59. As opposed to the overt racism he displays in *Chamber* through repeated use of the derogatory and highly insulting term "mudblood."
60. Elaine Ostry, "Accepting Mudbloods: The Ambivalent Social Vision of J. K. Rowling's Fairy Tales," *Reading Harry Potter: Critical Essays*, ed. Giselle Liza Anatol (Westport, CT: Praeger, 2003), 95.
61. Rowling, *Prisoner of Azkaban*, 346.
62. Hermione merely exclaims, "*He's a werewolf!*" while Ron gasps, "*Get away from me, werewolf!*" (Rowling, *Azkaban*, 345).
63. Ibid., 359.
64. Ibid., 361.
65. Ibid., 423.
66. *Goblet of Fire*, 434.
67. *Order of the Phoenix*, 170–1.
68. Ibid., 107.
69. Karin E. Westman, "Specters of Thatcherism: Contemporary British Culture in J. K. Rowling's Harry Potter Series," *The Ivory Tower and Harry Potter: Perspectives on a Literary Phenomenon*, ed. Lana A. Whited (Columbia: University of Missouri Press, 2002), 323.
70. Rowling, *Order of the Phoenix*, 488.
71. Ibid., 243.
72. Ibid., 302.
73. If Hagrid and Fleur Delacour are good examples, half-giants and part-Veelas would have a difficult time completely blending in.
74. Ostry, "Accepting Mudbloods," 95.
75. Westman, "Specters of Thatcherism," 306.
76. Rowling, *Prisoner of Azkaban*, 352.
77. The two potential problems for this assertion are brief moments in which Voldemort refers to werewolf cubs (*Azkaban* 311 and *Deathly Hallows* 10). That said, he is hardly reliable source of information. Even the birth of Ted Lupin does not help, since he is described as only half-werewolf — a half half-breed — whose mother is a metamorphmagus able to change her appearance at will and he does not display any wolf-ish characteristics.
78. M. Katherine Grimes and Lana A. Whited, "What Would Harry Do? J. K. Rowling and Lawrence Kohlberg's Theories of Moral Development," *The Ivory Tower and Harry Potter: Perspectives on a Literary Phenomenon*, ed. Lana A. Whited (Columbia: University of Missouri Press, 2002), 205.
79. Westman, "Specters of Thatcherism," 323.
80. Unfortunately, she also gets bogged down in, mistakenly, criticizing a perceived lack of non–British ethnic/racial diversity from the Patils, Cho Chang, Dean Thomas, Lee Jordan, and Angelina Johnson, ignoring the fact that, while they come from

Notes — Chapter 3

different immigrant communities, they are all ethnically British and that racial issues in the British Isles are not identical to those in the U.S.

81. Rowling, *Half-Blood Prince*, 624.

82. HPWiki, "Remus Lupin," 30 August 2007, 10 September 2007, http://harrypotterwiki.org/wiki/index.php/Remus_Lupin.

83. Some of these, from *Half-Blood Prince*, include "there is no cure for werewolf bites" (613), "We really don't know what the effects will be — I mean, Greyback being a werewolf, but not transformed at the time" (612), and "It is an odd case, possibly unique" (622).

84. Grimes and Whited, "What Would Harry Do?" 203.

85. Rowling, *Prisoner of Azkaban*, 138.

86. Ellen J. Goldner, "Monstrous Body, Tortured Soul: *Frankenstein* at the Juncture between Discourses," *Genealogy & Literature*, ed. Lee Quinby (Minneapolis: University of Minnesota Press, 1995), 31.

87. Green, "Interior/Exterior in the *Harry Potter* Series," 87.

88. Ibid., 105.

89. Rowling, *Prisoner of Azkaban*, 247.

90. Rowling, *Deathly Hallows*, 213.

91. Rowling, *Order of the Phoenix*, 94.

92. Roni Natov, "Harry Potter and the Extraordinariness of the Ordinary," *The Ivory Tower and Harry Potter: Perspectives on a Literary Phenomenon*, ed. Lana A. Whited (Columbia: University of Missouri Press, 2002), 136.

93. C. S. Lewis, *The Lion, the Witch, and the Wardrobe* (New York: Scholastic, 1987), 76.

94. Natov, "Harry Potter and the Extraordinariness," 136.

95. Rowling, *Prisoner of Azkaban*, 354.

96. Ibid., 157.

97. Rowling, *Half-Blood Prince*, 335.

98. Rowling, *Prisoner of Azkaban*, 356.

99. Rowling, *Half-Blood Prince*, 335.

100. Rowling, *Deathly Hallows*, 139.

101. The other three layers being her focus on (1) the relationship between Harry, Hermione, and Ron; (2) Harry's relationships with his surrogate family and secondary character friends, such as Hagrid, Luna Lovegood, Neville Longbottom, Ron's siblings, and the Gryffindor Quidditch team; and (3) Dumbledore's continued references to Voldemort's friendless state throughout *Half-Blood Prince*.

102. He lacks respect for Snape, at least, up until the end of *Deathly Hallows*. There is no evidence that he ever holds any real respect for Slughorn or Lockhart.

103. Terri Doughty, "Locating Harry Potter in the 'Boy's Book' Market," *The Ivory Tower and Harry Potter: Perspectives on a Literary Phenomenon*, ed. Lana A. Whited (Columbia: University of Missouri Press, 2002), 252.

104. Rowling, *Half-Blood Prince*, 614.

105. Rowling, *Prisoner of Azkaban*, 429.

106. Chantel Lavoie, "Safe as Houses: Sorting and School Houses at Hogwarts," *Reading Harry Potter: Critical Essays*, ed. Giselle Liza Anatol (Westport, CT: Praeger, 2003) 43.

107. Rowling, *Half-Blood Prince*, 105.

108. Rowling, *Order of the Phoenix*, 507.

109. Rowling, *Prisoner of Azkaban*, 386.

110. Rowling, *Half-Blood Prince*, 333.

111. Green, "Interior/Exterior in the *Harry Potter* Series," 102.

112. Rowling, *Deathly Hallows*, 441.

113. Rowling, *Order of the Phoenix*, 90.

114. Ibid., 170.

115. Giselle Liza Anatol, "The Fallen Empire: Exploring Ethnic Otherness in the World of Harry Potter," *Reading Harry Potter: Critical Essays*, ed. Giselle Liza Anatol (Westport, CT: Praeger, 2003), 178fn.

116. Rowling, *Prisoner of Azkaban*, 141.

117. Ibid.

118. Green, "Interior/Exterior in the *Harry Potter* Series," 104.

Notes — Chapter 4

119. A monster, miracle, marvel, portent, sign, or omen.
120. For example, Michael J. Fox's *Teen Wolf* (and MTV's recent *Teen Wolf* series), Charlaine Harris' Sookie Stackhouse novels, or Laurell K. Hamilton's Anita Blake novels (which also include a variety of non-wolf werebeings).

Chapter 4

1. Also called the Southern Vampire Mysteries or Southern Vampire series by both fans and Harris.
2. Notable changes include Lafayette does not survive far beyond the first novel; Sam has always been in touch with his family; the maenad only appears for a couple chapters of the first book; Sookie's friend Tara is Caucasian and owns a clothing shop (and breaks up with Eggs at the end of the first book, without him being killed); Bill never makes another vampire; Eric and Godric have never been in contact before (Godric is not Eric's maker); Jason never joined the Fellowship of the Sun; and Russell Edgington's lover is never killed nor does Edgington display any desire to take over the world.
3. Terry Pratchett, *The Fifth Elephant* (New York: HarperTorch, 2001), 88.
4. With few exceptions, human-to-animal transformation is used for punishment while human-to-plant transformation is used as a reward or form of aid in Ovid.
5. Leonard Barkan, *The Gods Made Flesh: Metamorphosis & the Pursuit of Paganism* (New Haven: Yale University Press, 1986), 69.
6. In many ways, pride (particularly male pride) is an important theme throughout the series, particularly with regard to Bill, Eric, Alcide, the various vampire kings and queens, Sam, and even Sookie to a certain extent. Often pride gets in their way or makes a plan of action more difficult, but sometimes their pride helps them achieve a goal or pass through a period of suffering.
7. Montague Summers, *The Werewolf in Lore and Legend* (1933; Mineola, NY: Dover, 2003), 65.
8. For example Jeremiah 5.6, Ezekiel 22.27, Matthew 10.16, John 10.12, and Acts 20.29.
9. Charlaine Harris, *Living Dead in Dallas* (New York: Ace, 2009), 180.
10. Ibid.
11. Charlaine Harris, *Dead as a Doornail* (New York: Ace, 2005), 268. In some ways, the word choice is odd because linguistically, "wereform" is literally "human-form," but the term is used for werewolves in wolf shape.
12. Ibid., 267.
13. Charlaine Harris, *Dead in the Family* (New York: Ace, 2010), 43.
14. Charlaine Harris, *Club Dead* (New York: Ace, 2003), 174–5.
15. At least until *Deadlocked* (book 12 of the series).
16. Barkan, *The Gods Made Flesh*, 66.
17. The term Harris uses for the person who "makes" a given vampire.
18. David Gilmore, *Monsters: Evil Beings, Mythical Beasts, and All Manner of Imaginary Terrors* (Philadelphia: University of Pennsylvania Press, 2003), 4.
19. See Brett D. Hirsch, "An Italian Werewolf in London: Lycanthropy and *The Duchess of Malfi*," *Early Modern Literary Studies* 11.2 (2005): 1–22.
20. Jane P. Davidson, "Wolves, Witches, and Werewolves: Lycanthropy and Witchcraft from 1423–1700," *Journal of the Fantastic in the Arts* 2.4/8 (1990): 47.
21. Presumably they are either twins or half-siblings, due to the nature of werewolf reproduction which will be discussed later.
22. Charlaine Harris, *Dead to the World* (New York: Ace, 2011), 81.
23. Ibid., 80–82.
24. Others include maenads, fae and fairies (including goblins, elves, and brownies), demons, and witches.
25. Harris, *Living Dead*, 181.
26. Charlaine Harris, *Definitely Dead* (New York: Ace, 2007), 18.

Notes — Chapter 4

27. Ursula K. Le Guin, *The Language of the Night: Essays on Fantasy and Science Fiction*, ed. Susan Wood (New York: Berkley, 1982), 54.
28. Charlaine Harris, *Dead and Gone* (New York: Ace, 2009), 12.
29. Ibid., 75.
30. Lillian Heldreth, "Tanith Lee's Werewolves Within: Reversals of Gothic Traditions," *Journal of the Fantastic in the Arts* 2 (Spring 1989): 15.
31. Victor was placed as regent over Eric (the only surviving sheriff in Louisiana after a hostile takeover) by the new king of Louisiana (and Nevada) and attempts to remove Eric several times often through attacking those close to him, including Sookie and Pam.
32. Bitten wereanimals are different from true wereanimals in that they only change at the full moon and do not become true animals. Instead they become a monstrous hybrid of man and beast.
33. Harris, *Club Dead*, 68.
34. Ibid., 67.
35. Sookie sought confirmation that it was not simply a woman's first child, but that each pairing counted separately (*Definitely Dead*, 82).
36. Charlaine Harris, *Dead As a Doornail* (New York: Ace, 2005), 87–8.
37. Ibid., 87.
38. Charlaine Harris, *Dead to the World* (New York: Ace, 2011), 101.
39. Harris, *Club Dead*, 67.
40. Harris, *Living Dead in Dallas*, 180.
41. Harris, *Dead as a Doornail*, 266.
42. Harris, *Club Dead*, 90.
43. Charlaine Harris, *Dead Reckoning* (New York: Ace, 2011), 122.
44. Harris, *Definitely Dead*, 3.
45. Harris, *Dead to the World*, 158.
46. Charlaine Harris, *From Dead to Worse* (New York: Ace, 2009), 134.
47. Harris, *Dead to the World*, 162.
48. Ibid.
49. Ibid., 179.
50. Harris, *Club Dead*, 146.
51. Charlaine Harris, *Dead in the Family* (New York: Ace, 2010), 43.
52. Ibid., 234.
53. Davidson, "Wolves, Witches," 57.
54. Harris, *Dead to the World*, 273.
55. Harris, *Club Dead*, 69.
56. Harris, *Definitely Dead*, 97–8.
57. Harris, *Dead to the World*, 229.
58. Harris, *From Dead to Worse*, 143.
59. Harris, *Club Dead*, 100.
60. Ibid., 100.
61. Harris mentions that Quinn, for instance, is one of a very few weretigers left in the world, indicating that they were often killed by tiger poachers who do not know their true nature.
62. Harris, *Dead as a Doornail*, 86. Of note here, in the books Debbie is a werefox whereas in *True Blood* she is a werewolf.
63. There is evidence to suggest that the werewolves in Gerald of Wales' *History and Topography of Ireland* are the kings of Ossory, Ireland. See John Carey, "Werewolves in Medieval Ireland," *Cambrian Celtic Medieval Studies* 44 (Winter 2002): 57.
64. Harris, *Living Dead in Dallas*, 180.
65. Ibid., 181.
66. Ibid., 180.
67. Harris, *Club Dead*, 17.
68. Ibid., 65.
69. Ibid., 100.
70. See Ovid's *Metamorphoses* and Petronius' *Satyricon*.
71. Marie de France, "Bisclavret," *The Lais of Marie de France*, trans. Robert Hanning and Joan Ferrante (Grand Rapids: Baker, 2002).
72. *A True Discourse. Declaring the Damnable Life and Death of One Stubbe Peeter, a Most Wicked Sorcerer, Who in the Likenes of a Woolfe, Committed many Murders, Continuing This Develish Practice 25 Yeeres, Killing and Devouring Men, Women, and Children* (London, 1590); Jean Grenier's trial is described in Sabine Baring-Gould, *The Book of Werewolves* (New York: Causeway, 1973), 89–97.
73. Harris, *Dead as a Doornail*, 58–9.

74. One exception might be the Hotshot werepanthers, but they are also a self-admittedly inbred extended family.
75. Harris, *Club Dead*, 99.
76. Harris, *Definitely Dead*, 58.
77. Harris, *Club Dead*, 59.
78. Harris, *Dead and Gone*, 10.
79. Ibid., 75.
80. Brett Hirsh, "An Italian Werewolf in London: Lycanthropy and *The Duchess of Malfi*," *Early Modern Literary Studies* 11.2 (September 2005): 30.
81. See Hirsh, "An Italian Werewolf," 34.
82. Heldreth, "Tanith Lee's Werewolves," 15.
83. Ibid., 20–1.
84. Harris, *Club Dead*, 100.
85. Reiterated throughout the series, but especially present in *Dead Reckoning*.
86. Harris, *Club Dead*, 146.
87. Ibid., 278.
88. Harris, *Dead in the Family*, 291.
89. Harris, *Definitely Dead*, 148–9.
90. Harris, *Dead to the World*, 98.
91. Ibid., 103.
92. Harris, *Dead in the Family*, 39.
93. Harris, *Living Dead in Dallas*, 182.
94. Ibid., 183.
95. This two word description is used several times throughout the series.
96. Harris, *Definitely Dead*, 180.
97. Charlaine Harris, *All Together Dead* (New York: Ace, 2007), 163.
98. Ibid., 230.
99. The closest that Remus Lupin comes to changing form in an urban environment, that we know of, is either his transformation on the Hogwarts grounds, near the Forbidden Forest, or his transformation in the Shrieking Shack, fairly close to Hogsmeade.

Chapter 5

1. According to the FAQ on his SF-Site profile: http://www.sfsite.com/charlesdelint/faq01.htm#newford2.
2. There is no *senex* as seen in Roman and Elizabethan drama, and only one negative parental figure (Tallyman, the twins' biological father) as commonly seen in, for instance, Roald Dahl's novels (or Rowling's). In fact, most of the adult figures (Miguel's father and the twins' stepfather) are reasonably supportive, with the exception of Johnny's father, who is apathetic.
3. From the romances *Arthur & Gorlagon* and *The Romance of William of Palerne*, respectively.
4. Charles De Lint, *Wolf Moon* (New York: Signet, 1988), 47.
5. Ibid.
6. All Bisclavret quotes come from Marie de France, *Bisclavret*, *The Lais of Marie de France*, trans. Robert Hanning and Joan Ferrante, (Grand Rapids: Baker, 2002).
7. De Lint, *Wolf Moon*, 130.
8. John Block Friedman, *The Monstrous Races in Medieval Art and Thought* (Cambridge: Harvard University Press, 1981), 29.
9. De Lint, *Wolf Moon*, 82.
10. Ibid., 9.
11. Ibid., 11.
12. Ibid., 116.
13. Ibid., 162.
14. Ibid., 199.
15. Ibid., 163.
16. Ibid., 34, 40.
17. Ibid., 39.
18. Ibid., 68.
19. Ibid., 47–8.
20. Ibid., 48–50.
21. Ibid., 82.
22. Ibid., 90.
23. Nicole Jacques-Lefevre, "Such an Impure, Cruel, and Savage Beast: Images of the Werewolf in Demonological Works," *Werewolves, Witches, and Wandering Spirits: Traditional Belief and Folklore in Early Modern Europe*, ed. Kathryn A. Edwards (Kirksville, MO: Truman State University Press, 2002), 181–195, 186.
24. De Lint, *Wolf Moon*, 8.
25. Ibid., 35.

26. Ibid., 87.
27. Ibid., 175.
28. Ibid., 41.
29. Ibid., 217.
30. "Now certainly, this beast is manlike. It cannot be otherwise. See the sorrow he suffers to save us two" (loose translation).
31. Walter W. Skeat, ed., *The Romance of William of Palerne* (1867; London: Elibron Classics, 2005).
32. In Marie's *Bisclavret*, after the werewolf-knight regains his human form, there is no indication of his being "cured" of lycanthropy. The court seems to accept that the change is part of who he is and he presumably carries on as he did at the start of the *lai*— spending four days of the week as a man and three as a wolf running harmlessly in the woods.
33. De Lint, *Wolf Moon*, 172.
34. Ibid., 51.
35. Ibid., 41.
36. Ibid., 50.
37. Those who are familiar with de Lint's other work likely expect a paranormal element and may not be taken in by the split personality explanation.
38. Albert the Great, *Man and the Beasts (De animalibus, books 22–26)*, trans. James J. Scanlan (Binghampton, N.Y.: Center for Medieval and Early Renaissance Studies, 1987), 66.
39. Augustine, *The City of God*, trans. Marcus Dods (New York: Modern Library, 1993), 16.8.
40. Charles de Lint, *Dingo* (New York: Firebird, 2008), 50.
41. Ibid., 146.
42. Ibid., 105.
43. For example, Barbee's first change in *Darker Than You Think* (chapter one of this work), all of the werewolf changes in the BBC's *Being Human*, and Remus Lupin's change in the *Harry Potter* books.
44. De Lint, *Dingo*, 129.
45. See Robert Bayfield (1663), Robert Burton (1621), John Deacon & John Walker (1601), Simon Goulart (1607), G. Havers (1661), James I (1597), and Reginald Scot (1584).
46. De Lint, *Dingo*, 46.
47. Ibid., 49.
48. Basil Sansom, "Irruptions of the Dreaming in Post-Colonial Australia," *Oceania* 72.1 (Sept. 2001): 1–32. 1.
49. De Lint is deliberately vague about which, if either, nation his Newford stories take place in. He does say that he draws elements of both countries, but uses U.S. laws.
50. Admittedly, we never see *Dingo*'s weres interacting with de Lint's other supernatural beings, so we have no idea how they get along with the various species with which he has populated the Newford world.
51. Specifically "a touch of corbae" and "a dram's drop of some kind of canid" (153).
52. De Lint, *Dingo*, 175.
53. Ibid., 76.
54. Ibid., 101.

Chapter 6

1. See the tale of Lycaon in Ovid's *Metamorphoses*, Virgil's "Eclogue VIII," Pausanias' *The Description of Greece*, St. Augustine's *The City of God*, Marie de France's "Bisclavret," the anonymous "Arthur and Gorlagon," and most of the early modern continental treatments of the figure (e.g., Jean Bodin, Henri Boguet, and *Malleus Maleficarum*).
2. See Jane Yolen and Martin H. Greenberg, eds., *Werewolves: A Collection of Original Stories* (New York: Harper & Row, 1988); Harlan Ellison, et al, eds., *The Ultimate Werewolf: New Stories by Some of the World's Leading Authors* (New York: Dell, 1991); Charlotte Otten, ed., *The Literary Werewolf: An Anthology* (Syracuse: Syracuse University Press, 2002); Martin H. Greenberg, ed., *Werewolves* (New York: Daw, 1995) as examples.
3. There are, of course, other movie takes on the werewolf throughout the

Notes — Chapter 6

twentieth and twenty-first centuries including Michael J. Fox's *Teen Wolf*, Hugh Jackman's *Van Helsing*, Kate Beckinsale's *Underworld*, and even Stephenie Meyer's *Twilight* as well as non-literary (at least in traditional terms) sources such as comic books, graphic novels, and role-playing games.

4. *Fox and Empire, King of the North, Prince of the North*, and *Werenight*. Only the first in the series, *Werenight*, actually has werecreatures appear, although the Werenight is referenced throughout the series.

5. Harry Turtledove, "Not All Werewolves," *Werewolves: A Collection of Original Stories*, eds. Jane Yolen and Martin H. Greenberg (New York: Harper & Row, 1988), 71.

6. The only exception being the werewolves in Gerald of Wales' account in *History and Topography of Ireland*.

7. Turtledove, "Not All Werewolves," 71.

8. Gervase was a thirteenth-century canon lawyer and the only writer before the eighteenth-century who made any connections between moon phase and werewolf changes.

9. Turtledove, "Not All Werewolves," 72.

10. Ibid., 70.

11. Ibid., 83.

12. Robert J. Randisi, "Partners," *The Ultimate Werewolf*, eds. Harlan Ellison et al. (New York: Dell, 1991), 275.

13. Ibid., 272.

14. Ibid., 273.

15. Ibid., 274–5.

16. Ibid., 274.

17. Ibid.

18. In Perrault's version of the story, the eponymous character is eaten because she transgressed rules of social propriety by entering a home with a strange male.

19. Robert E. Weinberg, "Wolf Watch," *The Ultimate Werewolf*, eds. Harlan Ellison et al. (New York: Dell, 1991), 334.

20. Ibid., 335.

21. Ibid., 337.

22. Ibid., 336.

23. John Block Friedman, *The Monstrous Races in Medieval Art and Thought* (Cambridge: Harvard University Press, 1981).

24. Weinberg, "Wolf Watch," 331.

25. Ibid., 328.

26. A.C. Crispin and Kathleen O'Malley, "Pure Silver," *The Ultimate Werewolf*, eds. Harlan Ellison et al. (New York: Dell, 1991), 231.

27. Ibid., 232–3.

28. Ibid., 240.

29. Ibid., 238.

30. Ibid., 244.

31. Philip José Farmer, "Wolf, Iron, and Moth," *The Ultimate Werewolf*, eds. Harlan Ellison et al. (New York: Dell, 1991), 49.

32. Ibid., 60.

33. Sabine Baring-Gould, *The Book of Werewolves* (New York: Causeway, 1973), 90.

34. Farmer, "Wolf, Iron, and Moth," 50.

35. Barbara Paul, "Never Moon a Werewolf," *Werewolves*, ed. Martin H. Greenberg (New York: Daw, 1995), 57.

36. Ibid., 55.

37. Ibid., 54.

38. Ibid., 54.

39. Ibid., 49.

40. Ibid., 48. Not to be confused with e-mail and other online emoticons.

41. Ibid., 54.

42. Ibid., 50–51.

43. Ibid., 60.

44. Ibid., 46.

45. Ibid., 48 and 60–61, respectively.

46. See the *Star Trek* (especially *DS9*), *Terminator*, and *Star Wars* (specifically Episode II) franchises at the very least. Also Hal Clement's *Cycle of Fire*.

47. Except, for instance, *ST:DS9's* Odo.

48. Jane Yolen, "Green Messiah," *The Literary Werewolf: An Anthology*, ed. Charlotte Otten (Syracuse: Syracuse University Press, 2002), 279.

49. Ibid, 284.

50. For another take, see Morning Glory Zell, "The Golden Egg," *Sword and Sorceress V*, ed. Marion Zimmer Bradley (New York: Daw, 1988), 263–271, in which a woman who slays a dragon is transformed into a dragon as both punishment and a means of preserving the original dragon's unhatched eggs.

51. Larry Niven, "There's a Wolf in My Time Machine," *The Ultimate Werewolf*, eds. Harlan Ellison et al. (New York: Dell, 1991), 174.

52. Ibid., 172.

53. Brad Strickland, "And the Moon Shines Full and Bright," *The Ultimate Werewolf*, eds. Harlan Ellison et al. (New York: Dell, 1991), 293.

54. Ibid., 306–7.

55. Ibid., 299.

56. Ibid., 304.

57. G. Havers, trans., *A General Collection of discourses of the Virtuosi of France, Upon Questions of all Sorts of Philosophy, and Other Natural Knowledge, Made in the Assembly of the* Beaux Esprits *at Paris, by the Most Ingenious Persons of that Nation* (London, 1664), 204.

58. Strickland, "And the Moon," 292.

59. Compare the revenge delivered in Crispin & O'Malley to the revenge that occurs in Michael J. Fox's *Teen Wolf*, where the werewolf's "vengeance" occurs through enhanced coordination and jumping on a basketball court, leading to popularity.

Final Thoughts

1. A few dozen main characters in his case from Vimes and the Watch as a whole to Granny Weatherwax and the witches to Rincewind and Cohen the Barbarian.

2. Pausanias, *The Description of Greece*.

3. Virgil, "Eclogue VIII," *Eclogues*.

4. Some sources place the earliest shape-shifter beliefs at around 75,000 or 6,000 B.C.E. while werewolves may go back as far as Gilgamesh (c. 2000 B.C.E.). See Adam Douglas, *The Beast Within: A History of the Werewolf* (New York: Avon, 1992).

5. Then meaning the tail of a fish. Other definitions appeared in 1608 and 1926, before Rowling's use of the term.

6. We can argue that dolphins, otters, and non-human primates, among others, also practice creativity in their games. But I will leave that discussion to animal behaviorists.

7. Recently in a Research Group on Manuscript Evidence sponsored session at the 43rd International Congress on Medieval Studies (2008) entitled "Bark at the Rune: Transforming the Medieval Werewolf."

8. Brad Steiger, *The Werewolf Book: The Encyclopedia of Shape-Shifting Beings* (Detroit: Visible Ink Press, 1999).

9. Brian J. Frost, *The Essential Guide to Werewolf Literature* (Madison: University of Wisconsin Press, 2003).

Bibliography

Aberth, John. *The Black Death: The Great Mortality of 1348–1350: A Brief History with Documents*. New York: Bedford, 2005.

Albert the Great. *Man and the Beasts (De animalibus, books 22–26)*. Translated by James J. Scanlan. Binghampton, N.Y.: Center for Medieval and Early Renaissance Studies, 1987.

Anatol, Giselle Liza. "The Fallen Empire: Exploring Ethnic Otherness in the World of Harry Potter." In *Reading Harry Potter: Critical Essays*, edited by Giselle Liza Anatol, 163–178. Westport, CT: Praeger, 2003.

Andriano, Joseph. *Immortal Monster: The Mythological Evolution of the Fantastic Beast in Modern Fiction and Film*. Westport, CT: Greenwood, 1999.

Ankarloo, Bengt, and Gustav Henningsen, eds. *Early Modern European Witchcraft: Centres and Peripheries*. Oxford: Clarendon, 1990.

Arden, Heather, and Kathryn Lorenz. "The Harry Potter Stories and French Arthurian Romance." *Arthuriana* 13.2 (2003): 54–68.

"Arthur & Gorlagon." In *Werewolves in Western Culture: A Lycanthropy Reader*, edited by Charlotte Otten, 234–255. New York: Dorset Press, 1989.

Augustine, St. *The City of God*. Translated by Marcus Dods. New York: Modern Library, 1993.

Bailey, H. W. "*Bisclavret* in Marie de France." *Cambridge Medieval Celtic Studies* 1 (1981): 95–97.

Baring-Gould, Sabine. *The Book of Werewolves*. New York: Causeway, 1973.

Barkan, Leonard. *The Gods Made Flesh: Metamorphosis & the Pursuit of Paganism*. New Haven: Yale University Press, 1986.

Bayfield, Robert. $Της\ Ιατρικης\ Καρτος$ or *A Treatise De Morborum Capitis Essentiis & Prognosticis*. London, 1663.

Benkov, Edith. "The Naked Beast: Clothing and Humanity in Bisclavret." *Chimeres* 19.2 (1998): 27–43.

Blount, Thomas. *Glossographia: Or a Dictionary, Interpreting all Such Hard Words of Whatsoever Language, Now Used in Our Refined English Tongue; With Etymologies, Definitions, and Historical Observations on the Same*. London, 1661.

The Book of Settlements; Landnámabók. Translated by Hermann Pálsson and Paul Edwards. Winnipeg: University of Manitoba Press, 1972.

Brinley, John. *A Discovery of the Impostures of Witches and Astrologers*. London, 1680.

Buchbinder, David. "The Orangutan in the Library: The Comfort of Strangeness in Terry Pratchett's Discworld Novels." In *Youth Cultures: Texts, Images, and Identities*, edited by Kerry Mallan and Sharyn Pearce, 169–182. Westport, CT: Praeger, 2003.

Burton, Robert. *Diseases of the Mind*. London, 1621.

Bynum, Caroline Walker. *Metamorphosis and Identity*. New York: Zone, 2005.

Carey, John. "Werewolves in Medieval Ireland." *Cambrian Celtic Medieval Studies* 44 (Winter 2002): 37–72.

Bibliography

Castiglione, Baldesar. *The Book of the Courtier.* Translated by George Bull. New York: Penguin, 1976.

Cheilik, Michael. "The Werewolf." In *Mythical and Fabulous Creatures: A Source Book and Research Guide*, edited by Malcolm South, 265–289. New York: Bedrick, 1988.

Chopin, Kate. "Desiree's Baby." In *The Awakening and Selected Stories*, edited by Sandra M. Gilbert, 189–94. New York: Penguin, 1984.

Clement, Hal. *Cycle of Fire.* New York: Ballantine, 1981.

Cockrell, Amanda. "Where the Falling Angel Meets the Rising Ape: Terry Pratchett's Discworld." *The Hollins Critic* 43.1 (February 2006): 1–11.

Cohen, Jeffrey Jerome. "Monster Theory (Seven Theses)." In *Monster Theory: Reading Culture*, edited by Jeffrey Jerome Cohen, 3–25. Minneapolis: University of Minnesota Press, 1996.

Crispin, A.C., and Kathleen O'Malley. "Pure Silver." In *The Ultimate Werewolf*, edited by Harlan Ellison et al., 227–247. New York: Dell, 1991.

Davidson, Jane P. "Wolves, Witches, and Werewolves: Lycanthropy and Witchcraft from 1423–1700." *Journal of the Fantastic in the Arts* 2.4/8 (1990): 47–68.

Deacon, John, and John Walker. *Dialogicall Discourses of Spirits and Divels.* London, 1601.

De Lint, Charles. *Dingo.* New York: Firebird, 2008.

_____. *SFSite.* "FAQ." Accessed on April 29, 2012. http://www.sfsite.com/charles delint/faq01.htm#newford2.

_____. *Wolf Moon.* New York: Signet, 1988.

Doughty, Terri. "Locating Harry Potter in the 'Boy's Book' Market." In *The Ivory Tower and Harry Potter: Perspectives on a Literary Phenomenon*, edited by Lana A. Whited, 243–257. Columbia: University of Missouri Press, 2002.

Douglas, Adam. *The Beast Within: A History of the Werewolf.* New York: Avon, 1992.

Eccleshare, Julia. *A Guide to the Harry Potter Novels.* London: Continuum, 2002.

Egil's Saga. Translated by Hermann Palsson and Paul Edwards. New York: Penguin, 1976.

Elms, Alan C. "Darker Than He Thought: Jack Williamson's Fictionalization of His Psychoanalysis." *Extrapolation* 30.2 (1989): 205–218.

Enterline, Lynn. "'Hairy on the In-side': *The Duchess of Malfi* and the Body of Lycanthropy." *The Yale Journal of Criticism* 7.2 (1994): 85–129.

Farmer, Philip José. "Wolf, Iron, and Moth." In *The Ultimate Werewolf*, edited by Harlan Ellison et al., 49–62. New York: Dell, 1991.

Freud, Sigmund. *The Wolf-Man and Other Cases.* Translated by Louise Adey Huish. New York: Penguin Classics, 2003.

Friedman, John Block. *The Monstrous Races in Medieval Art and Thought.* Cambridge: Harvard University Press, 1981.

Frost, Brian J. *The Essential Guide to Werewolf Literature.* Madison: University of Wisconsin Press, 2003.

Gerald of Wales. *The History and Topography of Ireland.* Translated by John J. O'Meara. New York: Penguin, 1988.

Gervase of Tilbury. *Otia Imperialia: Recreation for an Emperor.* Translated by S.E. Banks and J.W. Binns. Oxford: Clarendon Press, 2002.

"Gilgamesh." In *Myths from Mesopotamia: Creation, The Flood, Gilgamesh, and Others*, translated by Stephanie Dalley, 39–135. New York: Oxford University Press, 1989.

Gilmore, David. *Monsters: Evil Beings, Mythical Beasts, and All Manner of Imaginary Terrors.* Philadelphia: University of Pennsylvania Press, 2003.

Goldner, Ellen J. "Monstrous Body, Tortured Soul: *Frankenstein* at the Juncture Between Discourses." In *Genealogy &*

Bibliography

Literature, edited by Lee Quinby, 28–47. Minneapolis: University of Minnesota Press, 1995.

Goulart, Simon. "Admirable Histories." In *A Lycanthropy Reader: Werewolves in Western Culture*, edited by Charlotte Otten, 41–44. Syracuse: Syracuse University Press, 1986.

Green, Amy. "Interior/Exterior in the *Harry Potter* Series: Duality Expressed in Sirius Black and Remus Lupin." *Papers on Language & Literature* 44.1 (Winter 2008): 87–108.

Grimes, M. Katherine, and Lana A. Whited. "What Would Harry Do? J. K. Rowling and Lawrence Kohlberg's Theories of Moral Development." In *The Ivory Tower and Harry Potter: Perspectives on a Literary Phenomenon*, edited by Lana A. Whited, 182–208. Columbia: University of Missouri Press, 2002.

Gupta, Suman. *Re-Reading Harry Potter*. New York: Palgrave MacMillan, 2003.

Harris, Charlaine. *All Together Dead*. New York: Ace, 2007.

_____. *Club Dead*. New York: Ace, 2003.

_____. *Dead and Gone*. New York: Ace, 2009.

_____. *Dead as a Doornail*. New York: Ace, 2005.

_____. *Dead in the Family*. New York: Ace, 2010.

_____. *Dead Reckoning*. New York: Ace, 2011.

_____. *Dead to the World*. New York: Ace, 2011.

_____. *Deadlocked*. New York: Ace, 2012.

_____. *Definitely Dead*. New York: Ace, 2007.

_____. *Living Dead in Dallas*. New York: Ace, 2009.

Havers, G., trans. *A General Collection of Discourses of the Virtuosi of France Upon Questions of all Sorts of Philosophy, and Other Natural Knowledge*. London, 1664.

Heldreth, Lillian. "Tanith Lee's Werewolves Within: Reversals of Gothic Traditions." *Journal of the Fantastic in the Arts* 2 (Spring 1989): 15–23.

Hirsh, Brett. "An Italian Werewolf in London: Lycanthropy and *The Duchess of Malfi*." *Early Modern Literary Studies* 11.2 (September 2005): 1–43.

HPWiki. "Remus Lupin." Accessed on Sept. 10, 2007. http://harrypotterwiki.org/wiki/index.php/Remus_Lupin.

Jacques-Lefevre, Nicole. "Such an Impure, Cruel, and Savage Beast: Images of the Werewolf in Demonological Works." In *Werewolves, Witches, and Wandering Spirits: Traditional Belief and Folklore in Early Modern Europe*, edited by Kathryn A. Edwards, 181–195. Kirksville, MO: Truman State University Press, 2002.

James I. "Men-Woolfes." In *Werewolves in Western Culture: A Lycanthropy Reader*, edited by Charlotte Otten, 127–128. New York: Dorset Press, 1989.

Johnson, Sharon P. "The Toleration and Eroticization of Rape: Interpreting Charles Perrault's 'Le Petit Chaperon Rouge' within Seventeenth- and Eighteenth-Century Jurisprudence." *Women's Studies* 32 (2003): 325–352.

Jung, Carl G. *Four Archetypes*. Princeton: Princeton University Press, 1992.

Karkov, Catherine. "Tales of the Ancients: Colonial Werewolves and the Mapping of Postcolonial Ireland." In *Postcolonial Moves: Medieval Through Modern*, edited by Patricia Clare Ingham and Michelle R. Warren, 93–109. New York: Macmillan, 2003.

Kratz, Dennis. "*Fictus Lupus*: The Werewolf in Christian Thought." *Classical Folia* 30.1 (1976): 57–80.

Lavoie, Chantel. "Safe as Houses: Sorting and School Houses at Hogwarts." In *Reading Harry Potter: Critical Essays*, edited by Giselle Liza Anatol, 35–49. Westport, CT: Praeger, 2003.

Le Guin, Ursula K. *The Language of the Night: Essays on Fantasy and Science Fiction*. Edited by Susan Wood. New York: Berkley, 1982.

Lewis, C. S. *The Lion, the Witch, and*

Bibliography

the Wardrobe. New York: Scholastic, 1987.

Lspace: *Discworld & Pratchett Wiki*. "Bibliography." Accessed on March 27, 2012. http://wiki.lspace.org/wiki/Bibliography#Novels.

Maier, Sarah E. "Educating Harry Potter: A Muggle's Perspective on Magic and Knowledge in the Wizard World of J. K. Rowling." In *Scholarly Studies in Harry Potter*, edited by Cynthia Whitney Hallett, 7–25. Lewiston, NY: Edwin Mellen Press, 2006.

Malory, Thomas. *Complete Works*, edited by Eugene Vinaver. New York: Oxford University Press, 1971.

Marie de France. "Bisclavret." *The Lais of Marie de France*. Translated by Robert Hanning and Joan Ferrante. Grand Rapids: Baker, 2002.

Massey, Irving. *The Gaping Pig: Literature and Metamorphosis*. Berkeley: University of California Press, 1976.

Massey, Jeffry A. "*Corpus Lupi*: The Medieval Werewolf and Popular Theology." Ph.D. diss. Emory, 2003.

Melion and Biclarel: Two Old French Werwolf Lays. Translated by Amanda Hopkins. Liverpool: University of Liverpool, 2005. Accessed on Oct. 17, 2012. http://www.liv.ac.uk/soclas/los/Werwolf.pdf.

Mittman, Asa Simon. "The Other Close at Hand: Gerald of Wales and the 'Marvels of the West.'" In *The Monstrous Middle Ages*, edited by Bettina Bildhauer and Robert Mills, 97–112. Toronto: University of Toronto Press, 2003.

Natov, Roni. "Harry Potter and the Extraordinariness of the Ordinary." In *The Ivory Tower and Harry Potter: Perspectives on a Literary Phenomenon*, edited by Lana A. Whited, 125–139. Columbia: University of Missouri Press, 2002.

Niven, Larry. "There's a Wolf in My Time Machine." In *The Ultimate Werewolf*, edited by Harlan Ellison et al., 167–186. New York: Dell, 1991.

Njal's Saga. Translated by Magnus Magnusson and Hermann Palsson. New York: Penguin, 1960.

O'Leary, Crystal L. "Transcending Monstrous Flesh: A Revision of the Hero's Mythic Quest." *Journal of the Fantastic in the Arts* 13.3 (2003): 239–249.

Ostry, Elaine. "Accepting Mudbloods: The Ambivalent Social Vision of J. K. Rowling's Fairy Tales." In *Reading Harry Potter: Critical Essays*, edited by Giselle Liza Anatol, 89–101. Westport, CT: Praeger, 2003.

Otten, Charlotte, ed. *The Literary Werewolf: An Anthology*. Syracuse: Syracuse University Press, 2002.

_____. ed. *A Lycanthropy Reader: Werewolves in Western Culture*. New York: Dorset Press, 1989.

Ovid. *Metamorphoses*. Translated by Rolfe Humphries. Bloomington: Indiana University Press, 1983.

Pappa, Joseph. "The Bewildering Bounded/Bounding Bisclavret, or Lycanthropy, Lieges, and a Lotta Leeway in Marie de France." *Crossings* 4 (2000): 117–143.

Paul, Barbara. "Never Moon a Werewolf." In *Werewolves*, edited by Martin H. Greenberg, 46–61. New York: Daw, 1995.

Pausanias. *The Description of Greece*. n.t. London: Richard Priestley, 1824. http://books.google.com/books?id=OJMINAAACAAJ&dq=Pausanias+The+Description+of+Greece+Richard+Priestley,+1824.

Perrault, Charles. "Little Red Riding Hood." In *Perrault's Complete Fairy Tales*, translated by A. E. Johnson, 66–69. New York: Puffin, 1999.

Petronius. *The Satyricon*. Translated by J.P. Sullivan. New York: Penguin, 1979.

Pratchett, Terry. *The Fifth Elephant*. New York: HarperTorch, 2001.

_____. "Imaginary Worlds, Real Stories." *Folklore* 111 (2000): 159–168.

_____. *Thud!* New York: HarperCollins, 2005.

Randisi, Robert J. "Partners." In *The Ul-*

timate Werewolf, edited by Harlan Ellison et al., 263–275. New York: Dell, 1991.

The Romance of William of Palerne. Edited by Walter W. Skeat. London: Elibron Classics, 2005.

Routledge, Gregory E. "Science Fiction and the Black Power/Arts Movements: The Transpositional Cosmology of Samuel R. Delany, Jr." *Extrapolation* 41.2 (Summer 2000): 127–142.

Rowling, J.K. *Harry Potter and the Chamber of Secrets*. New York: Scholastic, 1999.

_____. *Harry Potter and the Deathly Hallows*. New York: Scholastic, 2007.

_____. *Harry Potter and the Goblet of Fire*. New York: Scholastic, 2000.

_____. *Harry Potter and the Half-Blood Prince*. New York: Scholastic, 2005.

_____. *Harry Potter and the Order of the Phoenix*. New York: Scholastic, 2003.

_____. *Harry Potter and the Prisoner of Azkaban*. New York: Scholastic, 1999.

_____. *Harry Potter and the Sorcerer's Stone*. New York: Scholastic, 1998.

The Saga of the Volsungs: The Norse Epic of Sigurd the Dragon Slayer. Translated by Jesse L. Byock. New York: Penguin, 1999.

Salisbury, Joyce E. *The Beast Within: Animals in the Middle Ages*. New York: Routledge, 1994.

Sansom, Basil. "Irruptions of the Dreaming in Post-Colonial Australia." *Oceania* 72.1 (September 2001): 1–32.

Sayers, William. "*Bisclavret* in Marie de France: A Reply." *Cambridge Medieval Celtic Studies* 4 (1982): 77–82.

Scamander, Newt. (J.K. Rowling). *Fantastic Beasts and Where to Find Them*. New York: Scholastic, 2001.

Scot, Reginald. *The Discoverie of Witchcraft*. London, 1584.

Shakespeare, William. *A Midsummer Night's Dream*. Edited by R.A. Foakes. New York: Cambridge University Press, 2003.

Smith, Kirby. "An Historical Study of the Werwolf in Literature." *PMLA* 9 (1894): 1–42.

Smith, Norman R. "Portentous Births and the Monstrous Imagination in Renaissance Culture." In *Marvels, Monsters, and Miracles: Studies in the Medieval and Early Modern Imagination*, edited by Timothy S. Jones and David A Sprunger, 267–283. Kalamazoo, MI: Medieval Institute Publications, 2002.

South, Malcolm. "Introduction." In *Mythical and Fabulous Creatures: A Source Book and Research Guide*, edited by Malcolm South, xix–xxix. New York: Greenwood Press, 1987.

Spenser, Edmund. *The Faerie Queene*. New York: Penguin, 1987.

Steiger, Brad. *The Werewolf Book: The Encyclopedia of Shape-Shifting Beings*. Detroit: Visible Ink Press, 1999.

Strickland, Brad. "And the Moon Shines Full and Bright." In *The Ultimate Werewolf*, edited by Harlan Ellison et al., 291–309. New York: Dell, 1991.

Summers, Montague. *The Werewolf in Lore and Legend*. Mineola, NY: Dover, 2003.

A True Discourse. Declaring the Damnable Life and Death of One Stubbe Peeter, a Most Wicked Sorcerer, Who in the Likenes of a Woolfe, Committed many Murders, Continuing This Develish Practice 25 Yeeres, Kiling and Devouring Men, Women, and Children. London, 1590.

Turtledove, Harry. "Not All Werewolves." In *Werewolves: A Collection of Original Stories*, edited by Jane Yolen and Martin H. Greenberg, 70–83. New York: Harper & Row, 1988.

Virgil. "Eclogue VIII." *Eclogues*. Translated by H. R. Fairclough. Cambridge: Harvard University Press, 1916. http://www.theoi.com/Text/VirgilEclogues.html.

Webster, John. *The Duchess of Malfi and Other Plays*. New York: Oxford University Press, 1998.

Weinberg, Robert E. "Wolf Watch." In *The Ultimate Werewolf*, edited by Harlan Ellison et al., 327–339. New York: Dell, 1991.

Bibliography

Westman, Karin E. "Specters of Thatcherism: Contemporary British Culture in J. K. Rowling's Harry Potter Series." In *The Ivory Tower and Harry Potter: Perspectives on a Literary Phenomenon*, edited by Lana A. Whited, 305–328. Columbia: University of Missouri Press, 2002.

Williamson, Jack. *Darker Than You Think*. New York: Berkeley Medallion, 1969.

Wiseman, S.J. "Hairy on the Inside: Metamorphosis and Civility in English Werewolf Texts." In *Renaissance Beasts*, edited by Erica Fudge, 50–69. Urbana: University of Illinois Press, 2004.

Yolen, Jane. "Green Messiah." In *The Literary Werewolf: An Anthology*, edited by Charlotte Otten, 278–284. Syracuse: Syracuse University Press, 2002.

———. *Touch Magic*. Little Rock: August House, 2000.

Index

Al Saud, Basim (Harris) 110, 131, 184
Albert the Great 39, 41, 110, 153
Alphouns (*William of Palerne*) 5, 12, 14, 21, 29, 42, 48, 70, 75, 78, 87, 112, 126, 138, 139, 140, 153, 154, 166, 174, 176, 184
Anatol, Gisele 95, 104
"And the Moon Shines Full and Bright" (Strickland) 180–182
Andriano, Joseph 73, 74, 92
Angua, Constable/Sergeant (Pratchett) 3, 36, 39–71, 84, 107, 108, 134, 140, 142, 143, 146, 148, 155, 158, 159, 161, 164, 165, 169, 184, 185
Arden, Heather 74, 77
Arthur and Gorlagon 20, 43, 44, 72, 111, 112, 177
Augustine, Saint 6, 17, 19, 20, 23, 110, 111, 113, 117, 153, 163, 164, 172, 174, 177

Barbee, Will (Williamson) 17–36, 169, 175, 185
Baring-Gould, Sabine 8
Barkan, Leonard 33, 110, 112
The Baron (Pratchett) 40, 43, 45, 47, 48, 53, 56, 57, 58, 62, 66, 67, 68
Bayfield, Robert 24
Bell, April (Williamson) 19–29, 31–35, 185
Benkov, Edith 27, 68
Bible 6, 110
bisclavret 39, 42, 74, 77, 99, 127
Bisclavret (character, Marie de France) 5, 8, 12, 13, 14, 21, 29, 42, 48, 55, 68, 70, 75, 76–77, 87, 100, 103, 112, 126, 138, 139, 141, 147, 153, 154, 163, 166, 174
"Bisclavret" (Marie de France) 4, 111, 163
Black, Sirius (Rowling) 73, 76, 78, 79, 80, 84, 86, 87, 89, 90, 91, 94, 95, 97, 98, 100–104, 149, 184
Blount, Thomas 24, 80
Bodin, Jean 80, 142, 185
Boguet, Henri 25, 49, 80, 142, 185
The Book of Werewolves (Baring-Gould) 8
Buchbinder, David 60
Burton, Robert 24

Butler, Andrew 37
Bynum, Caroline Walker 6, 7, 19, 38, 46, 79

cannibalism 8, 13, 17, 22, 25, 40, 41, 75, 82, 111, 127, 167–168, 172
Carrot, Captain (Pratchett) 41–43, 46–49, 55, 61–66, 69, 158
Castiglione, Baldesar 4, 85, 86
Chelik, Michael 13
Chopin, Kate 130
City of God (Augustine, Saint) 6, 19, 110
clothing 40, 41, 45, 51, 54, 75–76, 122, 140, 155, 167, 174, 180
Club Dead (Harris) 111, 115
Cockrill, Amanda 38, 60
Cohen, Jeffrey Jerome 12, 38
collective unconscious 2, 9, 28, 38, 67, 70, 105, 117, 187
Compton, Bill (Harris) 108, 112, 113, 117
Cooper, Marie-Star (Harris) 121, 132
Crispin, A.C. 5, 161, 162, 164, 169–171

Darker Than You Think (Williamson) 3, 17–36
Darwin, Charles 30, 31
Davidson, H.R. Ellis 8, 9
Davidson, Jane 22, 114, 124
Dawson, Trey (Harris) 112, 116
Deacon, John 24
Definitely Dead (Harris) 116, 133
de Lint, Charles 1, 2, 5, 11, 56, 120, 135, 136–160, 169; see also *Dingo*; *Wolf Moon*
Demarchus (Pausanias) 185
Dialogicall Discourses of Spirits and Divels (Deacon, Walker) 24
Dingo (de Lint) 1, 5, 11, 135, 136, 137, 150–160
The Discoverie of Witchcraft (Scot) 24
disease 4, 8, 24, 61, 73, 91, 93, 95, 96, 124–125
Diseases of the Mind (Burton) 24
dogs 3, 5, 12, 21, 24, 25, 27, 31, 33–34, 38, 47, 48, 56, 57–59, 61, 65–68, 70, 79, 111, 142, 146, 148, 153, 156, 169, 174, 178

Index

Doughty, Terri 100
Douglas, Adam 75
Dreamtime 136, 150, 151, 152, 156
The Duchess of Malfi (Webster) 24, 185
Dumbledore, Albus (Rowling) 73, 77, 78, 80, 86, 95, 97, 98, 101–104

Egil's Saga 9
Elms, Alan 29, 31, 32, 33
Em (de Lint, *Dingo*) 150, 151, 152, 153, 154, 155, 156, 157, 159
environmentalism 177, 178, 179
Epic of Gilgamesh 1, 2, 15
eroticism 5, 14
ethnicity 60, 61, 69, 92
evolution 3, 18, 68, 177, 178, 179, 180

fairy tales 2, 3, 37, 70, 185, 187; *see also* folklore; legends; mythology
Fantastic Beasts and Where to Find Them (Rowling) 83
fantasy genre 11, 23, 38, 50, 105, 122, 136, 137, 160, 176, 185, 187
Farmer, Philip José 5, 162, 171–173, 175, 177, 178
Ferdinand (Webster) 13, 24, 25, 49
The Fifth Elephant (Pratchett) 3, 38, 40, 41, 42, 43, 44, 47, 48, 49, 50, 52, 53, 57, 59, 60, 63, 65, 68, 69
fire 24, 31, 54, 163
Flood, Colonel (Harris) 115, 122, 126
folklore 2, 3, 10, 19, 26, 29, 37, 38, 39, 42, 56, 70, 128, 132, 136, 137, 143, 156, 163, 187; *see also* fairy tales; legends; mythology
Freud, Sigmund 8, 18, 27, 30
Friedman, John Block 45, 46, 140, 167
Furnan, Patrick (Harris) 110, 120, 121, 126

garvulf 39, 42, 74, 77, 81, 99
Gaspode (Pratchett) 5, 43, 57, 61, 62, 66, 148
General Discourse of the Virtuosi of France (Havers) 181
genetics 18, 21, 27, 28, 31, 33, 34, 55, 85, 89, 108, 118–120, 124, 173, 177
Gerald of Wales 7, 15, 20, 39, 42, 44, 47, 61, 75, 109, 110, 111, 153, 163, 185
germ theory 124–125
Gervase of Tilbury 17, 49, 121, 163, 165, 169, 171, 174, 180
Gilmore, David 13, 34, 68, 113
Glossographia (Blount) 24
Goldner, Ellen 97
Gorlagon (*Arthur and Gorlagon*) 5, 21, 42, 48, 70, 112, 126, 138, 139, 146, 163, 166
Goulart, Simon 8, 23, 24, 25

Granger, Hermione (Rowling) 73, 84, 87, 91, 92, 93, 94, 95, 96
Green, Amy 10, 77, 97, 102, 104
"Green Messiah" (Yolen) 177–178
Grenier, Jean 14, 25, 80, 82, 127, 142, 172, 177, 185
Greyback, Fenrir (Rowling) 12, 25, 71, 72, 73, 74–75, 76, 77, 80, 81–83, 95, 86–89, 90, 91, 92, 93, 96, 97, 99, 101, 103, 105, 171, 175
Grimes, Katherine 95, 96

Hagrid (Rowling) 73, 85, 89, 93
Harris, Charlaine 2, 4–5, 11, 26, 56, 107–135, 175, 184, 185; *see also* specific titles
Harry Potter and the Chamber of Secrets (Rowling) 83, 85
Harry Potter and the Deathly Hallows (Rowling) 4, 76, 77–78, 80, 82, 86, 96
Harry Potter and the Goblet of Fire (Rowling) 89
Harry Potter and the Half-Blood Prince (Rowling) 4, 75, 76, 77, 80, 82, 96
Harry Potter and the Order of the Phoenix (Rowling) 4, 77, 80, 84, 86, 89, 95–96
Harry Potter and the Prisoner of Azkaban (Rowling) 4, 75, 79, 84, 96, 123
Havers, G. 187
Heisenberg, Werner 18, 24, 30, 31, 32
Heldreth, Lillian 130, 189
heredity *see* genetics
Hevereaux, Alcide (Harris) 110, 111, 112, 115, 118, 119, 120, 123, 124, 126, 127, 130, 131, 185
Hirsh, Brett 129
History and Topography of Ireland (Gerald of Wales) 109, 110
horror genre 3, 7, 12, 19, 23, 43, 44, 50, 55, 64, 122, 134, 176, 185, 186, 187

Της Ιατρικης Καρτος or *A Treatise De Morborum Capitis Essentiis & Prognosticis* (Bayfield) 24
identity 45, 46–47, 56, 63, 70
illness *see* disease
insanity 6, 8, 17, 21, 22, 24, 25, 33, 48, 81, 153, 155–156, 186

Jacques-Lefèvre, Nicole 144
Jake (Harris) 133–134, 184
James I 8, 24
Jannalynn (Harris) 110, 112, 114, 116, 121, 132, 184
Johnny (de Lint, *Dingo*) 151, 152, 155, 157, 158, 159
Jung, Carl 9, 12, 14, 18, 27, 28, 117, 184

Index

Karkov, Catherine 7
Kern (de Lint, *Wolf Moon*) 136, 137, 138, 141, 142–143, 144–149, 150, 155, 169
Kramer, Heinrich 25, 80, 142, 185
Kratz, M. 74

Lainey (de Lint, *Dingo*) 150, 151, 152, 153, 154, 155, 156, 157, 158–159
Landnamabok 9
Lavoie, Chantel 101
Lee, Tanith 130, 188
legends 29, 37, 38, 56, 70, 109, 128, 142, 156, 187; *see also* fairy tales; folklore; mythology
Le Guin, Ursula K. 116
The Literary Werewolf (Otten) 15, 189
"Little Red Riding Hood" (Perrault) 97, 166, 185
Living Dead in Dallas (Harris) 115
Lorenz, Kathryn 74, 77
Lupin, Remus (Rowling) 3, 4, 13, 35, 71, 72, 73, 74–75, 76–78, 79, 80, 81, 82, 83, 84, 85–90, 91, 92, 93, 94, 95, 96, 97, 98, 99–105, 107, 119, 120, 123, 129, 137, 143, 148, 149, 150, 155, 157–158, 159, 167, 171, 175, 184, 185
Lupin, Ted (Rowling) 80, 85
lycanthropy 17, 19, 22, 24, 25, 26, 48, 55, 72, 75, 79, 83, 84, 93, 94, 95, 96, 100, 153, 154, 155, 175
Lycaon (Ovid) 6, 8, 19, 72, 75, 76, 127, 185, 186

Machiavelli, Niccolò 85
madness *see* insanity
Magnus, Albertus *see* Albert the Great
Malfoy, Draco (Rowling) 73, 81, 92, 93, 101, 104
Malleus Maleficarum (Kramer & Sprenger) 142
Malory, Thomas 12, 14, 188
Marie de France 4, 8, 10, 12, 13, 14, 15, 20, 39, 40, 41, 43, 44, 50, 72, 74, 76, 77, 81, 112, 127, 134, 138, 141, 161, 163, 185, 186; *see also* "Bisclavret"; Bisclavret (character)
Massey, Irving 13, 14
Massey, Jeffry 6, 20
melancholy 17, 24, 29, 155
Melion (*William of Palerne*) 146, 154
Men at Arms (Pratchett) 63
"Men-Woolfes" (James I) 24
mental illness *see* insanity
Merlotte, Sam (Harris) 108, 110, 116, 117, 127, 128
Merlyn (Malory) 12, 14, 188
Metamorphoses (Ovid) 15, 109
metamorphosis 3, 4, 7, 13, 23, 33, 38, 89

Metamorphosis and Identity (Bynum) 7
"Metamorphosis, or Gerald and the Werewolf" (Bynum) 7
Miguel (de Lint, *Dingo*) 151, 152, 153, 154, 155, 156, 157, 158–159
Mittman, Asa 90
Moeris (Virgil) 185
Mondrick, Dr. (Williamson) 21, 24, 25, 26, 27, 33, 35
Mondrick, Rowena 21, 25, 27, 28, 29, 32
monsters 2, 4, 6, 7, 12, 13, 17, 19, 21, 22, 23, 36, 38, 45, 48, 49, 50, 58, 63, 67, 68–69, 72, 73, 74, 75, 80, 81, 82, 83, 85, 86, 89, 90, 92, 101, 105, 113, 114, 138, 140, 141, 143, 145, 155, 165, 169, 183, 186
moon 17, 49, 64, 96, 120–121, 123, 143, 163, 165, 169, 171, 174, 180, 182
morality 91, 96, 97, 98, 99, 104
mystery genre 11, 107, 134; *see also* police procedural
mythology 2, 9, 10, 18, 19, 37, 56, 70, 141; *see also* fairy tales; folklore; legends

Natov, Roni 98, 99
natural selection 30–31, 131
nature-versus-nurture debate 12, 39, 50, 60, 64, 66–67, 88–89
"Never Moon a Werewolf" (Paul) 173–176
Niceros (Petronius) 109
Niven, Larry 5, 162, 177, 178–179, 180
Njal's Saga 9
Northman, Eric (Harris) 108, 112, 113, 114, 117, 133
"Not All Wolves" (Turtledove) 162–164

"Of the Metamorphosis of Men into Beasts" (Boguet) 142
O'Leary, Crystal L. 90
O'Malley, Kathleen 5, 161, 162, 164, 169–171
Ossory 42, 52, 70, 109
Ostry, Elaine 92, 94–95
Otten, Charlotte 15, 189
Ovid 2, 7, 8, 15, 17, 19, 64, 72, 74, 76, 108, 109, 110, 127, 134, 185, 186

paranormal romance genre 2, 11
"Partners" (Randisi) 164–166
passing 129–130
Paul, Barbara 5, 162, 173–176
Pausanias 185
Peeter, Stubbe 5, 8, 14, 33, 80, 127, 142, 185
Pelt, Debbie (Harris) 112, 126, 127
Perrault, Charles 10, 15, 97, 99, 166, 168, 185
Petronius 2, 15, 19, 40, 41, 64, 72, 74, 75, 76, 108, 109, 122, 127, 134, 185; *see also Satyricon*

Index

Pettigrew, Peter (Rowling) 78, 79, 84, 90, 123
Platonic forms 9, 187
Pliny, Plinian races 19, 61
police procedural 11; *see also* mystery genre
Potter, Harry (Rowling) 4, 73, 76, 77, 79, 80, 81, 82, 84, 85, 86, 87, 88, 89, 90, 91, 92, 93, 95, 9, 97, 98, 99, 100, 101, 01, 103, 104, 105, 150, 157–158, 159
Potter, James (Rowling) 76, 79, 86, 90, 98, 100, 102, 103, 149, 158, 184
Pratchett, Terry 2, 3, 4, 5, 11, 14, 17, 36, 37–71, 72, 73, 83, 105, 106, 107, 108, 109, 120, 122, 132, 134, 136, 140, 142, 143, 146, 148, 150, 154, 155, 156, 158, 161, 164, 169, 184, 185, 186
prejudice, 61, 62, 63, 73, 91, 93–94, 104, 164, 175; *see also* specific titles
psychoanalysis, 8, 9, 18, 27, 29, 30, 31, 32, 33, 53, 108
"Pure Silver" (Crispin & O'Malley) 169–171

Quain, Sam (Williamson) 21, 25, 26, 27, 30, 31, 34, 35
Quinn (Harris) 128, 131

racism 39, 59, 60, 62, 73, 90, 91, 93–95
Randisi, Robert 5, 161, 162, 164, 166
rebirth 14, 29, 52
Rowling, J.K. 1, 2, 4, 5, 11, 12, 13, 15, 25, 35, 54, 55, 56, 61, 64, 71, 72–106, 107, 120, 123, 125, 134, 137, 143, 144, 148, 150, 154, 155, 156, 157, 158, 159, 171, 175, 184, 185, 188, 189; *see also* specific titles

Saint Augustine *see* Augustine, Saint
Salisbury, Joyce 3
Sally (Pratchett) 42, 44, 64, 65, 66, 67, 69
Sansom, Basil 156
Satyricon (Petronius) 15, 109, 177
Sawyer, Andy 37
science fiction genre 5, 18, 23, 161, 176–177, 178, 181, 182
Scot, Reginald 8, 24
self-fashioning 4, 8, 45, 49, 66, 72, 80, 85, 88, 93, 98
Serafine (Pratchett) 40, 43, 45, 47, 51, 53, 56, 60, 67
shadow (Jung) 12, 14, 18, 26, 27, 28, 32, 34, 35, 47, 50, 53, 61, 67, 73, 76, 83, 86, 87, 88, 90, 99, 101, 115, 116, 117, 121, 132, 143, 144, 145
Shakespeare, William 14, 186
silver 17, 24, 26, 31, 54, 55, 72, 143, 163, 171, 181
Smith, Kirby 10

Smith, Norman 23
Snape, Severus (Rowling) 74, 78, 80, 84, 89, 92, 93, 94, 95, 96, 102, 104, 105
socialization 42, 46, 67, 73, 77, 86, 87, 91–92, 93, 95, 104, 105
South, Malcolm 2, 53
Spenser, Edmund 12, 14, 188
Sprenger, James 25, 80, 142, 185
Stackhouse, Jason (Harris) 117, 118, 124
Stackhouse, Sookie (Harris) 108, 109, 110, 111, 112, 113, 114, 115, 116, 117, 118, 119, 120, 121, 122, 123, 125, 127, 129, 133
Stonebrook, Hallow 14, 118, 122
Stonebrook, Mark (Harris) 114, 118, 122
Strickland, Brad 5, 162, 177, 179–182
Stubbe, Peeter *see* Peeter, Stubbe
Summers, Montague 110
Sybil, Lady (Pratchett) 45, 51, 58, 60

Tallyman (de Lint, *Dingo*) 152, 154, 159
"Tanith Lee's Werewolves Within" (Heldreth) 189
Tesla, Nikola 31
"There's a Wolf in My Time Machine" (Niven) 178–179
Thud! (Pratchett) 3, 38, 40, 41, 42, 43, 44–45, 46, 47, 52, 53, 54, 57, 58, 60, 64, 65, 68, 69
Tonks, Nymphadora (Rowling) 80, 85, 100, 149
Topographica Hibernica (Gerald of Wales) *see* *History and Topography of Ireland*
transformation 23, 42–44, 54, 70, 122–123, 143, 154, 173
Της Ιατρικης Καρτος or *A Treatise De Morborum Capitis Essentiis & Prognosticis* (Bayfield) 24
trickster, trickster archetype 10, 12, 13, 14, 15, 169, 184–185, 186
True Blood 108
Tuiloch the Harper (de Lint, *Wolf Moon*) 138, 139, 141–142, 145, 146, 147–148
Turtledove, Harry 161, 162–164
The Ultimate Werewolf 180

Umbridge, Dolores (Rowling) 89, 91, 94, 96
Uncertainty Principle 18, 24, 30, 31, 32
Underworld 124, 125, 132, 189

vampires 17, 26, 29, 60, 62, 63, 64–65, 66, 68, 108, 109, 111, 113, 114, 115, 117, 120, 128, 129, 132–134, 135, 168
vibration 24, 31
Vimes, Samuel, Commander (Pratchett) 42, 43, 46, 49, 51, 53, 54, 55, 56, 57, 58, 59, 60, 66, 67, 68, 69, 158

Index

Virgil 185
Voldemort (Rowling) 79, 80, 82, 83, 85, 86, 87, 88, 94, 96, 98, 101, 104
Volsunga Saga 9
von Überwald family (Pratchett) 40, 48, 58; *see also* Angua, Constable; The Baron; Serafine; Wolfgang

Walker, John 24
Warrigal (de Lint, *Dingo*) 151, 152, 157, 159
Weasley, Bill (Rowling) 80, 82, 96
Weasley, Molly (Rowling) 74, 94, 103
Weasley, Ron (Rowling) 73, 74, 81, 87, 91, 92, 93, 94, 95, 104, 158
Webster, John 10, 13, 15, 24, 25, 49, 185
Weinberg, Robert 5, 161, 162, 164, 166–169
weredingo 5, 137, 150–160
werepanthers 118, 119, 124, 126, 128
weretigers 15, 126, 128
Westman, Karin 93–94, 94–95
Whited, Lana 95, 96
William (*William of Palerne*) 78, 146, 154, 184

William of Palerne 4, 12, 14, 20, 39, 43, 44, 72, 74, 78, 111, 112, 146, 184
Williamson, Jack 2, 3, 5, 13, 17–36, 134, 169, 170, 175, 177, 181, 184, 185; *see also Darker Than You Think*
Wiseman, S.J. 7–8, 33
witches 14, 17, 21, 22, 24, 28, 29, 30, 31, 32, 33, 34, 48, 83, 108, 114, 186
"Wolf, Iron, and Moth" (Farmer) 171–173
Wolf Moon (de Lint) 5, 135, 136, 137, 138–149, 159
"Wolf Watch" (Weinberg) 166–169
Wolfgang (Pratchett) 39, 40, 41, 42, 43, 44, 45, 46, 47, 48, 49, 50, 51, 53, 54, 55, 56, 57, 59, 60, 62, 65, 66, 68, 69, 134, 186
wolves 3, 5, 9, 12, 15, 38, 41, 47, 49, 51, 56, 57–59, 60, 61, 62, 63, 65, 66, 67, 68, 70, 84, 117, 130, 141, 142, 144, 146, 147, 149, 167–168, 169, 177, 178, 179

Yolen, Jane 5, 61, 162, 177–178, 180
young adult fiction 1–2, 137

www.ingramcontent.com/pod-product-compliance
Ingram Content Group UK Ltd.
Pitfield, Milton Keynes, MK11 3LW, UK
UKHW041955140426
5217IPUK00015B/812